Nest in the Wind

Second Edition

Second Edition

Nest in the Wind

Adventures in Anthropology on a Tropical Island

Martha Ward

University of New Orleans

WAVELAND

PRESS, INC.

Long Grove, Illinois

For information about this book, contact:
　　Waveland Press, Inc.
　　4180 IL Route 83, Suite 101
　　Long Grove, IL　60047-9580
　　(847) 634-0081
　　info@waveland.com
　　www.waveland.com

Illustrations by Nancy Zoder Dawes

This book is dedicated to men I love,

Dr. John L. Fischer
Anthropologist, mentor, colleague, and friend

and

Hugh Coonfield
Teacher, counselor, craftsman, and my father

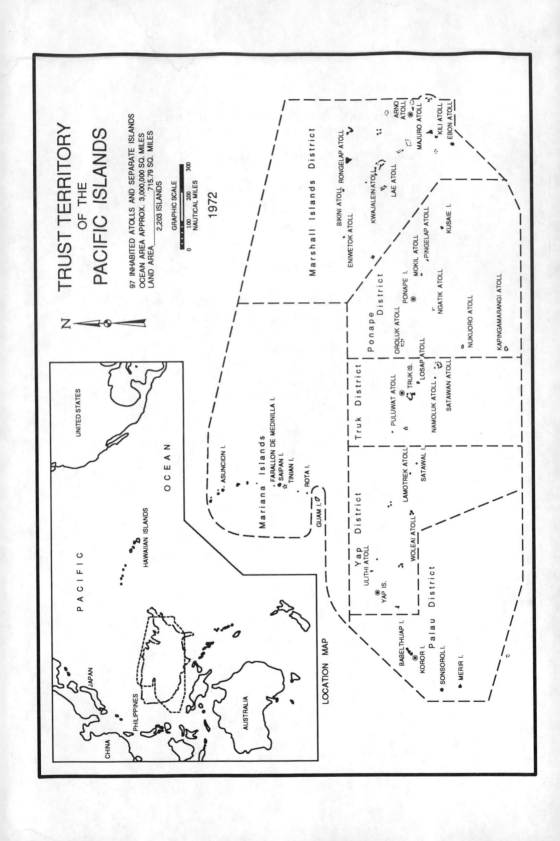

TRUST TERRITORY
OF THE
PACIFIC ISLANDS

97 INHABITED ATOLLS AND SEPARATE ISLANDS
OCEAN AREA APPROX. 3,000,000 SQ. MILES
LAND AREA   715.79 SQ. MILES
                   2,203 ISLANDS

GRAPHIC SCALE

0   100   200   300
     NAUTICAL MILES

1972

N

LOCATION MAP

UNITED STATES

PACIFIC

OCEAN

HAWAIIAN ISLANDS

JAPAN

CHINA

PHILIPPINES

AUSTRALIA

Mariana Islands

ASUNCION I.

FARALLON DE MEDINILLA I.
SAIPAN I.
TINIAN I.
ROTA I.

GUAM I.

Yap District

ULITHI ATOLL

YAP IS.

BABELTHUAP I.
KOROR I.

Palau District

SONSOROL I.

MERIR I.

WOLEAI ATOLL

LAMOTREK ATOLL

SATAWAL

Truk District

PULUWAT ATOLL

TRUK IS.

LOSAP ATOLL

NAMOLUK ATOLL

SATAWAN ATOLL

Ponape District

OROLUK ATOLL

PONAPE I.

MOKIL ATOLL

PINGELAP ATOLL

NGATIK ATOLL

KUSAIE I.

NUKUORO ATOLL

KAPINGAMARANGI ATOLL

Marshall Islands District

ENIWETOK ATOLL

BIKINI ATOLL

RONGELAP ATOLL

KWAJALEIN ATOLL

LAE ATOLL

ARNO ATOLL

MAJURO ATOLL

KILI ATOLL

EBON ATOLL

Contents

Contents

Acknowledgments

I am indebted to friends and colleagues—Professor Ann Edwards who teaches through the book each semester, and Dr. Glenn Petersen and Dr. Michael Lieber who shared their theoretical sophistication with me. In the decades since my first visit, four women have completed fieldwork research and dissertations about Pohnpei—Dr. Suzanne Falgout, Dr. Eve Pinsker, Dr. Elizabeth Keating, and Dr. Kimberlee Kihleng. Anthropology is a craft practiced and passed on like family traditions or genes. All of us, related to each other and to Pohnpeians through extended family and professional ties, acknowledge the founding generation of our anthropological lineage—Saul Riesenberg, John Fischer, Ann Fischer, William Bascom, Daniel Hughes, and the other leaders of Micronesian anthropology whose students we are.

On my return trip to Pohnpei in 2003 I discovered beautiful air-conditioned libraries and archives. In 1972, the year we finished the blood pressure research and left, the Catholic Church had founded Micronesian Seminar or MicSem, a social research and public service institute for community education, and appointed historian and Jesuit Father Francis Hezel to head the organization. The videos MicSem has produced, Hezel's prolific research, and the collections at their headquarters are a stunning contribution to all the people of Micronesia. At the beautiful, new Library of the College of Micronesia I found Iris Falcom and Jean Thoulag surrounded by piles of consultants' reports, proceedings of meetings, and the materials a new nation acquires in its birthing process. I want to thank them, Fran Hezel and MicSem's staff, and all the other people who smoothed my professional path. Maria Donre, Catalina Donre, their husbands, children, and circle of family members welcomed me back, invited me to feasts, and took me around the island—to each of you, *Kalahngan en komwi*.

The illustrations that grace this book are the work of Nancy Zoder Dawes, whose lines and pens and paper capture another spirit of truth. I would particularly like to thank Tom Curtin at Waveland Press for his belief in humanistic and creative anthropology, and Dr. Jeffrey Ehrenreich, chair of the Department of Anthropology at the University of New Orleans, who encouraged me to return and found some money for my trip. At the end I have included a list of books and articles on Pohnpei. This is to honor colleagues who slog through mud, verbs, and kinship systems and to assure you that my tale is only one view of a complex society. All of us who have worked on Pohnpei enjoy a special fellowship, even as, among ourselves, we gossip, debate alternative interpretations, mourn our dead, and remember the smell of coconut husk fires on a humid morning. We accept that no single person can explain an island culture as dynamic as Pohnpei.

ABOUT THE AUTHOR

Martha Ward is University Research Professor of Anthropology and Urban Studies at the University of New Orleans. Among other books she has written are *Them Children: A Study in Language Learning; Poor Women, Powerful Men: America's Great Experiment in Family Planning; The Hidden Life of Tirol; A World Full of Women;* and *Voodoo Queen: The Spirited Lives of Marie Laveau.*

Nest in the Wind

Second Edition

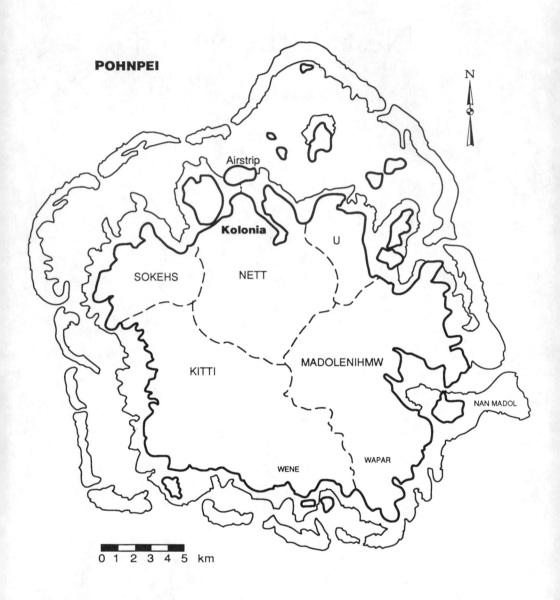

POHNPEI

N

Airstrip

Kolonia

U

SOKEHS

NETT

KITTI

MADOLENIHMW

NAN MADOL

WENE

WAPAR

0 1 2 3 4 5 km

Introduction

Once Upon a Time— And Back Again

The tale is about quarter-ton yams, sex, sorcery, tin shacks, feasts, heart disease, and a beverage called kava. On the island of Pohnpei (pronounced *Pone-pay*) in the middle of the Pacific Ocean, I ate dog; I got pregnant; I was lost on the lagoon. In 1970 I had moved to Micronesia as part of a large medical research team studying blood pressure and social change. A decade and a half after the project ended, I wrote the first edition of *Nest in the Wind* with the shameless goal of enticing students into the romance of anthropology, of making readers part of the smells, tastes, and sensations of the island culture I had come to love. In 2003, three decades after my return to the United States, I went back to discover what had happened and learned what none of us had predicted. Therefore the first seven chapters of this new edition are the original edition, rephrased and edited in parts; the eighth chapter provides the bridge to three new chapters, which describe the trajectories of island culture that have taken shape since the early 1970s.

Many people have South Pacific fantasies of bare-breasted maidens, pristine beaches, and waving palms. Most know nothing about Micronesia, "small islands" scattered randomly over three million square miles of ocean, an area as large as the continental United States that stretches between Hawaii and the Philippines in the northern Pacific. The 2,141 tiny islands combined are no larger than the state of Rhode Island; they do not register in popular consciousness. In school Americans seldom learn that in 1946, at the end of World War II, the United States government began to administer Micronesia as a Trust Territory of the United Nations.

Pohnpei is a high island of volcanoes forged millennia ago. Located near the center of Micronesia, it lies equidistant in nautical miles between the cities of Honolulu and Manila. The main island, which retains its volcanic

1

ancestry, has a roughly pentagonal shape and a maximum diameter of thirteen miles. A fringing coral reef encircles the volcanic core, forming a loose protection and a line between lagoon and open ocean beyond. Within the lagoon, the coral bottom is a world of deep beauty that only divers and rare tropical fish can visit. Although there are low coral islets with sandy beaches in the lagoon, dense mangrove swamps surround the main island and provide wood, food, and protection from erosion. Visitors are surprised to see so few beaches, yet the towering cliffs of Sokehs Island, mountain forests, dramatic vegetation, and the textures of tropical life strike them with awe. Pohnpei is one of most beautiful islands in the world.

The island creates its own rain system by collecting the clouds as they pass, and so it rains most of the time. More than 200 inches a year fall on the lowlands, and the uninhabited mountain center receives about 400 inches. The rain creates unbelievable humidity, magnificent waterfalls tumbling down basaltic cliffs, and rivers of clean, cool water. Since the heat feels intense, few inhabitants are grateful for cloudless days.

The National Institutes of Health had given Dr. John Cassel, dean of the University of North Carolina School of Public Health and a well-respected scholar, a large grant to study the complex relationships between social change and modernization, and the high blood pressure that leads to heart attacks. Most Westerners know about the danger of heart attacks; we understand that blood pressure rises with age. Researchers believed that lifestyle, heredity, and many factors in the way Westerners lived or thought or felt influenced their health. But many pieces of the puzzle remained unclear, and were even disputed. So Cassel and his colleagues wanted to test new theories. They asked, how does blood pressure work in a completely different place? The island of Pohnpei was a natural experiment, as perfect a laboratory as human cultures offer.

Dr. John "Jack" Fischer, who had worked in Micronesia after the United States Navy inherited it from the Japanese at the end of World War II, was a senior member of our research team. Among other languages, he spoke Japanese and Pohnpeian, and had been District Anthropologist in Pohnpei when its name was still spelled Ponape (pronounced *Pon-a-pay*). Jack, a former Marine with three degrees from Harvard University, had been my professor at Tulane University and helped me finish my doctorate the year before we arrived. During our first summer, his job was to develop contacts, establish the project, and lend credibility to its success.

My husband, Roger, a graduate student doing dissertation research, wanted to study traditional medical systems and the diagnosis and curing of disease as Pohnpeians experienced them. When the grant for the project was approved, I took a research leave from my teaching post at the University of New Orleans, intending to be absent only for a year. My job in the field was hiring, training, and supervising interviewers to administer the census, sample, and questionnaires. Roger and I had to learn the language as soon as possible so we could manage the entire field portion of the project through to the completion of the medical examinations. Other members of the professional team, including a psychologist, a cardiologist, an epidemiologist, and several nurse-administrators, joined us for brief periods.

But this is not a book about science or blood pressure. The research project was the reason I moved there and explains why at some moment I happened to be arguing about the price of pigs, sleeping in a rat-filled feast house, or carrying sugar cane stalks over one shoulder. This book is a personal encounter with a team of researchers, unfamiliar customs, a demanding environment, and my own personality. Written accounts from other anthropologists, Roger's and my letters, field notes, and reports from government agencies from this period provide the framework. I changed some personal names—people on Pohnpei often change their own names on important occasions of personal and professional growth—and probably imparted more wisdom to myself in recounting these events than I deserve. The only sin I have not knowingly committed is to distort the lives and customs of the people of this island. Through mere words I want to convey my respect for the integrity of this culture and trust that the people of Pohnpei will see the fruits of what they taught me and appreciate how much an understanding of their lives and culture has to offer.

This book is only an impressionist painting. As in the art I admire so much, I wish to evoke images, a sense of immediacy, and the feeling that you are there with me—that you are also a participant and an observer. I hint at the realities between the dots of the painting and make no effort to analyze each dot. This is not an official ethnography or history. It is only a true story about the doing of fieldwork and the doing of anthropology.

Chapter 1

Fruit in the
Hands of the Gods

Once upon a time, a man named Sapkini built a large canoe. He knew that the sky is a roof that touches the sea at its edges. His people, sailing in their fine canoe to the place where the sky meets the sea, would find land there. On the way, they met an octopus who showed them a shallow reef in the ocean. The people brought rocks and stones from faraway lands to make the reef higher. But the waves broke up the stones. So they planted mangrove trees to protect the island. But still the ocean was too close. So they built a fringing reef around the island. Two women brought soil and the island grew larger. On its top the people built a shrine to the spirits and named their new land—*Pohn-Pei*, Upon-the-Altar.

The feast house of the High Chief of Nett was quiet. Men and women sat cross-legged on raised platforms along the three sides below the thatched roof. The fourth side was open to a view of stars in a clear sky. On the rocky ground between the platforms rested large flat stones. The men seated beside the stones removed their shirts; women rubbed scented coconut oil on their bare backs and placed flower wreaths in their hair.

At a signal, the men began to pound the broken roots and twigs heaped on the stones in front of them. The rocks they held in their hands made deep ringing sounds as they struck. When the roots and twigs were broken down by the pounding, the men spread them with slow and practiced gestures into a long bundle of fibers. One man picked up the ends of the bundle and began to twist, much as a wet towel is wrung. With gentle strength he continued to coil the bundle against itself until a thick brown liquid oozed from it. Another man caught the flow with a round bottomed coconut cup. Rising to his feet, he approached the High Chief, seated on the woven mats at the head of the

U-shaped feast house. Averting his gaze, the servitor extended the cup across his bent forearm, offering it to his Chief who drank the viscous liquid.

As turns came around, I had my first taste of kava. Astringent and slimy, it resembled strings of swarthy mucus and tasted as though the strong roots our ancestors used for medicine had been mixed together. The first sip numbed my lips, tongue, and throat. Pretending that no one could see me, I picked pieces of woody debris from my teeth.

Although I understood none of the speeches, I savored the smell of fresh flowers and coconut oil, the shadows kerosene lanterns cast on the gathering, and the serenity of gestures. I had read about the pepper plant whose roots are pounded on basaltic stones selected for their acoustic properties and knew that the communal drinking of kava is the heart of ceremonial life, much as communion is for Christians. The sources said that sipping too much would induce sleepiness but never intoxication or hallucination. I had yet to understand that kava has the power to promote communal harmony and peaceful social relationships. I had yet to need its healing powers.

A man moved next to Jack, Roger, and me; he sat cross-legged and began to tell the story about the octopus and the reef. Another translated it into English. I took notes—here was a genuine origin myth recounted by genuine natives. I had not asked any questions, but he seemed to be giving me answers. As the kava cup circulated again through prescribed ritual sequences, the enormity of understanding the ancient meanings of this culture swept over me.

Later, we adjourned to a Western-style house for a buffet. The tables were laden with breadfruit, taro, and yams cooked in different ways; dishes seasoned with coconut milk or mashed bananas; and pork cooked in soy sauce. Some younger men spoke excellent English and, as I later learned, had earned graduate degrees from American universities. The conversation revolved around economic development prospects for the island, the pros and cons of the nascent tourist boom, the hope for a Pohnpeian-owned fishing industry, and the excitement surrounding the newly inaugurated Continental Air Micronesia Airlines jet flight to the islands. The men gossiped about Trust Territory politics and recent High Court decisions.

The week before, Jack Fischer had met Roger and me at what was fondly called an airport. The landing of the 727 jet on the small islet in the lagoon was still a novelty to the Pohnpeians. Before the bare coral landing strip was built through a flattened mangrove swamp running between the watery ends of the islet, only seaplanes could land—and only if the lagoon was calm. There were no lights, no tower, no radio contact between plane and ground, and no ground services of any kind. Jets, each carrying a mechanic and spare parts, landed in Pohnpei three times a week when the weather was favorable, treating passengers to a view of the spectacular Sokehs cliffs towering beyond iridescent bays and lagoons.

My first glimpse of Kolonia, capital of Pohnpei and my new home, was not promising. The shanty town, an example of urbanization, ethnic diversity, and development, was home for out-islanders, those who come from other islands of Micronesia, and foreigners, mostly a handful of Americans in the Trust Territory government. Tropical vegetation had gone on a rampage; weeds, mildew, and a jungle of plants concealed entire neighborhoods as well as the population density. So-called "civilization" had gone berserk as well. Huge piles of rusting, rotting trash stood outside the thatch-roofed shed at the airport, the local hospital on the hill, and the headquarters of the district administration. Women drew water from outdoor spigots while abandoned cars rusted nearby. Newer cars that had not yet succumbed to the hardships of the tropics were parked anywhere; old dead vehicles rested and rusted wherever they had stopped. The few miles of unpaved roads turned to dust in dry spells and mud after rains.

The stores and businesses displayed no signs because local people knew their names. The town had a Protestant church, a Catholic mission, the ruins of a Spanish fort, the district hospital, administrative offices, several good restaurants, and nineteen bars. But there were no zoning laws, building codes, city planning schemes, or attempts to build an urban life. The tropics are a great equalizer, and even new cinder-block construction had begun to rot and age. Cheap tin rusted in the incessant rains, changing in color to earth tones of red, ochre, and brown.

Jack had rented an appalling shack on a side road leading from Kolonia's main street. The roof of the lean-to kitchen had collapsed, and the walls came only halfway up to the rusty tin roof. The only door had to be lifted into place. Mosquitos, flies, geckos, lizards, mice, and—to my special horror—rats were the shanty's main tenants. With no justification that I could see, he was proud of the dump that would be his home for three months. The thought of sleeping on the floor, animals or no, unnerved Roger, while I was disgusted to leave my rubber thongs outside and walk across the floor in my bare feet. To placate me, Jack agreed to refer to the rats as ground squirrels and to run an illegal electrical line from the jail on the hill so there could be some light in the dark hut.

Jack, who needed the hovel to house two researchers yet to arrive, Floyd and Ian, arranged for Roger and me to live in a "real" house that a Peace Corps administrator usually occupied. My senses had not yet acculturated, so I judged this house by Western standards and took appliances, electricity, beds, indoor plumbing, and a kitchen sink for granted. I did time-consuming chores, reflecting standards of housekeeping learned at my mother's knee, that Jack could ignore in his shack. Although termites had eaten everything but the paint and the house was sifting into dust, and despite having to shake our sheets free of termite dust in the morning and again at night, I needed the illusion of home—tables, chairs, couches, beds, and desks. Every cell in my body urged me to live at waist level, use counters and reach up to cabinets— not sit on the floor to cook as I saw Micronesian women doing. Even the front yard with its flower-edged sidewalk—landscaped as only those descended from European cultures see space—reassured me.

The house gave Roger and me breathing space to experience full culture shock. Anthropologists, travelers, or others cut off from the daily comfort of their own culture and language react in strange and unpredictable ways. We lose our tempers or retreat into alcohol, prejudice, and a dozen forms of escapism. Simple yet absolute things we take for granted—the taste of food, how to sit and stand, words for yes and no—are gone. I understood cultural relativism from an intellectual perspective, but the gut reality turns out to be something else. My brain claims, for example, that the British drive on the left-hand side of the road, opposite to that of Americans, by cultural choice; it's a variation of many possibilities and no more God-given than the "right" side of the road Americans have chosen. All my senses, however, scream at me when I drive or am with another driver to get over on the safe side, the "right" side of the road, before we are all killed.

An objective observer or therapist would have recognized the forms our culture shock was taking. Roger wrote postcards to 200 people to whom we had not even sent Christmas cards. He also lurked behind trees trying to take pictures of exposed maidenly breasts; he ordered useless items to be sent from his hometown. He said that these were perfectly normal behaviors under the circumstances and that I was the one who did weird things. It is true I read ten-year-old magazines like *Boys' Life* and trashy novels from cover to cover—when I could find anything to read. I made up anxious lists that included unrelated or long-term tasks: hire interviewers, eat mango for breakfast, learn to speak Pohnpeian, and find that bobby pin. I cleaned house more than necessary for someone who had cheerfully given up material goods and the American mania for possessions. Jack had his own ideas of what we needed to learn. He taught me how to fill, clean, and cook on a smelly kerosene camp stove and graciously ate the raw or burned results. As he demonstrated the proper way to trim the wick, he lectured us on linguistics or folklore.

"Somewhere there is a sound like 'h.' It may be very important. Write down all the occurrences you hear." I never heard any.

"Here are some questions you will need: How is this thing like that thing? How is this thing different from that thing?" Too sophisticated for someone still pondering what to eat.

"Listen for stories about eating forbidden animals or horned fish or twins or sibling rivalry." I could barely say hello.

Our first challenge—other than oppressive heat, transportation, housing, adjustment, and learning a new language—was to set up the research project. When the United States Navy began to administer the island in 1946 after the defeat of the Japanese in World War II, doctors aboard the U.S. Navy ship, the *Whidby*, conducted a health survey of the island. This baseline, the foundation of our research, was the reason why John Cassel and the School of Public Health had selected Pohnpei. The Navy doctors found that islanders had consistently low blood pressure with no rise as people grew older. Whether blood pressure readings had risen in the quarter century since the original study or remained low and stable, our research team had a natural laboratory in which to test sophisticated hypotheses and to collect data that addressed the dilemmas and underlying causes of heart disease in a population. The grant application stated our goals:

> to investigate the dependent variable, possible cardiovascular disease as manifested by high blood pressure, and the independent variable, individual response to social stress and change as related to personality types, degree of modernization, and the sense of belonging to organized groups in the social structure.

But the concept of and words for "heart disease" did not exist in traditional Pohnpeian medicine. The language had no term for "blood pressure," much less words for "variable" or "hypothesis." Spirit sickness, yes; heart attacks, no. Westerners believe that high blood pressure is a silent killer; English is a language that insists on causation.

Jack wrote out an explanation and asked the director of the District Hospital, a respected Pohnpeian doctor, to broadcast it on the island radio. Translated into English, it read:

> The movement of blood through the body can be strong or weak. Strong movement taxes the heart and eventually causes sickness and death. This is happening increasingly in America and in countries where people's lives are like those of Americans. A physical examination can reveal the strong movement of blood in a person's body.
>
> The strong rather than the weak movement of the blood through the body can be caused by age, weight, diet, smoking, too much salt, lack of exercise, pregnancy, and some diseases. However, this important disease is also related to worries and feelings that people have about their responsibilities, opportunities, and the swift changes occurring in Pohnpei. Being overworked, burdened with heavy responsibilities, or simply worried is not enough to cause this strong movement of blood we call high blood pressure. All of these feelings occurred among your ancestors in Pohnpei without a rise in blood pressure or similar sicknesses.
>
> We conclude that not all Pohnpeians are prepared for the demands of a modern Micronesian nation, business, schools, economic and community development, and new social problems. This is why the first interview asks for your feelings about change: "Would you rather your children learn about the time-honored traditions of Pohnpei or learn modern customs brought by the Americans?" You will be asked about your feelings of belonging: "Who would you turn to in times of trouble? What type of organizations do you belong to?" Other feelings that you have are also important: "Do you mind having your work interrupted? Are you impatient about having to wait?"

The broadcast answered other questions: Who was sponsoring this research? Why were some people included and others not? Why were healthy and sick people included together? What were the benefits for Pohnpei and those who participated? Jack, Roger, and I began to visit officials in the traditional system of government and in the American administration; we enlisted the support of Peace Corps volunteers whom the islanders trusted, and we established a base of operation with the cooperative personnel at the island's rudimentary hospital.

Computers, copying machines, electric typewriters, and other staples of research were in North Carolina. For any practical purposes there was not a telegraph or telephone system, and few written records existed—no house or telephone directories, social security or precinct registrations, censuses, marriage licenses, birth certificates, land deeds, or other statistical documents for us to use. On the mountainous island, with a population estimated to be about 17,000, people often shifted residences and changed their names. The research team would have to conduct our own census of the areas we had selected for sampling and hope to find the 1,200 or 1,300 participants we needed.

Pohnpei is divided into five districts shaped like pieces of a pie. Cut up in this fashion, each district includes high mountains, forests, coastal plains, shorelines, and lagoons. The five districts, called Madolenihmw, U, Nett, Kitti, and Sokehs, have distinctive personalities. Each tells its own stories about wars, rebellions, boundary changes, unique events, and histories of succession to chiefly ranks. Each one has reasons to believe itself special and to compete with other districts. In the olden days, the men of the districts went to war against each other; since colonial occupation, however, competition centers on less bloody encounters.

Before we left the United States for Pohnpei, team members decided to concentrate on three areas of the island where we believed modernization and the stresses of change were having different health results. In an excess of optimism we labeled the town of Kolonia as our urban zone. With a shifting population of about 3,000, it was the epicenter of massive changes affecting Pohnpeian society, many of which the American administration had introduced. The second zone, in the district of U, was near enough to Kolonia for commuting to school or work, but far enough away to make traditional ways of living off the land possible. The third zone, the rural area of Wene in the district of Kitti, was on the opposite side of the island from Kolonia; we could reach it by boat in three to six hours, depending on the tides. The residents of Wene prided themselves on preserving classical tradition better than their friends and relatives in the other areas had. But the price of cultural preservation was economic isolation and little chance to earn money. We imagined that the residents of urbanizing Kolonia would feel the stresses of change and modernization more than people living closer to Pohnpei's past.

The first step was a census of households in the three areas. While we were doing that, we would also write and pretest a long questionnaire that asked about social, cultural, and psychological features related to blood pressure. While these questionnaires were being printed and sent from North Carolina, we planned to train interviewers to administer them. In the final stage, a medical team from New Zealand and Australia planned to give thorough physical examinations to the more than 1,200 Pohnpeians in the sample.

The results of the medical exams would be correlated with anthropological findings, census data, and questionnaires.

As a break from my awkward, tasteless cooking that first summer, the research team ate at Stewo's Restaurant, a gathering spot for Americans, Micronesians, and interesting visitors—a good place to meet and exchange gossip. The chief topic of conversation was economic development: How can islanders earn their living? Where is the money going to come from? Tied to finances, real and imagined, was the political future of the islands: What was going to happen with the negotiations with the United States government about the status of Micronesia?

I had sworn to avoid politics, either Micronesian or American—the lure of the Paramount Chiefs and their machinations to high office or the gossip about the U.S. politicians who controlled the destiny of Micronesia. The grant was paying me to research blood pressure while giving me time and resources to do my own investigations on language and social organization. When we asked about people's feelings and the pressures they felt, however, they wanted to talk about politics. Every conversation either centered on or returned again and again to political maneuvering.

The beginning of the 1970s was neither the time nor the place to be proud of being an American. The Vietnam War had tested my naive patriotism, and I left the United States a few days after the shooting deaths of students at Kent State University. A college professor, I had been embroiled in protests sweeping over American universities. Although I had looked forward to escaping from the political strife and materialism of my culture, it proved impossible to avoid the impact of U.S. foreign policy in Micronesia, the corrosive terms of trusteeship government, and my country's colonial control of such distant islands. Colonialism in Micronesia was benign—there were no beatings, political imprisonment, or violations of human rights. Yet when Pohnpeians questioned us about the United States' involvement in the Southeast Asian war and the implications of the negotiations with the United States over independence for Micronesia, I wanted to side with them.

In 1947, the United Nations had given political and military control of Micronesia (except for Guam, which the United States already possessed) to the United States and enjoined it to exercise all due speed in moving this protected area into independence or some form of self-government with cooperative ties to the United States. Until the late 1960s, however, the U.S. had ignored the far-flung islands under their control. But Micronesia's strategic position along the eastern arc of Asia and the war in Vietnam gave them new significance and ended two decades of neglect.

Budgets increased and money for jobs poured into the Trust Territory. The infusion of money in the absence of sensible development projects was beginning to create a systematic dependency upon U.S. money. To buy consumer goods in increasing amounts, Micronesians demanded more jobs—even if the jobs were only make-work. That meant that cash flow was not a product of economic development, but of colonialism. Among other problems, this caused a generation gap between older men raised in the Japanese system, which emphasized respect for elders and strict obedience, and the younger ones with dreams of cash and easy jobs.

Even with increased budgets and bureaucratic jobs, however, the basic tasks of colonial administration did not get done. The U.S. administration built little infrastructure of public services or economic development. No one collected trash or maintained the few sewer and water systems the Japanese had built. Except for a few Americans, no one I knew had a telephone or had ever completed a call on or off the island.

Gossip at Stewo's Restaurant often centered on the CIA, the U.S. Central Intelligence Agency and their agents operating in Micronesia, on Department of Defense operatives, on Americans posing as researchers, on officials bugging Micronesians' meetings, or on U.S. bureaucrats maneuvering to undermine the status talks. On occasion social science research has provided a convenient cover for spying or covert activities, and anthropologists at the time were going through a period of painful self-criticism and active disassociation with government agencies such as the CIA and the Department of Defense, whose policies were seen as injurious to the native peoples we studied and whose trust we tried to earn. Although islanders questioned everyone, Roger and I felt safe under the umbrella of Jack's reputation and our eccentric clothing. Spies were said to be single men, have short hair, and wear business suits—spies never studied the local language as we did.

Kolonia may have had foreign espionage agents, but it had nothing resembling a food market. Shopping for something to eat was a constant challenge, and learning the system absorbed much of my adjustment energy. A half-dozen small stores stocked very expensive imported goods. Next to the canned mackerel and corned beef, staples of our diet, were bolts of brightly colored Japanese cloth, hundred-pound sacks of rice, sugar, and flour, and imported canned soda pop. Only one store had refrigeration or freezer facilities. Another, owned by a family that came from Belgium in the early part of the century, carried such unpredictable treasures as genuine Scottish oatmeal and, once, a sheet of Formica. Ordinary objects—batteries, film, deodorant, razor blades—had to be ordered. Thanks to colonialism, however, Micronesia had a U.S. zip code, 96941, and sending away for what we needed was inexpensive.

If there was any organizing principle for the arrival of ships from Japan, Australia, the United States, or European countries or for the cargoes they carried, I never discovered it. Beer and soft drinks flowed off the ships, but toilet paper was irregular. One ship brought only ketchup. When I saw canned tomato sauce, I bought it; three weeks later, another ship might bring noodles. If hamburger meat came in, spaghetti was possible. If not, I substituted canned corned beef.

Fresh produce should have been easily available in this lush tropical environment where plants grow easily. But the distribution and marketing system was full of kinks. No one could predict what would be available at the small produce market from hour to hour. Sometimes I found fresh fish in the late afternoon at the dock where the boats tied up; other times no one went fishing or had done so early in the morning and sold their catch by nine o'clock. Although Japanese and U.S. fishing fleets caught hundreds of tons of fish only miles from the island, the fish was processed thousands of miles away and reached Pohnpei in expensive cans. No one was in danger of going hungry, but Pohnpeians, like anyone else, had developed food preferences. They liked the ease and status of canned food. Amid the bounty of the ocean, they chose canned mackerel. From the Japanese, they had acquired a love of white rice, and from the Americans, sugar, salt, and white processed flour.

I haunted the public market for my favorite island food—breadfruit. The tree on which this treasure grows is botanically related to fig and mulberry. Broad, deep green, and serrated leaves filter sunlight against trunk and branches, reminiscent of temperate-zone oaks. Children climb the trees and gather the beach-ball-shaped fruit. Beneath the rough green peel is a hard, ivory center; cooked breadfruit is one of the world's most nourishing and tasty carbohydrate foods. I have eaten it boiled, baked, fried, dried in strips as candy, preserved in pits, and fermented. If allowed to ripen until soft and then baked, it tastes like the ultimate Fig Newton. Little wonder Pohnpeians call it "fruit in the hands of the gods." It was difficult to appreciate rice and canned mackerel when breadfruit was in season.

Just as I was learning how to cook and keep house in a strange culture, another member of our team arrived. Floyd, the team's psychologist, took one look at Jack's dump, pronounced it a slum dwelling, and refused to set foot, much less sleep, on its floor. Declaring Jack's happy domesticity in the face of deplorable housing conditions to be simple madness, he moved in with Roger and me.

Assigned to the project for his special abilities in writing a questionnaire that would tap the social and psychological dimensions relating to high or low blood pressure, Floyd was a good husband, a good father, a good Christian, a good citizen of the United States, a good teacher, a good psychologist, and a bad person to watch going through culture shock. He had an absolutist view of culture. Some things are right; some things are wrong; Floyd was willing to explain the absolute differences to us at each meal.

Cultural influences, belief systems, and customs might be interesting, he conceded, but they did not explain why people behaved in a certain way. Human behavior can be understood by looking at individuals' feelings and opinions. Floyd possessed the naive belief that our common humanity made everyone on the planet predictable. Therefore, he was able to apply the concepts of Western psychological sciences to anyone anywhere. He also believed in world-wide natural laws.

The main part of his laws was that women "naturally" waited on men. The first week Floyd lived with us included many adjustments and, without much thought, I acted as hostess and provided some of the same domestic services my husband took for granted. I got breakfast, straightened up the house, cooked, and made daily rounds of small stores. Jack, who had strong domestic skills and a wife who was a professional anthropologist, also helped, even though he did not live with us. But a week after his arrival, Floyd brought me his laundry and asked when it would be finished. Although there was a washing machine in the Peace Corps house, it was broken, and I had been washing my personal things by hand. Without thinking, I fixed the machine and did the men's laundry. Such is the force of natural law.

I am ashamed to admit that I might have continued to wait on him, but his dependency interfered with my work. It was the little assumptions and the small tasks that ate into my time and energy: coffee, toast, and constant patronage. He could not apologize for the messes he made because he just "naturally" made them, and could not be expected to cook because only wives knew how. Despite the equivalence of our degrees and titles, he refused to accept me as a partner in research and communicated with me only about what was to him my real work—taking care of men.

One night at supper, in discussing a party for key Americans in Kolonia, it became obvious that I was going to do the work and he was going to receive the credit. In my first act of feminist rebellion, I wrote down the jobs connected to domestic management as well as to the party. After each job, I wrote one of our names. Then, as anger welled inside me, I posted the duty roster on the termite-ridden wall. Jack was accustomed to the same system of shared duties in his household, and Roger had borne his own share of our guest's demands. Floyd was aghast—first, he fumed and reasoned, then he resorted to natural law: I am a professional, sent to do an important job, my wife treats me with proper respect, and so forth. He tried unsuccessfully to convince Roger to bring his wife in line.

Our conflicts about gender, professionalism, and the division of labor were quite apart from Floyd's misgivings about anthropologists and the concept of cultural relativism we practiced. Pohnpeian religion struck at the heart of his absolutist moral code. Floyd believed, for example, that the disciples of Jesus truly had seen their teacher returned from the dead, but that Micronesians who claimed to have witnessed ghosts on the path or to have spoken with spirits of departed relatives and ancestors had only superstitions and a strong delusional structure. More to the point, the questionnaire we were writing together included an important section on clan membership. Everyone on Pohnpei, as in many traditional societies, is conscious of clan membership. It steers marriage choices, since marrying someone of the same clan is incest. Titles and social status are handed down through the clans; being born into or marrying into a prestigious clan is a pathway of social advancement.

In common with kinship systems in many world societies, Pohnpeian clans are matrilineal. That means clan membership is reckoned through the female line. All Pohnpeians, male and female, acquire their clan status from their mother who got it from her mother and so on back to a mythical ancestress. This means that men cannot pass on clan membership to their sons or daughters, but everyone shares a common clan with their mother's brother.

Floyd was horrified—such severe social deviance was not possible, he insisted. But he had heard "matriarchal," not "matrilineal"; he thought we had said women were in control, the dominant sex—a clear violation of natural law. He had never once questioned the Western practice of wives and children taking on their husband's and father's name and status, and he was appalled when I pointed out how reasonable a custom matrilineal descent is in light of the fact that people can always be certain who their mother is but are never certain about their father's identity. Furthermore, in matrilineal societies, children automatically take their mother's name and inherit from them, so illegitimacy as Westerners understand it does not occur. I am not sure we convinced Floyd that just as people choose to trace descent through the father's line, they can equally choose to trace it through their mother's line. But I did succeed in keeping clan membership in the questionnaire.

The grant-writers who designed the research and calculated a budget assumed, as I did, that we could hire bilingual young men as interviewers, the local equivalent of American college students who work for minimum wages and the opportunity to get experience. The first people Roger and I hired, however, were disasters. One ran off with the typewriter. Another giggled and stared at his toes when we mentioned the questionnaire. A third had desires for status and money, which surpassed his abilities. None had what Americans or Pohnpeians consider good work habits.

As I was to discover, males in Pohnpei stay youths and are not accorded adult status until they reach their forties and earn the high titles by which respect is measured. Paralyzed by lack of standing in a society that values the wisdom of age, youngsters with no titles cannot ask personal questions of high-ranking or older people. Nor would anyone with more years or status listen when a youngster spoke in public; a job was not important if callow youths were sent to do it. Where were we going to find interviewers?

One evening after Floyd's merciful departure, a visitor arrived at the end of a well-cooked, therefore rare, dinner of sweet and sour pork. Dressed in dark trousers, a short-sleeved white shirt, and navy blue baseball cap, he spoke at length with Jack, a conversation I intuited in tiny random chunks. Jack decided to check out some notebooks this man had written; a few adult men on the island were known to keep diaries, records, or written accounts. Since little of Pohnpeian life has been written down and men were so reticent about sharing certain kinds of information, Jack always watched for these kinds of documents. These notebooks, however, proved to be of less value than the man's literacy; he knew one of the conflicting orthographies—alphabets or scripts—for writing Pohnpeian.

Sohn Alpet—John Albert in English—was in his middle sixties and held a socially prominent or high title in the district of Madolenihmw. He also spoke and wrote Japanese, whose army had conscripted and sent him to fight in New Guinea during World War II. Of his group of conscripts, he was the only one to return and was, therefore, a war hero on Pohnpei. Jack was impressed with Sohn Alpet and urged us to hire him. I was hesitant. The man spoke no English and, as far as I could tell, knew nothing about the conduct of social science research. He had never worked with Americans, been to regular school, or held a regular job. Roger and I continued to look for our ideal college student—Jack eased the older man into the job.

Sohn Alpet took his tasks seriously. He started to carry a black plastic briefcase and within two weeks showed up for work with his own assistant. From within his kinship network he hired an obedient youth, Roswel, whom he intended to use as interpreter and secretary until Roger and I developed better language skills. In an unorthodox but successful solution, Sohn Alpet supervised his assistant and we paid him.

Imagine learning a language without the help of dictionaries, grammar books, classes, or teachers, in full sight of your fluent major professor. Roger and I had a mimeographed introduction to Pohnpeian, which the Peace Corps had produced for their first cohort of volunteers. To start, we learned a few fixed phrases:

> Hello, goodbye
> Yes, no, right, wrong, excuse me
> Thank you, please
> My name is _____. What is your name?
> What is this called in Pohnpeian? How do you say this?
> Where is _____?

Then we collected nouns. "What is the name for this?" Body parts; objects in nature such as trees, flowers, sun, moon, and stars; names of buildings; terms for relatives; types of machines; doors and roof; roads, rocks, and fish. With a growing number of nouns, adjectives were added: colors, quantities (how many), qualities (good, bad, big, little), and descriptions. Soon it was possible to make short sentences based on simple patterns:

> the fish, the red fish
> the small red fish, two small red fishes
> The fish is red. The fish is small.
> Here is the fish. There is the fish. Where is the fish?
> The fish is not red. This is not a fish.

Substitute other nouns, numbers, colors, or qualities and the number of sentences that can be produced increases exponentially.

The sound of Pohnpeian that gives English speakers trouble is a consonant, "t," for which there is no English equivalent. For us, the resulting sound is more like a "ch." In English there is a nasal sound at the end of words like sing or ring. Pohnpeians have the same sound, but use it at the beginning of words. Dogs bark—*ngong*, bite—*ngalis*, and cast shadows—*ngehn*. At first it was difficult to hear words with long and short vowel sounds—*ma* means "if" and *mah* means "old," "aged," or "ripe"; the *h* is a writing symbol signifying that in speech the vowel is held longer, like maa. *Man* is an intransitive verb meaning "to take hold or be effective." *Mahn*, with a slightly longer vowel, is an animal or insect.

Sometimes scholars claim that the deepest meanings a culture holds about itself are imbedded in the structure of its language. For example, English emphasizes time—past, present, future, and subtle permutations of each. Its precision about tenses is said to contribute to the scientific mentality that marks English-speaking culture. If this theory is correct, then pronouns reveal important properties of Pohnpeian worldview.

English speakers say "they" meaning any group of two or more that does not include the speaker. Pohnpeians say one "they" for a general group of three or more, and have another "they" for just two things or people. The same is true for "you": there is "you" [singular], "you all" [plural], and "the two of you" or "you two" [the dual]. English speakers just say, "We are going swimming." Pohnpeian speakers say, "We [all of us including you] are going swimming." Or, "We [exclusive of the persons being addressed, that is, not including you] are going swimming." Or, "We [just the two of us] are going swimming." "Our boat" is a bit vague in English because the person we are speaking to may not be a partner in the boat. In Pohnpeian, "our boat" has two forms, one if everybody owns the boat and one for speaking to others about a boat in which they do not share ownership.

Pronouns of ownership—"my, our, your, his, their"—depend on the noun being possessed. Personal things such as clothes, parents, or spouses belong in one category. A second group takes in plants, animals, children, and small objects. But if you discuss something to eat, you use another set of possessive pronouns, and still another for something to drink. Forms of transportation, such as scooters, cars, canoes, or boats, require their special forms. "My brothers and sisters" or "his sacred objects" have special categories. Why in a culture in which cooperation and sharing are so emphasized would there be two dozen ways of showing possession? Or perhaps a better question, what impulses cause humans to use language to divide up the real world into such arbitrary categories?

I may have made this business of learning another language sound easy. It was not. I cannot omit the frustration of early stages when even dogs understood more than I did, and three-year-olds did better on simple sentences than I did. The subtleties and innuendo I wanted to express—and was able to in English—had become impossible. For months, whenever I carried on a conversation in Pohnpeian, the sweat of hard, dirty work soaked my clothes and ran down my face.

Nonetheless, I will never forget the elation of deciphering and using relative clauses or personal pronouns. Nor will I forget the agony of stepping on a woman's toes. Instead of asking forgiveness, I blurted out, "His canoe is blue."

To celebrate our progress in setting up the research project, learning the language, and making our first adjustments, Jack took us on a holiday trip to Nan Madol, the largest archaeological site in the Pacific Ocean. In the shallow lagoon between the island of Temwen and the fringing reef, the ancestors of the Pohnpeians had, more than a thousand years before, built a walled city of canals, a tropical Venice, covering nine square miles. They stacked multiton polygonal basaltic crystals that look like Lincoln Logs into more than one hundred artificial islands, citadels, shrines, or fortresses, some twenty feet high.

What inspired ancient Pohnpeians to labor so long and hard to build temple complexes through which only water traffic may pass? It is hard to believe that such regular forms occur in nature and harder to understand how people moved so many tons of stone from quarries high in the mountains to the lagoon floor—yet they did. Islanders had to abandon ceremonial use of the site in the nineteenth century when as many as half of the population died in a smallpox epidemic. But the remains, the most awe-inspiring ruins in the island Pacific, continue to hold their cultural memories. The contrast of this gracious planned city to the randomness and dirt of Kolonia stunned me.

A letter from the field:

Dearest Ones,

It is hot, hot, hot. We are sweltering. I feel mildewed all over. Yesterday, as on most days, it rained. The leather stuff we brought has begun to rot, and there is a thickening layer of green goo over sandals, belts, camera case, and so forth. The aspirin tablets have disintegrated into a fine powder.

Everyone wears those rubber thongs you use for beach or showers at home. They are called *zories* because the Japanese introduced them. Also, the Japanese custom of removing your shoes before entering any house is followed here. You don't have to leave your zories outside churches, the hospital, government offices, or stores. But private residences have a stack outside, and it is just good manners to take yours off. I laugh about those signs in the USA against barefooted or bare-chested hippies.

Roger and I love our new Suzuki 70 motor scooter. For various reasons, the grant can't buy a Jeep or a boat. The motor scooter is much more practical. The 30-mile-per-hour speed limit on Main Street is just a dare. Only a foolish person would try to drive that fast. Some of the roads are so rocky and full of potholes from incessant rains that we have to push the bike. Did you know that you can ride a motor scooter and carry an umbrella at the same time?

Last weekend we hiked up into the mountains of the district of Nett. We saw the ruins of the Japanese-built hydroelectric generating plant (sure beats the kerosene-fueled monster that provides intermittent electricity for Kolonia). Our destination was several lovely waterfalls at about 2,000 feet. Here the tropical rain forest vegetation is even more extraordinary than along the shore. Many trees and rocks were covered with a cushion of green moss. Kolonia seemed cool and sophisticated when we returned.

Jack's daughter, Mary Ann, born here when he was District Anthropologist in the 1950s, has just joined us. She has adjusted to the trash heap he lives in, although her slumber has been interrupted by peeping Toms, young boys who spy at the windows. One of her peepers was a kid from the jail; security is lax, to say the least, and boys from there wander around at night. Jack reported this petty crime, but no one seems concerned. When she and I went up to the police station yesterday to register the motor scooter, we heard giggling and shuffling. Looking down through the wide cracks in the floor of the veranda, we saw a group of teenage boys peering up at us. American women are objects of great curiosity. Jack says that I should ignore the stares and ride the motor scooter astride rather than sidesaddle. He laughed and said that if we are seen together on the motor scooter, people will think we are having an affair.

Working with Jack is a constant delight. It will be very difficult to follow in his footsteps. At a meeting with the hospital staff last week, he gave a long lecture on blood pressure and heart disease in Pohnpeian and only needed to ask for the Pohnpeian word for "kidney." All the senior people know and respect him. Jack is the official fresh-food purchaser for our little group, a task he takes very seriously. Yesterday he returned with mangos, papayas, and a pineapple. He sniffed each carefully and laid them out on the windowsill. Then he announced that the mango would be ripe in time for supper, but that the papayas would be at their peak about 3:00 in the morning.

Mother, your lessons in baking did not cover a lemon cake mix with a coupon on the back that said you must redeem it before March 30, 1959. The cake mix was a strange gray color and I had to beat it with a hammer before I could add the eggs. Incidentally, eggs are scarce, and I got two only by following some chickens. It was Jack's birthday, and the cake was widely judged a success.

We eat out at least once a day. Organizing cooking while learning all these new foods and customs is too difficult to do three times a day. Anyway, it is a chance to meet people and to try new foods. I love the raw tuna fish with hot horseradish sauce and the bland local foods, such as breadfruit, taro, yams, and bananas of many varieties.

For amusement, we went to the movies the other night. You have to be a desperate moviegoer like Roger to appreciate the *Sports Highlights of 1949* and *Jason and the Argonauts*. We sat on backless wooden benches while the rain beat heavily on the old tin roof and kids and babies took over the floor. Usually the projector, the only one on the island, fails to perform or provides only the sound, only the picture, or bits of each. But it costs only a quarter, and the enthusiastic response and audience participation makes it all the more enjoyable.

Yes, you can send us something. How about 10 plastic coat hangers (the wire ones rust over everything) and an egg carton (one of those cardboard ones your eggs come in from the store). I can't buy a dozen eggs until I have something to carry them in on the motor scooter. Also, some germicidal soap like Phisohex because a bite or blister can so quickly become infected here, and Americans have horrible tropical ulcers when they don't take care of their skin. Thank you for all the stuff you sent last week.

Kaselehlie. That means goodbye—and hello—in Pohnpeian.

Chapter 2

Green Leaves on Stories

Kava here is what the cross is to Christians; it fell from heaven and is the only means of communication with their spirits; they hold a cup of this drink, always in their hands, when addressing the object of prayer.

—The missionary Sturgis, 1856

*S*unrise was spectacular the morning our trip began; the air was filled with sounds and smells unique to an island dawn. Jack had made arrangements to visit the remote community of Wene in the district of Kitti. The design of the project called for 300 people from this community on the opposite end of the island from Kolonia to represent the rural component. Ian Prior, a cardiologist from New Zealand and head of the medical team scheduled to arrive the following summer, had just landed in Pohnpei and wanted to survey local conditions. Ian was a phenomenon, a whirlwind; we suspended other work during his stay. Without speaking a word of their language, he coopted the attention of the four Pohnpeians who accompanied us: Sohn Alpet, his son-in-law, Pedro Kihleng, and two health aides the hospital had assigned to the project.

There were no roads in the heavily forested and mountainous regions outside Kolonia and walking that far and back would take days. So Jack rented an open whale boat, a type that has replaced the single outrigger canoes of olden days. Nineteenth-century whalers brought the design from New England, and skilled boat builders of Micronesia duplicated the sturdy, wide-bellied craft that could carry eight to ten people on routine trips. Two men navigated, one in the back with the outboard motor and one in front with a pole or oars to guide the boat over shallow reefs and through the circuitous channels.

The eight of us boated into the Kolonia harbor, past the derelict, rusty landing craft abandoned by the American Navy at the end of World War II.

21

At each harbor marker in the lagoon, I turned around to look at Pohnpei from the water. Clouds hung over central peaks rising almost 3,000 feet above sea level, and tropical vegetation appeared denser from this viewpoint than it did on land. The salty smell and the sounds of gulls and terns celebrated in sea songs and poems thrilled my land senses. Every vista looked like *National Geographic*.

As the ship channeled through coral, I put on a hat, long-sleeved shirt, and sun screen. Direct rays of the sun only a few degrees north of the equator burned with a vengeance, even as they illuminated the exotic coral formations waving only a few feet below the surface of the turquoise water. We approached the fringing reef that protects the island and the lagoon from the ocean's relentless moods. A ship, wrecked in a storm and impaled on the coral, inspired thoughts of novels about the sea I have loved. Romantic thoughts occupied me as the boat driver sped through the turbulent transitional zone between lagoon and open sea and into the deeper hues and broad swells of the Pacific. From this distance, no signs of human occupation on Pohnpei were visible.

Under normal conditions I hate even to think about riding in a tiny boat on a vast ocean. But I was captive that morning to stories of the navigational genius of Polynesians and Micronesians; I believed myself safely in the hands of descendants of the "Vikings of the sunrise." In the greatest seafaring achievements of all time, the argonauts of the western Pacific settled the far archipelagoes on the world's largest ocean while my European ancestors were still clinging to the shores of the Mediterranean in leaky boats. Micronesian navigators sailed by the stars and the subtle rhythm of currents as they broke against the hull of their canoes. Through accidental and planned voyaging, their ancestors had colonized the habitable islands of the Pacific thousands of years before the first European arrived. Adapted to a seagoing life, their sturdy canoes carried families, pigs, chickens, dogs, seeds, and plantings for pioneering new lands. Voyaging on the ocean was their inheritance. I felt safe.

Ian, serious about blood pressure, produced his portable cuff and took readings.

"Amazing," he said to me, "you have the lowest pressure and pulse on the boat. Aren't you nervous or excited at all?"

"Why should I be?" I explained my historic sense of security with the Vikings of the Pacific.

Through Jack's tactful translations of the conversation that followed, I began to intuit the purpose of an extra outboard motor, cans of gasoline, bottled water, and food supplies on the floor of the boat.

"I never go outside the reef in a boat unless I have no other choice," revealed Sohn Alpet as he clutched his seat. "It is too dangerous. We have planned for emergencies, but you can never tell. I leave travel on the ocean to out-islanders who understand it."

Pohnpeian fear of open ocean was as great as mine! True, they had many legends about fleets of ocean-going canoes venturing to and from the islands.

But that ancient knowledge had since been lost. Contemporary Pohnpeians are landlubbers who use the lagoon only when necessary. They take pride in farming skills and the fertility of land, and they depend on people who came from atolls to preserve and practice seafaring habits. We took the boat into the ocean because lagoon passage to our destination would have been impossible to navigate at low tide. Sailing beyond the reef and back into the lagoon shortened our trip. I dropped my fantasy life, vowed never to enter the open ocean again, and prayed to the gods who protect naive anthropologists. Ian reported that my pulse rate was climbing.

Grateful to be on rocky ground, I hiked mountain paths with the men as Jack paid ceremonial visits, scouted areas for our research, and sought out old friends. Wene had no village center, no central public area. Homesteads, churches, the dispensary, docks, stores, and feast houses were scattered throughout the tropical forest with, to me, only random and winding paths to connect them. We often stopped to ask for green coconuts—a more thirst-quenching beverage than the soft drinks and sugar water islanders prefer. Standards of Pohnpeian hospitality are high, and they honor the requests of strangers. As we walked, our guides pointed out specific locations and explained various plants. I only saw green jungle, wild and uninhabited but for the occasional oasis of a homestead and surrounding clearing. Because of terrain or the force of tradition, Pohnpeians do not build what Westerners think of as communities. The farms of which Pohnpeians are justifiably proud were not visible to my Western eye—no plowed fields, no fenced gardens, no rows of crops. Coconut palms looked as though they grew wild; each one, however, had an owner whose rights to its produce others respected.

On Pohnpei, every place has a name, an owner, and traditional stories about its special spirits or genealogical history. Pohnpeian eyes see gardens, boundaries, and a complex system of land tenure where I see only jungle. As Pohnpeians talked to me, I began to feel a growing pressure to understand and master these place names. The stories and legends I heard were less the tales of human passions I yearned for than lists of place names. When legendary lovers succumb to passion, the storyteller names the place.

"The hero came from this place and went to that place and there in that place met another person who came from such-and-such a place. Together they go off to a series of different places." Each place is fully described.

The first grammar lesson I learned was locatives—words and word endings that told where we were going, where we had been, and whether the directions were up or down, over or under. As we walked, Sohn Alpet commented, "Now we are leaving X and entering Y." But how could he tell, and how could he expect me to remember when landmarks were as absent as on the ocean? A casual assortment of rocks along the shore had significance—a marker or code for a historical event that explains why people are the way they are and why their relationships must be conducted in certain ways. Pohnpeians are enmeshed in a web of kinship, titles, obligations, social relationships, and stories that ground them to place.

My tendency was to describe a place as down the path from that church, not far from this house, or over the next hill where the big rocks are. But all places, however bereft of identifying characteristics to me, have a name. As a lay minister explained, "What was the first job that God instructed Adam to do? Name everything!" When I protested that God meant for Adam to name animate objects, such as plants and animals, my instructor told me to reread the Genesis account and report back when I acquired greater wisdom. He told me that a baby adopted from another clan can be made part of the adopter's clan by feeding it breadfruit from the adopter's land. So, people are in places, but places are also in people. Each must be named.

For Pohnpeians, places have personalities and spiritual characteristics just as Westerners believe people do. At one lovely high mountain pool below a waterfall, Sohn Alpet pointed to eels swimming there and recounted the founding myth of Lasialap, the Great Eel Clan, which he had inherited from his mother. The story cycle of the clan's beginning tells of the adventures of a generation of eels that gives birth to the female ancestors of the clan through magical means. Since land-faring and lagoon-going eels traveled to and from many places, I suspected the full story would take days to tell. Because of the heroism and sacrifice of eels, members of the Lasialap clan are prohibited from eating the sacred creature. Breaking the taboo against eating the clan totem can bring down the punishment of the spirit world; Jack believed that guilt over breaking such a taboo could induce a psychosomatic allergy or illness.

Our time in Wene gave no hint of the problems we were to encounter later. We stayed in the house of a prominent citizen, the health aide at the dispensary. Dr. Franko's house had an elaborate water catchment system for cold showers, and reminded me of Hansel and Gretel's, a lone dwelling in a primordial forest. "Be careful," my host warned as I rose with the 5:30 dawn to take a walk before breakfast. "Ghosts may be on the path. Watch for a woman who carries a basket of breadfruit on her left arm. You may look at her but do not speak. If you talk to her, she will have the power to take you away to the underworld where spirits live." To my disappointment, she never appeared and I wondered if local spirits avoid foreigners.

Some places are so wondrous, some events are so difficult to explain, some happenings are so magical—how can we understand what we cannot see? Sometimes people fall ill for no apparent reason. On Pohnpei there are spirits of the dead, clan spirits, spirits of particular places, spirits who hang around, and spirits who are arranged in a systematic hierarchy just as people are. Magical incantations honor and control them; to make kava grow, insure a good catch in the fishing nets, make rain, and stop rain require a blessing. Some practices are aimed at placating the spirit of deceased relatives. Others are love magic for successful amorous adventures. Spells protect people, houses, crops, canoes, or dangerous ventures against natural or supernatural diseases and disasters. When relatives leave and return from a trip, they are anointed with oil. The ceremony looks like an ordinary welcome-home party or prelude to a feast, but it is a cleansing ritual to rid travelers of foreign spirits.

Many spirits are local—they live in specially named places. Others like the mangrove demon have a more extensive realm. Tiny trolls live in the high grasses of the rain forest. Because they come from wild, unsettled places outside the boundaries of daily life, spirits help people define themselves as cultured, civilized, or ordinary. Place names tame the wildness, explain spirit interventions, and bring order to green chaos. The spiritual universes of Pohnpei exist beside the expansion of Christianity and have accommodated to, not receded from, the presence of Western religion. The God of Thunder still speaks with a mighty voice and brings good fortune to those who respect him, and mangrove demons still cause illness and death if crossed.

Human beings with their dogs and sneaky rats were the first land mammals. Nothing that is dangerous inhabits the island—no snakes or deadly insects. Some fish are poisonous; a few types of plants are said to be dangerous if prepared by a sorcerer. Repulsive creatures, however, have established a foothold. Japanese farmers introduced giant African snails after World War I as a possible food source. Pohnpeians refused to eat them, and the snails multiplied in an ecology that had no natural predators to hold them in check. The Japanese colonial administration organized school children to collect and destroy them and brought in a predator in hope of retarding their advance. The aggressive horned toads, however, soon discovered a more appetizing source of nourishment. Instead of eating snails, toads dine well on mounds of pig dung that litter paths. Although I carried a flashlight at night, stepping on toads was unavoidable. The combination of spiky toads and squishy pig dung underfoot was not fatal or painful; it was revolting.

On the first visit to Wene, with little spoken Pohnpeian at my command, I learned to listen better. Despite Ian's public health protests about dread diseases kava drinking might cause—he was up to number eleven by then—I discovered that nightly gatherings provided the best opportunity to practice speaking. In the relaxed atmosphere of pounding kava, we met people, talked about the project, and spoke the language with less strain.

Sohn Alpet had a talent for phrasing simple sentences appropriate to my language skills; he offered spontaneous stories during the evening sessions, though he warned me that not everyone told stories in the correct manner. He insisted that any storyteller—himself included—embellished stories much as yams and other foods are decorated with leaves to make them look better. A proper oft-told tale, however, is better for the flourishes of greenery. One evening he recounted the age-old story of the origin of kava:

> Islanders noticed that when rats ate from the base of a certain plant, they could no longer run about but would stagger to sugar cane, eat some, and fall asleep. People tried some of this plant and grew light-headed; they liked the sweet sugar cane as well. Then two women from Heaven spied on the people of the Land and decided to try some too, so they stole a cutting and gave it to the Lords of the Eel, who planted it in the garden plot of Heaven. They harvested it, but as they prepared it, a piece of the root bounced out and fell onto the island where it multiplied.

With the first sip of kava, the lips and tongue grow numb. Speech is slowed, but the head remains clear. Although heavy consumption may result in some weakness or loss of control in the legs, the drink is not hallucinogenic, nor do drinkers become drunk as with alcohol. The main effect is serenity and peacefulness. People say, "You cannot drink kava and stay angry." When people are mad at each other, even when murder, adultery, or other serious offenses have been committed, they will drink kava together at special feasts of apology or propitiation. Because kava symbolizes public forgiveness and the granting of pardons, no one who drinks can take revenge. Early Christian missionaries tried to stamp out the practice; so Protestant elders like Sohn Alpet grow kava, prepare it as a sacrament for others, but will not drink it. Sohn Alpet affirmed the spiritual value of kava to me each time he encouraged me to drink, although he had taken an oath of abstinence himself.

The kava ritual is hypnotic. One need not partake to appreciate its beauty. The stones on which the roots of fresh kava plants are pounded are three to four feet in diameter and resound with a clear bell sound when struck. At formal feasts, ancient rhythms mark special parts of the ceremony. When kava is made in homesteads on ordinary evenings, sounds of pounding carry through the air, inviting any within hearing distance to participate. The gestures of men who pound, squeeze, and serve are deliberate with the accumulated custom of centuries. The rituals of presenting kava to guests in coconut-shell cups follows the etiquette and traditions of respect, even in simple households. Women nurse children who fall asleep by the light of kerosene lanterns and the sounds of sharing. Others bring bits of food and stay to talk, snacking on popcorn, fruit, sugar cane, candy, or little snacks through the evening as the quietness of kava takes over.

Because kava induces heavy salivation and because spitting is an art form, many drinkers spit between the cracks in the floorboards or over the sides of the feast houses. After several slippery episodes I learned to stash my zories safely out of range.

One day the research team received an invitation to a household in the hills. The owner excavated a rock-lined pit about five feet deep and six feet in diameter that contained aged breadfruit. He had wrapped breadfruit in leaves years before and left it in the pit to ferment. Like the casks of good bourbon, the age of the pit dated from the oldest portion, and keeping a pit going through several generations was a way to acquire status. Preserved breadfruit was famine food in the past. Jack lectured us on the history of this custom; Sohn Alpet added comments on the proper manners for presenting it at feasts. Ian speculated on the public health implications and vitamin content. I ate some. Preserved breadfruit tastes like exotic, very ripe cheese and will never replace Hershey bars.

Ian's charisma and Jack's stature among the islanders put our research project on firm ground. With the trip to Wene, we laid the groundwork taking a census, administering the sociological-psychological interviews, and assisting the visit of the medical team—all to be spaced across the year to follow.

Meanwhile, Roger and I needed to move. The relatively luxurious living in the Peace Corps house in Kolonia ended as Floyd left and Ian's visit was complete. Sohn Alpet arranged for us to move in with one of his daughters, Kioko Kihleng, and her husband, Pedro. The house was a new, four-room cinder block, tin-roofed, slab construction that bureaucrats in Washington had designed to be suitable for the tropics; they are, however, hotter, dirtier, and less attractive than raised, thatched, and open stilt houses built of native woods.

The temporary living arrangement was a valuable opportunity to live in the Pohnpeian style and to work on our language development. In the house, set close to other houses of similar construction, lived Kioko, Pedro, their ten children and a Peace Corps volunteer, Mike. Mike had been moved out of his room on our behalf, acknowledgment of the family's acceptance of him, and, Roger and I imagined, covert permission to court one of their beautiful daughters. Family members came into Kolonia and stayed with Kioko and Pedro for periods of days, weeks, or months; they took some of the ten children to their home district when they left. Despite the nuclear-family appearance of cinder-block houses, the cooking areas, feast houses, outhouses, and other shared facilities for sleeping and eating were based on older, extended-family patterns.

We washed from a rain barrel next to the house or from a community spigot across the muddy path and used the communal latrines or "little houses." During the day, women gathered around a spring emerging from the rocky hillside to wash clothes, children, dishes, and themselves. Men usually went after dark for greater privacy. We ate a Pohnpeian breakfast—a few bites of cold leftovers or ship biscuits (unsalted, unleavened hard crackers that originated as a staple on sailing ships), and bananas—fat, short, sweet, tart, red, orange, and other varieties, all tasty and filling. Lunch was canned mackerel and rice. I had dietary difficulty with the high-prestige drink made from equal amounts of water, sugar, and food coloring. Finally, in desperation, I announced that I was getting "sugar sickness" or diabetes.

Roger and I carried on simple conversations with women working in the open cooking houses, island substitutes for porches. We needed to practice speaking; they were filled with curious questions.

"Who is watching your children while you are here?"

"Roger and I don't have any children yet."

"But you said that you were married in church. Why would you want to get married in church if you don't have any children?

"It is the custom of our religion to get married first and then have children."

"It is better to wait until you have children before you get married."

I was uncomfortable justifying customs I followed but did not always accept, or customs I accepted but did not observe.

"Who is watching your pigs while you are here?"

"I don't have any pigs."

Childless, I was a target for sympathy and help, but pigless and landless, I was not a proper adult. They kept repeating the question until I gave them a satisfactory answer.

"Who is watching your pigs and land while you are here?"

"My mother [may she forgive me] is watching my pigs."

"Good, they are reproducing, and so you will have more of them when you return."

My companions of the cookhouses were no more attuned to cultural relativism or any less ethnocentric than Floyd had been. Although being an inkblot for Floyd's misconceptions about anthropology was aggravating, being an inkblot for Pohnpeians was data, information, and a way to do fieldwork. Nor could I maintain my notions of privacy when I wanted to ask them the same kinds of questions they asked me.

The conversations about having children grew more pointed. Concern for our childlessness increased among men and women.

"You should adopt a baby like other Americans who can't seem to have children. We will help you find one. What kind do you want? A boy? A girl? Newborn, toddler, teenager?"

Their repeated offer was serious. Pohnpeians adopt each other's children or give children for adoption to foreigners with a generous spirit.

Women regularly offered me magical spells or chants believed to enhance fertility. They said people in olden times knew spells for making babies and for preventing them, and then quickly added, "Of course, we ourselves are Christians now, and we don't use spells anymore. But we know some people who use them." Women without children wanted them; women with too many children asked me about birth control. Everyone, male and female, agreed that we needed children. I could feel the pressure building, "Babies are life's greatest blessing. We are going to have to help you. Don't you know that the ropes of marriage can part, but the ropes that bind children to parents are forever?"

Pohnpeians, like many other peoples in the world, regard sex with more fun and less seriousness than most Westerners do. The openness about sex in this island society reminded me of Margaret Mead's famous book, *Coming of Age in Samoa*. But Samoans have not been happy with what Mead wrote about them, and an occasional anthropologist thinks she misinterpreted the culture. Not all anthropologists on Samoa have collected the same information or reached the same conclusions about sexual life that she did. Each anthropologist who has worked on Pohnpei has a different feel for the island. Some have far more lurid details than I to report; others choose to emphasize the Pohnpeians' public view of themselves as modest, discrete, and rule abiding. Pohnpeians are aware that Japanese, Americans, and the church officials with whom they have lived for many years have different standards for sex and family life. In public, some insist that things have changed and that Pohnpeians are now abiding by the rules imposed by foreign influences. In private, however, they laugh, joke, and gossip about sex. In private, I think they are having ribald, exuberant, enthusiastic, playful sex lives. Learning about the clan system or the title system requires long extensive interviewing and cross-checking as anthropological research techniques. Learning about family life started the first time my childlessness was a topic for speculation; learning about sex started the second night I heard the peepers.

The crunch of footsteps outside the window after midnight and a loose giggle in the dark signaled their presence. When I asked questions around the neighborhood, I learned the curious young boys posed no danger. Although their nocturnal activities were not officially approved, they were tolerated. Pohnpeian has a word that translates as "night-crawling" or "walking about at night." A young man must brave a girl's sleeping household to rendezvous with her. Sometimes, they have made arrangements to meet in this romantic fashion. At other times, the boy has heard about her charms but has no way to make her acquaintance. A boy who succeeds at night-crawling will be admired. Young men brag to each other of their intimate conquests as they plan the next one and compare strategies. Although trysts are supposed to be secret, calculated revelation and controlled gossip adds spice. Young women want to be courted, want romance and suitors, yet want to control what is said of them. Their dilemma is to attract the right man on the right night and to appear modest in public yet exciting in private. Favorite folktales and songs speak of a boy who pines after a girl and overcomes great difficulties to be with her. Girls are thrilled to be the focus of such romance and bravery—or so the stories claim.

Judging from the gossip, the girl's relatives may abet the couple's conspiracy or place obstacles in their way. In Pohnpeian households, one arranges his or her mat on the floor of the central room; a girl may choose to sleep in the middle of wakeful babies and watchful elders or near a convenient entrance. With the tacit permission of her relatives, she may sleep in another part of the household or frequent the path to the "little house" during the moonlight hours of the night.

Night-crawling is reserved for the young. But older men tell fond stories about their experiences. They claim that in the past, boys bought spells or chants to keep the dogs from barking and revealing their presence to the sleeping household. Girls acquired love magic to lure boys and make them fall in love. One man told me about stringing dry, unhusked coconuts together to use as flotation devices so he could cross the lagoon to his lover at night. Another told me that, by accident, he woke up his true love's uncle, her mother's brother, who demanded an explanation. The youth replied, "Do you have a light for my cigarette?" The uncle gave him some matches and went back to sleep. Night-crawlers need an appropriate excuse to be prowling a strange house at night, he claimed. To me, it illustrated the connivance of custom.

A German anthropologist named Hambruch visited Pohnpei in 1910 and reported that "sexual intercourse begins very early . . . before marriage there is complete freedom in sexual intercourse" (7ii:76). He implies that there are no rules, only sexual freedom. But rules exist, they are just different from the ones Hambruch knew in turn-of-the-century Germany. I heard criticism of American standards of sexual behavior, irresponsible Peace Corps or military men fathering children with young girls, clothing, or styles of walking or sitting, all of which were interpreted as lewd and immodest. Even carrying a sleeping mat down the street would be worthy of comment. Sexual freedom for romantic youth on Pohnpei has limits. Couples who have arranged successful midnight trysts do not date, go out to eat, or go to the movies together. In keeping with strong Pohnpeian feelings about public displays of affection, they will not hold hands, hug, or go on a picnic with each other. If families approve, the couple may have sex in the yard at night. But when the couple adds board to bed, they are married. Pohnpeians may tolerate a foreign male (like the Peace Corps worker) moving in with their daughter and behaving like a son-in-law. They are scandalized and fear for their daughter's reputation if she accompanies him to the movies or to a restaurant.

While parents may accept nocturnal excursions, premarital intercourse, and an occasional baby, they value marriage and want to prevent undesirable unions. Marriage is a gradual process growing from adolescent years of freedom and experimentation. A man and a woman become a couple when they openly establish a joint residence. If families of both partners recognize this fact, the relationship is a marriage. The same is true for divorce. People say that if the couple has been living together (or apart) for six months or so, then the changed terms of the relationship make it legal. In the past, it was rare for young couples to set up housekeeping on their own and rarer still if the woman had no children. This is why many Pohnpeians questioned me.

Church leaders, both native and foreign, have wielded considerable pressure on officials to regularize and enforce marriage and divorce laws. But the terms for "true marriage" (married with the blessing of the church) and "vain marriage" (what is called common law marriage in the United States) show the reality in practice. The ancient customs, missionary teachings, Japanese law, and U.S.-imposed civil customs are confused and mutually contradictory. There is no question that marriage in a church or a civil ceremony or a certificate of divorce from a judge establishes a legal relationship. But many marriages and divorces are binding, though, like birth and death records, not always registered.

The decision of a couple to live together is determined by family pressures, romantic love, and religious loyalties. Families may oppose a prospective spouse on the grounds that he or she is of lower rank, is of higher rank, is lazy, is an outlander, drinks too much, or may be a drag on the family resources. Occasionally, the power of romantic love is so strong that a couple will brave the pressures of family and church to live openly with each other, raise children, and consider themselves married.

Sexual permissiveness, however, changes after marriage. The public party line about extramarital sex is that married couples are straight, modest, fruitful, and relatively faithful. By all accounts, however, adultery is as frequent as it is disruptive or attractive. In the past, adultery, betrayal, and sexual jealousy caused clan wars and local feuding. Again and again, listening to gossip, I was aware of attitudes about sexuality that permeated Pohnpeian customs. When two people of the opposite sex are left alone, the inevitable will happen. The couple will shrug, "What can we do, how can we help themselves?" A glimpse of an inner knee, a liquid look, and making love must begin—their solution is not increased internal control but avoidance of occasions for incest or adultery.

When I collected material about incest, many stories concerned unusual combinations of forbidden relatives who find themselves alone together on a deserted path, up a coconut tree, or in a sinking canoe. The drive that will bring two people together in carnal knowledge is stronger than the fear of gossip or of breaking a taboo. Islanders watch each other, wise in the ways of physical attraction. If you do not wish to be gossiped about, stay near others. When a male and a female are seen together, the suspicion of intimacy will arise. I was chided several times for being seen alone with one of the men working on the project. The interviewers made nervous jokes if we found ourselves alone together. The bottom line is that no matter what a man and a woman do or avoid doing, someone will find reasons to suspect an affair. When a man and a woman want to be alone together, they will hide the fact. If two people are avoiding each other, then they have something planned! Yet again, they may *not* be avoiding each other to throw off suspicion in case someone should notice them avoiding each other.

The corollary to the principle of sexual opportunism is the principle of sexual necessity. Micronesians in general believe that everyone must have sex regularly. They also believe that no matter what anybody says, human beings cannot remain faithful or go without sex for extended periods of time. The third principle is mutuality. Women and men equally find pleasure in sex and in one other.

Pohnpeian has a word that translates as "it is said," or "they claim." Placed at the front of the sentence—"it is claimed that men get bent penises from that activity"—the phrase absolves the speaker of responsibility. In Pohnpei, as in small-scale societies everywhere, the strongest control over sex or any other area of human life is not law or formal control of governments, but gossip, public shame, and fear of ridicule. Gossip is not a trivial activity, but one to which anthropologists pay close attention. In the United States, Jack never gossiped. But in the field, he often noted the power of gossip and recounted, then analyzed, the stories we heard. The statistics that Americans consider research do not exist in a place like Pohnpei. Attitudes and practices about sex cannot be collected by asking random subjects to fill out questionnaires. Only if an anthropologist lives in the community, speaks the language, hangs out with different groups, attends rituals, asks questions, answers questions, and listens, will he or she learn. Only then is it possible to know that, for Pohnpeians, "virginity" does not carry the same meaning or economic value it does in patrilineal societies. Only then is it possible to understand that members of the same clan help each other erect houses, give feasts, and discipline wayward clanmates.

Roger was like sticky fly paper for gossip about sex. Perhaps his innocent air or his study on healing attracted disclosures. On the other hand, it may have been his avid curiosity. His field notes are full of material, sometimes recorded as hearsay, but frequently as direct confessions or personal revelations. Some Peace Corps volunteers used Roger as an older brother or confidante; one volunteer confessed that he made arrangements through a go-between to visit his lady love late at night. But, first mistake, he carried a flashlight. Second, he had not scouted in advance the paths leading to her house. A local prankster, himself on the prowl, hid in the foliage and jumped out suddenly with machete in hand. Terrified, the volunteer youth ran wildly, fell, and tore his trousers and one knee. He limped for weeks as the prankster told the story with glee.

A Pohnpeian man, sophisticated and educated, had squired a Peace Corps woman in American style to movies, restaurants, and other public occasions. That meant only one thing—they were married. Then, as the woman finished her tour of duty and departed, she kissed him good-bye at the airport. By the time we heard the tragic tale, the embellishments and green leaves were abundant. They had been star-crossed lovers who could never be reunited. She had joined a convent, died of a broken heart or an incurable disease, committed suicide, or succumbed to parental disapproval. Once I heard she was locked in a tower. All the young man's subsequent actions—a regular island marriage, a job, and cute kids—were explained by the tragic loss of his American "wife."

Another U.S. Peace Corps volunteer had been living with a Pohnpeian man with the approval of his family—in local eyes they were married. Then people saw her in Kolonia in the company of other men, colleagues in the Peace Corps, and Micronesians with whom she worked. The family was incensed and broke up the relationship. The young man, forced to accept his family's evaluation of her conduct, wrote bitter love songs. Each time a song aired on the radio, I heard another version of their legend of lost love.

Living in a Pohnpeian household showed me that sexual lives are not hidden from children. Sleeping arrangements lack privacy. Babies and toddlers do not wear clothes; naked children play in groups. As long as the taboos about discussing sex in front of certain relatives are followed, adult conversations in the inevitable presence of children are frank. A young girl named Maria began exhibiting the habits of a boy as she grew into her teens. She went walking about at night looking for girls. The activity was acceptable, but that a girl was doing it caused consternation. Family and neighbors held a meeting to discuss the problem; they brought it up with Maria. Then they held a feast and declared for all to hear that Maria was henceforth a boy named Mario. They cut his hair and presented the new male with appropriate clothing. I heard that Mario had became a responsible citizen, married with a wife and children.

The important fact about the story is not the biological or psychological roots of Maria's shift in gender. Sometimes in human societies children are assigned to the wrong gender category and confusion results. What fascinates me is the ease with which Pohnpeians repaired whatever had gone wrong; they found a sensible social solution to a sexual dilemma.

Some things, however, are considered to be wrong. A principal sexual offense in Pohnpei is called "spying at the water"; young boys hide and spy on women as they bathe in pools or streams. The occasions on which boys spy on females are limited only by their imagination. All the women I talked with heard peepers dozens of times and caught groups or individuals in the act of spying. When I went to a remote pool in Wene to bathe, I could be certain boys were hidden in nearby groves of trees. But their behavior is shameful—it is said to involve solitary sexual activity and to indicate an inadequacy in the males' ability to attract women. It is also considered shameful for a man to take a woman by force. Something is seriously wrong with a man who has to do that. Although, in every society there are a few rotten eggs whose behavior cannot be condoned, on a small island most people know who the bad characters are and avoid them. In a culture in which men gain sexual favors through good manners and do not reward their peers for aggression against women, rape is rarer than in the United States. It is also permissible, even necessary, for Pohnpeian women to be explicit in rejection—saying "you stink" or making disparaging references to an offending man's private parts is also recommended.

A Pohnpeian word meaning "to pick too young" refers to the appropriate age for intercourse to begin. The lower limit of sexual activity for girls was variously placed at eleven to fourteen years of age, certainly by fifteen to nineteen for conservative folk. It is generally assumed that intercourse is appropriate if a girl has started to menstruate and is not exposed to any situation that would harm her, emotionally or physically. Boys usually begin their sexual lives later than girls as their bodies are believed to mature more slowly.

Foreigners ask, "But what if she gets pregnant?" In Pohnpei, children automatically belong to their mother's clan and illegitimacy is not a word. Children have many males and females in their extended family to love and care for them. Pregnancy is a good reason for a couple to regularize their union and settle down. A century and a half of contact between islanders and foreigners resulted in babies absorbed into their clans and families, even if the couple didn't settle down together.

Pohnpeian society before Western contact was a politically sophisticated, hierarchically organized society with overseas trade links with the islands to the west and atolls to the east. Nan Madol is an eloquent testimony to ancient Pohnpeian feats of engineering and organizational skills. After foreign contacts in the early nineteenth century, the islanders incorporated new iron technologies, Western goods such as guns and alcohol, monetary trade, and most profoundly, the messages and organizational structure of Christianity.

The United States has not been the only colonist on the island. The rule of the Spanish from 1886 to 1899 produced little change, as they seemed frightened of natives and stayed in the fort whose ruins still grace Kolonia. The German administration, which lasted until the outbreak of World War I, reduced the powers of the Paramount or High Chiefs through the prohibition of warfare and changed the ways people owned and inherited land. The Japanese influence over their colonial possessions in Micronesia lasted until their defeat at the end of World War II. U.S. influence, however, does not date only from 1945 and the trusteeship. Americans were in Micronesia in the 1830s when whaling ships and trading ships stopped in Pohnpei. Despite two centuries of contact with foreigners, Pohnpeians have not given up their traditional politics, language, or family organization. Adjusting to the succession of colonial governments, they have absorbed large numbers of other Micronesians into their cultural vision.

Foreigners brought new and deadly diseases—a smallpox epidemic in 1854 wiped out at least half of the population. Venereal diseases that sailors and traders transmitted are still endemic. Tuberculosis, leprosy, respiratory infections, and such childhood diseases as measles wreaked havoc on the health of islanders who had no natural immunity to the pathogens.

Even the material goods that islanders coveted from contact with whalers and traders altered traditional culture. Tobacco, firearms, knives, and alcohol brought germs of destruction as dangerous as diseases. Pohnpeians are comfortable with and sophisticated about Western technology. They move easily back and forth between modern things and ideas and older traditions, often weaving complex new patterns. That does not mean, however, that people who wear the same clothes or drink the same beer as Westerners do think the same way.

Sometimes Westerners refer to places such as Micronesia as "primitive" or simple. Sometimes the Pohnpeians blame their current problems on U.S. colonialism. Westerners and Pohnpeians alike tell anthropologists that the past was a golden time of rich rituals and reverence for custom, when life's meanings were clear and all children respected their elders. None of these folk beliefs is true. They are green leaves on stories.

A letter from the field:

Dear Len and all University of North Carolina supporters of high blood pressure,

The questionnaire development is going very well and we have started preparations for the census. A separate budget sheet is attached. Thanks for all your efficiency in calling Washington to find out how we can buy pigs out of our budget. Glad you know how to switch budget categories so the project can make appropriate contributions.

I have had to change my manner of dressing. Thank goodness for the Sears catalogue. Those mini-dresses and short skirts you all are wearing in the States cause quite a stir here. It seems that breasts are only normal female equipment for feeding babies. Clothing for many women consists of a large towel or three-yard length of brightly colored cloth. This is worn around the waist inside the house or in the yard, but is pulled up to cover your breasts for walking in the road. More formal dress is a one-piece dress with gathered waist (no doubt missionary inspired). The back zipper is rarely used except for church and community gatherings. If you have on a bra, you don't need a blouse. If you wear a blouse, then you don't need a bra. In fact, bras are considered proper public dress for women. Those black Maidenforms with the heavily stitched pointed cups are particularly valued.

When foreigners are not around, it is sufficient to cover oneself only from the waist down. Jack says I should do what I feel comfortable with. I hope he means for me to follow my Oklahoma-born inclinations and stay dressed. The Pohnpeians ask, "Why do you wear a blouse and a bra at the same time?" I hope they are just teasing me.

Breasts are not particularly erogenous, but legs are—particularly that sexy place on the inside of the knees. No more miniskirts for me. Fitting in and observing local custom means that I have unfashionably lengthened my skirts to below the knee. I have a proper slip that has a two-inch layer of hand crocheted embroidery on the bottom. Bright blue, red, and yellow flowers. The slip is designed to show below my dress. Later I will tell you other practical uses for this slip.

American men watch women with nothing on above the waist. The Pohnpeian men comment on American women with short skirts and eye our knees. I am now dressed to please the standards of two cultures. You would love it here. Both women and men say that I am too skinny—downright scrawny for a proper woman. They expect women to eat a lot, gain weight, keep weight on after each pregnancy, and stay on the large side of pleasantly plump. They say, "Women eat to bear children." Women accentuate their posture to make them look substantial. Men are compared to brown doves, a bird that eats a bite of fruit, leaves it and goes to another, always to nibble sparingly. Warriors in the olden days went to battle with an empty stomach. To die with food in one's stomach would have been humiliating. So men are noticeably thinner. Men who eat too much are subject to ridicule, and women who are rotund, Rubenesque, and roly-poly are objects of sexual interest.

You may think this discussion is about sex (again). Not so. File this information away. We will need it for the medical questionnaires and interpretations about blood pressures, weight, eating habits, and values.

I hear the plane coming in to land. If I hop on the motor scooter and hurry down to the airport, I can get this letter off the island.

Kaselehlie.

Chapter 3

Water Running under Boulders

Evil magic, which the people of Pohnpei perform among themselves when they are feeling ill towards each other, have their origin in the supernatural power of people. Destruction: bury magical objects under the corner of an enemy's house. Making blood flow: people will die. Swimming fire: send flames from burning coconut leaves to one's enemy. Clouding the water: magical infusion and spells in the streams where a victim bathes may cause blindness.

—from Luelen Bernart

A home at last. After months of shifting about Roger and I moved into Jack's spacious, shady, private house with relief. With the departure of Jack, Ian, and Floyd, we were alone to run the research project until the arrival of the medical team the following summer. I began to see Jack's former abode as less a decrepit hut and more a nest that needed repairs.

The wooden, tin-roofed house was one room about eighteen feet by eighteen feet with partitions to create visual privacy. Roger and I slept on mats and used a low Japanese table for working and eating. Although I never learned to cook sitting down, as Pohnpeian women do with such skill, I was adjusting to life on the floor. Sohn Alpet brought relatives who explained each of the plants in the yard, an invaluable language lesson. We had papaya, breadfruit, coconut, and lemon-lime trees; flowers; bushes; taro, the delicious Pacific root crop; and a plant that yielded tiny red hot peppers. Yard chickens that feasted on them tasted spicier than other chickens. Each food-bearing tree had a private owner, that is, the person or his or her descendants who planted the tree. Although we rented the homestead, we also had to

negotiate for rights of use from tree owners who returned at random intervals to gather produce.

When the electricity—one light socket and a plug wired from the jail on
the hill above the house—worked, we operated a fan. The Japanese administration had built a telephone system, but along with other public works, it
had fallen into disrepair. Our shower was a tin shed about five-feet square,
paved with pieces of coral rock; a raised piece in the center served for pounding clothes. Water for the shower and a small tin sink in the kitchen lean-to
came from the rudimentary Kolonia system. Pipes ran at random; no one
billed us; and we drank the water without boiling it because all the Americans did. Used water from bathing and washing ran under the house and out
into the yard because the town had no drainage system for our neighborhood.
If we wanted hot water, we heated some in a sauce pan on the two burner
butane stove in the kitchen. A gas stove was a major improvement over cooking with kerosene camp stoves—no smells or messes and more ease of temperature regulation. A square biscuit tin placed on one of the burners made
do as an oven. The cakes I continued to bake tasted awful, but homesick
Americans appreciated them.

Because the medical team needed refrigeration for laboratory materials
and blood and urine samples, Ian had sent a kerosene refrigerator and freezer
manufactured in Norway. We used it pending the team's arrival, sacrificing
valuable floor space to accommodate the bulky piece and struggling to understand directions for installation and maintenance in Norwegian. One of us,
usually Roger, had to be constantly vigilant to care for wicks and fuel levels;
the appliance required babysitting when we were out of town. On top of that,
kerosene stinks. Why bother? Because it made cooking in the tropics easier,
and above all, the thing made ice. Beautiful, cold, crystal ice. We had taken
ice for granted and, like many Americans in the tropics, were having trouble
adjusting to ice deprivation.

But the pièce de résistance, a marvel of Yankee ingenuity, was our toilet.
Only a few privileged households and offices in town had flush toilets; islanders built outhouses. But the public health saying, "flies, fingers, food, feces,"
the four-cornered cause and effect for the spread of disease in places without
adequate sanitation or running water, held true in Pohnpei. Outhouses with
constant flies that respected no boundaries were a source of dysentery and
other illnesses that had plagued the islands since contact. Municipal authorities discharged raw sewerage into the harbor; hepatitis, parasitic infestations,
and other waterborne diseases were common.

Jack, devoted to practical solutions, had ordered a pamphlet from the
U.S. Government Printing Office on water seal toilets and convinced Roger
and me to build one. We hired workers to dig a hole about the size of a fifty-
gallon drum; they filled it with rocks graded in size from small at the bottom
to large at the top, an excellent filtration system that needed no chemicals or
other drainage. As per instructions, the workers capped the rock-filled hole
with a tin lid and a layer of dirt, then ran a pipe to the third lean-to addi-

tion—the toilet room. There was no ceramic appliance—the floor was a square of concrete with an almond-shaped hole in the middle. A U-shaped pipe connected the hole to the filtration system outside. Fresh water in the base of the U-pipe prevented smells from backing up from the rocky filter. Our toilet, sealed with water against odor, was flushed with rainwater stored in a fifty-gallon drum next to the house and syphoned down the hole with a twenty-cent length of rubber hose. To use the toilet, one squatted, then sucked on the end of the hose to bring water from the rain barrel. No flies, no smell, no plumbing bills, no walks in the rain to the outhouse, and no public health hazards.

Everyone hated it. Pohnpeians excused themselves and went across the road to an outhouse. Americans whose government was promoting the projects urged us to build a wooden seat or paint footprints on either side of the hole; they demanded sturdy handles to hoist themselves to their feet.

After a prisoner from the jail broke into the house, Sohn Alpet brought us a black and white spotted puppy whom I named Pwutak or "male youth." By guarding the house and eating leftovers, he earned his keep. A wild cat named Yapper lived in the rafters of the house and dealt harshly with rodents. With time and regular food, she came down from her perch, uttering her strange cry, and at night deposited dead rats and mice in the exact middle of the floor. A starved, flea-ridden orange cat called Oang-Oang or "yellow" wandered in and stayed to hunt the tiny mice Yapper missed. To our ecological regret, both cats caught geckos, harmless lizards with miniature suction cups on their feet who walk on ceilings and walls eating insects. The mosquito population increased, and we had to burn green mosquito coils at night.

The large yard held the framework of a classic Pohnpeian feast house, with platforms on three sides and a kava stone in the middle. But the thatched roof had rotted. So we negotiated with our landlord for a new thatched roof. Roger's field notes reveal righteous indignation over the transaction, so we may have offended people and paid too much. But it was worth the money just to watch a master craftsman weave and apply the ivory-palm thatch and later to sit under its cool rustle. Although I loved the sound of rain on its tin roof, our house was uncomfortable on sunny days. Much of Pohnpeian life is conducted in feast houses, and we began to use ours as they did: as office, guest room, dining room, study, and den; we began to rise with the sun each morning as Micronesians did.

Soon after the move into new quarters, Ioannes appeared and began to cut and weed the yard. "You need me," he said. True. Although I was also insecure about hiring people to wait on me, the demands of tropical gardening mystified me. Roger put him on the payroll when he discovered another talent of our adopted employee—Ioannes was an expert in traditional diagnosis and treatment of disease. His specialty, indeed his genius, was knowing how to use ancient Pacific techniques of healing massage—ideal for Roger's study of traditional medicine. Ioannes practiced on me as Roger took notes;

he demonstrated how to get rid of muscle spasms, cramps, indigestion, and other ordinary ailments. He had potions and oils for insect bites and an instant cure for centipede bite. Beyond practical folk remedies, he knew the theories of relationships between body and mind on which all native treatments of disease are based.

Sohn Alpet, with black briefcase and navy blue baseball cap pulled low, tried to look casual when he dropped by our homestead on weekends when we had no work scheduled. One evening, with his private agenda in mind, he complimented us on our diligence in studying Pohnpeian. "However," he commented, "you speak like children. You know the words and sentences, but you do not use the respect language for high people. I shall have to teach you."

He did not trust Akina, the linguistic informant we had been using. She was, for various complex reasons, beyond paying homage to men or to ceremonial customs from which she derived no benefit. Although she had lived on Pohnpei, married, worked, and raised her kids there, she had not been born on the island and was not connected to the local version of the old-boys' network. The sharp tongue and irrepressible intelligence that made her suitable for language study meant to Sohn Alpet that Roger and I were not learning the codes of deference Pohnpeians valued.

The Pohnpeian language has three levels of language usage—common, respectful, and honorific. The latter two levels are called "high language." Because the Pohnpeians value sophisticated oratory and skilled speech, subtle gradations operate between these levels. In high language ordinary actions—eat, speak, love, hate, die, come, go, sleep, think, weep, wash, and whisper—body parts, and nouns for common places like cookhouse, canoe, eating place, bathing place, pillows, and many others are different words depending on the level of honor the speaker must show and the listener deserves. Other words—terms of humility and exaltation—have no meaning except to show status. They elevate other people and their possessions while belittling yourself and your possessions. A loose translation, the only kind possible, may convey the flavor. "Would your honored self deign to give this unworthy person something to drink?" There is a special word for "drink" in high language.

It is not just a matter of convenient phrases such as "your exalted pig" and "my humble pig." High people do not wear crowns or jewels or drive fancier cars. The privileges of rank are evident in seating arrangements and distribution of food at feasts and, above all, in clever and sumptuous displays of language. Pohnpeians know each other's genealogies, recent title promotions, and other rationales for ranking. They know how to judge each social interaction on the relative status of those speaking—how you view your own social rank in relation to that of others, including those who are the topic of conversation. A thorough knowledge of the title system and related customs of respect is essential for Pohnpeian advancement into the high ranks of the society, yet not even older Pohnpeian men use the forms with equal facility. How could anyone expect me to know all this?

"I'm a mere woman," I insisted to Sohn Alpet, "who will have no occasion to speak with high-ranking people." Let Roger sweat it out, I thought; I will keep Sohn Alpet at my side to represent me. But Sohn Alpet was adamant, suggesting with great tact that I could not play the role of co-head of a medical research project one moment and a dutiful, retiring wife the next.

For example, to children or pets, you can say *menlau* or "hey, thanks." For younger people and peers, *kalahngan* or the phrase *mehn sahmwa* is appropriate. For older people and those with higher rank, depending on how you assess that, you say *kalahngan en kowmi*. Other more elevated phrases of gratitude must be used for the Paramount or High Chiefs, for God, and for the spirits. It is impossible to utter a worthwhile sentence without taking a stand on the amount of respect due those being addressed. Besides title and rank, questions of relative age and kinship are also important. Sohn Alpet insisted that we address him by his title, Nahnid Lapalap, and use respect language to him and others he designated. He did not care about teaching us nouns, verbs, or new sentence structures; he cared about the language of respect.

Roger and I spent days under the thatch roof of our feast house training Nahnid and his assistant Roswel in the strange mysteries of Western social science—how and why to do a household census, how and why we needed a sample, how and why blood pressure was related to people's feelings. We planned the next phase of the research project, completing the census and beginning the questionnaires in the municipalities of Kitti, U, and Madolenihmw. The first item on our agenda was a return trip to Wene; working out living arrangements and payments for room and board had been challenging. Sohn Alpet had a high title from Madolenihmw. If he stayed with anyone who had a lower title, the man would be obliged to sponsor an expensive feast. If he stayed as guest of someone with a higher title, we would have to pay for a feast. Moreover, Roger and I had been assigned a high status as foreigners—a canny assessment of the project's budget. On the previous visit, Jack, Roger, and I arranged—or thought we had—to pay room and board based on the rate the Peace Corps paid, a rate that was less than the hotel in Kolonia charged.

Although Roger, Sohn Alpet, Roswel, and I planned to leave on a Monday morning, a downpour, boat troubles, and missed appointments postponed our departure. Late Tuesday afternoon we at last arrived at our host's farmstead, sunburned, drenched, and hungry, to discover several hundred people filling house, feast house, and yard. A funeral for a high-ranking section chief, our host's mother's brother, had reached its four-day crescendo. The Paramount Chief of Kitti was already seated; other dignitaries were arriving. The feast, or *kamadipw*, was a triple celebration: a commemoration for the deceased man, a title repayment feast for his successor, and a housewarming called the "cleansing of worms" for the new feast house completed just days before the death.

Although I had attended kava poundings and family feasts, this was the largest and most formal event I had witnessed. The master of ceremonies assigned Sohn Alpet—as Nahnid Lapalap—a place close to the front with other high-titled Pohnpeians, and to Roger and me he indicated an opening in the far back. I could barely see the Paramount Chief of Kitti who sat against the wall at the head of the feast house with wife, retainers, and others of high rank arrayed below him. "Show respect to the high people and elders," Sohn Alpet managed to whisper to us before they whisked him away. "Always, no matter how uncomfortable you are, sit cross-legged on the platform and never, never, dangle your legs off the edge. Don't get up and leave because you don't know the right speeches to ask to be excused." In translation—sit there until I come to get you, all night if necessary.

Although I did not understand the long speeches, the feast was an excellent opportunity to observe and participate, if only on the edges of ritual life. Although I recognized the steps of kava preparation by that time, I could not yet appreciate the earth oven at the open front of the feast house or the many hand-woven baskets of food that were circulating. In the wake of so many funerals, however, agreements for the housing and meals we had negotiated were void; a funeral feast for a newborn baby held the previous Sunday night meant that few people in Wene had slept much; many mourners and their relatives filled the homesteads of Wene. Our project was swamped in ceremonies and we were homeless. Hurried arrangements for housing in a homestead about an hour's walk into the hills took advantage of our inexperience and need.

The morning after the triple feast, which lasted very late, the four of us met with Dr. Franko, health aide at the dispensary, to plan the census and logistics of the month's work. Sohn Alpet and Roswel departed with forms in hand. Two hours later, Roswel returned. An announcement on the radio called for relatives of his wife's sister to gather for her funeral. We loaned him travel money and he left.

Six days later, Roswel had not yet returned. Sohn Alpet was feeling ill; Roger had the flu, I was irritable and vexed, and none of us was eating well. Roswel had to walk back to Wene from Kolonia, a hard two-day hike—we need to be filled with mercy, Sohn Alpet pleaded. The poor youth has family troubles, a pretty young wife with a new baby, and a sick father.

On the evening of Roswel's return, we met again and mapped out our work for the following week. As we finished and began to compliment ourselves, another announcement came on the radio. A distant relative of Sohn Alpet had died; the funeral was at an in-law's house deep in the hills of Kitti. When he covered his face with his hands, it was clear that he had to attend. Roger and I looked at one another, deciding in that moment to go with him. "Oh no," Sohn Alpet responded, "the path is not suitable for foreigners." He was right—the track was rocky, precipitous, and muddy, and we had to ford several streams. However, our spontaneous decision led to the first good day's work in Wene and to a better solution for taking a census than homestead-to-homestead visits. With everyone from that section gathered in one place for the funeral, the four of us were able to complete the census for the entire area.

Two days later, when the broadcast from Kolonia announced another funeral and more obligations, Sohn Alpet gestured to Roswel—"we didn't hear that." During this time, twelve funerals intersected with our work. A flu epidemic, a frequent respiratory affliction Pohnpeians called the "sickness of foreigners," had hit newborns and old people hard. Sometimes when a ship had docked, a wave of sickness would pass through the island and then abate until the next ship arrived carrying a different set of germs, contagion from other countries around the world. Moreover, Pohnpeians have more kin-folk—reciprocal relationships with members of their mother's clan, father's clan, spouse's clan, people married into these groups, and other relatives—than most Westerners do. Funerals last a minimum of four days, some ten days, and the extent of personal grief a person feels is less important than the facts of kinship. Kinship ties also determine how large a contribution of purchased food or produce from the land a mourner brings.

In addition to funerals, lack of food, and make-shift housing, Roger and I needed more language skills than we had. No sooner had we stepped off the boat at the Wene dock and causeway through the swamp than Sohn Alpet began speaking high language to us. Our host and hostess used high language when speaking to the Peace Corps couple who lived with them and in front of their children. The speeches at the funerals were full of honorifics and terms for humility. At every homestead, at public gatherings, and on the paths between, I heard people proud of their linguistic virtuosity, marking themselves off from others by the skills of their tongues. In this verbal chess or poker, they scored points by speaking of themselves with humility and modesty while exalting their opponents to absurd levels of status. Sometimes I thought this was a game they played with each other and on clumsy foreigners—I could find no other reason for their speech displays. This game, if my view is correct, fits an ideal Pohnpeian personality—public modesty and private ambition.

In an arc over other difficulties were questions about financing our stays in Wene. "The Peace Corps has ruined Wene for the rest of us," Sohn Alpet ranted. Our hosts and the health aide, expecting the same standards from us, a new wave of rich foreigners, liked to compare the stingy blood pressure project with the generosity of American volunteers, the first class of whom trained in Wene. An invasion of free-spending Americans had infused the area with cash and unrealistic expectations. In Wene, people torn between their canons of hospitality to strangers and the sudden cash the Peace Corps brought craved both economic reciprocity and economic power; they sold their culture and spoiled the values of hospitality.

Wene had a Catholic mission, a Protestant church, a tiny dispensary, and a school that went up to the eighth grade, but no office jobs, motor vehicles, bars, roads, electricity, running water, restaurants, or tourist facilities of any kind. Copra, the dried meat of coconuts, was their major source of income; they scooped out the oily meat, left it in the sun to dry, then bagged and shipped the bales to the Philippines for processing. But the world price for copra was falling as better substitutes for the rich oils and residues was developed. On Pohnpei, whose climate for drying anything was poor, income from copra averaged only about $250 per harvester per year. Men could also go to Kolonia to work and send money back. But the customary obligations, farming, and feasting that gave their lives meaning could not be sustained from a distance, and few jobs were available for people without skills and knowledge of English. Only 44 percent of the men from this area had wage-labor employment compared to 85 percent in Kolonia.

Our failures in bargaining and money management were wearing out the four of us. As Roger commented, "We were strangers and they took us in." Agreements on which we shook hands fell through, and written contracts were subject to further wrangling. Funerals, financial problems, and the sicknesses we suffered during this visit cut into the amount of work we had hoped to achieve. I grew apprehensive about the difficulties of fielding and financing the medical team later in the year. Roger and I would have to negotiate every detail of housing, food, laundry, transportation, and the other services necessary to sustain a dozen people for a month. We were barely scrounging meals for ourselves.

We decided to cut our stay short and return to celebrate Christmas Day in Kolonia. As Roswel attached the outboard motor to the whaleboat, Sohn Alpet stood erect at the helm and pronounced in a perfect imitation of John Wayne's cowboy English—"I sho' will be happy to shake the dust of this gol-darn place off my boots"—the only English I ever heard him speak.

In the month following the working trip to Wene, I had nagging colds and a feeling of despondency. The project's work had not gone well. I worried about the accuracy of the census and the hidden frictions that we encountered. One morning, Sohn Alpet came by as usual to discuss the day's work and the Kolonia census. We talked about the feasts in Wene, and he explained aspects of the feasting system to me. In an off-hand manner, he announced that he and his family had decided to stage a demonstration that included appropriate foods, an earth oven, speech making, and proper manners for a Pohnpeian feast. Our feast house had a newly thatched roof that had not been dedicated—another reason for a feast, he said. He set a date, gave me a list of instructions, and departed.

Sohn Alpet negotiated the purchase of a pig without strain and tethered it in the yard for several days. On the appointed day, he brought yams and a kava plant, and Ioannes installed a special stick for husking the coconuts and dispatched some young boys up the coconut and breadfruit trees for leaves and fruit. Akina made irreverent jokes while she helped me cut up pineapple. Sohn Alpet's wife and daughters sat on the gnarled roots of the breadfruit trees and wove headdresses from the basins of sweet-smelling flowers they had gathered. Relaxed, they pulled the tops of their dresses down to their waists. When they realized that Roger and I had no traditional cups in which to serve kava, they picked up a thick piece of green Coke-bottle glass and began to scrape the halves of a coconut shell. Under their firm hands, the rich, walnut brown of a kava cup began to emerge. They laughed as I cleaned the kava stone—Pwutak, the dog, had marked territory he thought was his.

The men built a fire over the volcanic rocks below the eaves of thatch at the wide entrance. They grabbed the pig and stuck a knife in its throat, Sohn Alpet eyeing me to test the threshold of squeamishness. The pig squealed, bled, and died. They removed the internal organs and dragged its body across hot coals to singe off dirt and hair. Spreading out the hot coals and glowing rocks out with wooden tongs, they laid yams and breadfruit in the oven first, then the splayed pig—the elements of a proper earth oven. The men covered the food with broad leaves and anchored the edges of the oven with rocks. Wisps of smoke escaped through the leaves, seeping through the thatch and giving rich flavor to the food. When the steam from the earth oven began to rise, the men prepared to pound kava.

Sohn Alpet seated everyone on the platform of the feast house, then gave orders to open the earth oven, distribute the food, and serve the kava. Throughout the preparations, Sohn Alpet kept up his running commentary and I took notes. He explained what they were doing and why it accorded with tradition. He emphasized the proper manners to be observed even in a small family feast and made a simple speech emphasizing—I thought— points of etiquette and the history of our research project. He remarked on the classic Pohnpeian values of cooperation, humility, hard work, and respect to the high-titled people and elders.

I accepted his explanations at face value and the project entered a new and invigorating phase. Roger and I were working hard with language les- sons; my lassitude and colds disappeared. Weeks later, however, I began to hear unconnected comments about what happened at the little feast. I don't know when these references began to form a pattern or even when my West- ern consciousness admitted another reality. According to the low-keyed gos- sip, Sohn Alpet had staged the feast to lift the curses to which we had fallen prey in Wene. To him, the evidence was strong. We had more problems than random bad luck, coincidence, God's will, or poor planning could explain. Perhaps germs do cause colds or flu, but why to that particular person at that time? The project people were sicker than the people of Wene.

He never claimed, to me at least, that a sorcerer had put a spell on us or added something in our food to make us confused and sick. These are the classic methods of sorcerers in many parts of the world, including the Pohnpei of the past. But he mentioned from time to time that feeling jealousy or greed toward others was the same as sending a curse. By harboring bad feelings, you wished others evil and rejoiced in their bad fortune. In a society that places the value of cooperation above all others, sorcery is competition and rivalry unleashed. Sorcery fears feed on hidden rivalries, individual cha- risma, and a need to explain sudden sickness, death, or terrible accidents where no ordinary explanations suffice. It is said that sorcerers in the past had the power to send killing magic. The only way to cure this lethal curse was more powerful magic sent back on the head of the sorcerer. Sometimes the practice may misfire like a poorly loaded gun and rebound against the sorcerer or even injure the innocent. Naturally, sorcerers or their clients cannot brag about their successes or complain about their failures, and Pohnpeians begin conversations about sorcery by first denying even the existence of such practices.

By no scientific standards in American logic can I prove that we fell victim to sorcery. I have no evidence that anyone spiked our food or sent spells of misfortune upon us. Yet troublesome little things kept happening in Wene. I stepped on more of those repulsive toads than during all the rest of my time on Pohnpei. My feet were continually covered with pig dung and scratches. Ordinary objects were lost, then mysteriously found. Precious flashlight batteries refused to operate during those weeks. The mail was mislaid. We had strange dreams. It was not only the illnesses and frustrations of work. On some level, I came to believe in the power of jealousy, fear, competitiveness, and greed to cause illness and bad luck. The quiet conviction of the Pohnpeians that the explanatory models of Western science and Christianity were inadequate to account for all human feelings and events sifted through my consciousness.

If the four of us had been targets, then the curses were lifted by no deeds or counter-spells that I witnessed, but by a spirit of cooperation and mutual respect at the little feast. The blood pressure project would have been harmed had Sohn Alpet brought accusations of sorcery. In any case, he was too good a Christian to engage in a war of spells. Instead, in his serene way, he planned the feast and passed the word that our troubles were over. Let others draw conclusions.

Late one night, Michael, the only American doctor at the district hospital, drove up to the house, disheveled and frantic. A newborn baby with a birth problem required immediate surgery, but the baby's parents refused to give permission. If they did not sign within a few days and allow him to operate, the baby would die. Since the infant was in Sohn Alpet's extended family, Michael thought we could help.

Through the following day and into that night as the radio broadcast an open invitation to family members, they met and talked. In their view, the hospital had told them what was wrong with the baby, but not why. Although they trusted Western medicine to correct the defect, that would not solve the real problem. A Pohnpeian illness has a Pohnpeian cause and cure. Unless they themselves, working out of the traditions of island medicine, determined the cause of the sickness, the baby would later fall victim to it or not survive the operation. Such causes could include sorcery against some less-innocent family member that had ricocheted onto the baby. Perhaps an evil spirit had caused the illness—it could be placated and sent away. Unresolved frictions, jealousies, or arguments within the larger family network may have caused the baby's life-threatening condition.

The families consulted traditional curers inside and outside the hospital and could find no evidence of sorcery or spirit-caused illnesses; they thought family frictions were the root of the problem. In a process similar to group dynamics or family therapy in the West, the relatives began to speak about their actions and those of others that may have brought harm. Pressured by time and their love for the infant, they gave voice to their hurts, the petty recriminations of the past, and their continuing disagreements.

The failure to solve an argument stemming from a marriage contract and land dispute between two families had festered. The parties to the dispute had been gossiping about each other and had permitted hard feelings to prevent their participation in feasting and other traditional responsibilities of the extended family. The ill will they bore each other had been deflected onto the infant, an innocent hostage to their conflicts. This, then, was the cause. The cure was to renegotiate the dispute. Like skilled labor-management consultants or divorce mediators, they hammered out a new contract that addressed the accusations of all sides. The agreement meant that they would forgive, forget, and cooperate with each other in public. People's private feelings were neither revealed nor soothed. Exhausted and relieved, they signed the permission to operate. The time had come for Christian prayers and Western medicine. The baby lived and thrived.

The Pohnpeian treatment of illness involves the body and soul of patients, as well as the social configurations surrounding them. Hundreds of plant species are used in Pohnpeian recipes or therapies and carefully handed down to specialists in diagnosis and treatment. Western medicines, the logical treatment for diseases that Westerners brought to Micronesia, were grafted onto this extensive curing system. Roger sent me to curers so he could find out what they did and how they did it. They examined me, I drank potions reputed to cure one minor condition or another; I was a guinea pig for science.

One steamy day, Roger roared up to our homestead on the motorbike. He had been collecting traditional medical practices from a renowned curer we had named "the Pagan," because, unlike other men of his generation, he did not preface his remarks with pious statements about being a good Christian and renouncing the evil past.

"The Pagan claims that he can give me a magical spell that will guarantee the complete obedience of my wife for one year," Roger announced gleefully. "Only ninety dollars!"

I laughed. "It would take a lot more money than that, and how do you know it will work?" I had no intention of paying for my own obedience training.

But Roger and the Pagan had not given up. Another offer followed the next week.

"What about the same magical spell for six months and forty-five dollars?" Roger asked on behalf of the Pagan. But I still did not wish to be bewitched into docility.

Finally, Roger reported the last offer. "We will split the money and the results with Pedro and Kioko Kihleng"—the couple with whom we had lived. "Pedro knows this will work, and he needs it even more than I do. This will buy at least partial obedience from our wives." At the time I believed the

charm would not work unless Kioko and I agreed; yet the power of sugges-
tion coupled with a financial investment might have activated its power. Perhaps the Pagan's last offer was a cheap spell without our consent.

On one of our boat trips, I asked Sohn Alpet what Pohnpeians thought
about Americans. "Americans are very clever and very energetic. You have
invented so many things." He elaborated on the space program, machines,
cars, airplanes, outboard motors, and other items of technology. "Your political system is very strange. You have High Chiefs and men of wisdom like President Kennedy and Martin Luther King, but they are killed for it. Even in
pagan times, we did not behave like that. I hear that you put men in jail for
helping their brothers-in-law. Why should men go to jail for doing their duty to
help their relatives? What will your sisters do if their husbands are in trouble?"

I explained how nepotism and favoritism in awarding contracts and jobs
undermined our economic system. But I could not comprehend why leaders
like Kennedy and King were dead.

"It is good for us to know more Americans," he continued. "Your government was wise to send the Peace Corps, economic development people,
and our research project, which will help people in the world. But all of you
have one major problem. You smell funny and your feet are dirty."

"What?" I demanded. Like other Americans, I was prepared to be criti-
cized about my country's foreign policy, President Nixon, and the war in
Southeast Asia, but Americans spend millions of dollars on soaps, perfumes,
and preparations to cleanse the body and to disguise basic human odors. I
had never heard of another culture in history so obsessed with cleanliness.

"Then that is the reason why you smell funny," he retorted. "Moreover,
Americans do not know how to walk with zories in mud and dust without
getting dirty. No matter what they do, their feet are always dirty." As I contrived to hide my admittedly dirty feet, I realized how relative smell and dirt
must be, except within one's own culture where these standards are absolute. I
began to look at feet and, to be sure, American feet were stained by the omnipresent mud and the minerals of the volcanic soils yet Micronesian feet were
not. Although I vowed to scrub my feet with the hard brushes the Pohnpeians
used, they would not look clean until months after I left the island.

Because the research questionnaire was attempting to reveal how
Pohnpeians felt about their own lives and the stresses they perceived, I listened to how they talked. When I asked the kinds of questions anthropologists are supposed to ask, I often received answers that bore scant relationship
to my questions, answers that came in the form of myths or stories, the favorite of which was a long tale about a cultural hero named Lord Kelekel.

> Once upon a time a dynasty of ruthless men called the Lords of Deleur
> lived in the great city of Nan Madol and ruled over the island. Cruel
> and oppressive, they did as they wished and did not respect the high
> gods. It is claimed that they summoned people to their presence and ate
> them; it is said they required subjects to bring them head lice which they
> enjoyed eating.

Then a Lord of Deleur imprisoned the mighty God of Thunder, Nahnsapwe, who contrived to escape to an island upwind from Pohnpei. There the Thunder God gave a kinswoman a sour fruit like a lemon or lime to eat; she shuddered and in that moment became pregnant. She bore a son named Lord Kelekel. When Lord Kelekel reached manhood, he gathered his resources and supporters, 333 fighting men and assorted women and children, to stage an invasion of Pohnpei. On the atoll of Ant near Pohnpei, they stopped; a High Chief gave them 333 baskets of breadfruit seeds, taught them to speak the language and to know the customs of Pohnpei. After this, they launched their fleet into a harbor in Madolenihmw.

Lord Kelekel was extremely clever. His supporters took beautiful young women as wives. But he picked an old servant woman from whom he learned the food habits, work, geography, and customs of the island. He did not reveal his true status as a leader to the Lords of Deleur or any Pohnpeians. War broke out when the children of the two groups began fighting among themselves. The troops of Lord Kelekel were outnumbered and began to retreat when a brave man, of his own free will, speared his foot to the ground and refused to retreat. The invader troops rallied and won the battle. The reigning Lord of Deleur fell into a river and lives there today as a fish.

Many other stories about the exploits of the hero, magical creatures, spirits, and the cruelties of the lords are woven into this framework. The moral of the story changes from time to time. Sometimes they said that after this, Pohnpei changed and became peaceful. People valued hard work and quarreled less with each other. The successful resistance to tyranny brought a new order of peace comparable to the American struggles for independence and freedom. Sometimes they cite stories to support customs, such as respect for high people and elders. The stories in the myth cycle of Lord Kelekel give answers to such questions as: What kind of people are we? Why do we act and feel the way we do? What is really important to us?

Sometimes, answers to questions I had not asked came in the form of sayings, tidbits of verbal wisdom, and metaphors. English speakers say: "Don't sweat the small stuff." Pohnpeians say: "See, this is like water running under boulders. You can hear the water, but you cannot see it. You can complain about the actions of high people or the American administration, but nothing will come of it. They will still be doing the same thing tomorrow." The water will still be running under the boulders. Sorcery or the fears of it persist and cannot be dammed by the rocks of reason.

Dearest Ones,

Kolonia is temporarily out of sugar, and the donuts taste worse than ever. Some people must be hoarding because a very nice clerk at Carlos' store slipped me some from the back. We can't move the kerosene freezer out of the so-called bedroom until we fix the timbers in the kitchen floor. We can't do that without redoing the door. But all the two-by-fours or two-by-sixes in town are sitting out in the lagoon, waiting to be unloaded.

Another ship is tied up at the only dock. They are behind schedule because Friday is payday, and everything in Kolonia stops for two days while people go to bars, kava pounding, shopping, or to feasts. Apparently no financial inducement will convince stevedores to work around the clock, and the ships do not schedule their arrivals.

The MILI ship came last Friday with the lumber we need to build a door to the kitchen, and the carpenters were scheduled for Saturday. Alas, too late. After all the precautions we take when we leave the house with its meager belongings, we were robbed while we slept. They (or he) poked a hole in the screen. Sohn Alpet, Akina, and Ioannes were terribly upset because they thought the police would suspect them. But I cleared that up in another memorable trip to the constabulary.

About three times a week, at night, we have visitors who peer through the windows and through the cracks in the walls. That is how often we hear them; the quieter ones may come more often. Pete Hill, who is director for Community Action (whatever that is), says we must accept the fairness of reverse anthropology. After all, they are curious about Americans and we are the only ones living in the area. Now we are installing wire safety screens on all the so-called windows. I am making curtains by hand. That should solve the problem of peepers.

Public Works has taken a benevolent interest in the house. They raised the shower head from three feet to six feet off the ground. They know that foreigners shower standing up rather than sitting down (although I'm flexible). Now they are going to install an outdoor light, as it is widely gossiped that the nocturnal peeping has not abated in the least. I offered to pay the city for these services, but the workmen assured me that would be impossible because their record-keeping system is in hopeless confusion.

Our menagerie of animals is endearing. They work for a living and for this are rewarded with leftover rice and mackerel. We eat chicken several times a week because it's cheap and usually available from the last boat. The two cats and the dog line up beside us on the floor and wait their turns for the bones.

Dear Len and our Chapel Hill friends,

Public health is more than diet and heart disease. It is toilets, too. Last week I ran into a Peace Corps volunteer while on a hike into Nett. Who else would have a roll of toilet paper under one arm and a jar of peanut butter under the other? We chatted and shared a drinking coconut. He had just spent two years out in the wilds of Kitti working in what is euphemistically called "community development." That translates—build water seal toilets. With heroic effort, he had succeeded in convincing two families to build them.

His theory for the reluctance of islanders to construct the toilets is the price of toilet paper. Traditionally, they used leaves, which are abundant and cost nothing. Leaves, however soft, do not flush down the water seal toilet, and toilet paper, assuming it is available, is expensive relative to income. He is depressed at the failure of his efforts. We speculated about the kinds of people who, with the best of intentions, design projects for the yet-to-be developed world but who have never examined fundamental assumptions about their own world.

Yes, our last letter was right. Pohnpeians do eat dogs at their feasts. Dogs were a major source of protein, along with fish, for Pohnpeians and other Pacific Islanders before contact with Westerners. Now only ritual specialists know how to wrap them in a certain type of leaf binding and cut the meat in prescribed ways, so cooked dogs mark occasions of high honor. Nowadays, pork is served at family gatherings and pigs have an economic importance dogs do not have. But dog remains a ceremonial option—Pohnpeians know that Westerners do not eat the flesh of dogs and offer us the choice to partake or not, in their usual courteous manner. O.K., I know what you're asking. It tastes like roast beef.

Thank you for the Maidenform bra in your last shipment. Where did you ever find a red one with heavy stitched cups?

Menlau and Kalahngan—that means thanks for everything.

Chapter 4

Smoke Follows the High People

We were seated in the center of the canoe house, upon mats; and yams, breadfruit, plantains, fish, bits of cold game of some sort were brought to us. Parties of two or three would come down to where we sat, walking with their bodies bent almost double. They took hold of our persons very familiarly, women and men, and gave frequent clucks of admiration at the blue veins marked through our skins on parts of the body which had not been bronzed by the sun. My comrades feared the Indians were Cannibals, and this examination was to discover whether we were in good roasting case.

—From the 1826 diary of a shipwrecked sailor, James O'Connell

"Hello there, empty nest," Sohn Alpet called out as he approached our homestead one muggy Sunday afternoon. When I heard the respectful form of greeting used when one is not certain who is inside a house, I knew something was about to happen. He added other honorifics, a rare compliment, and the promise to tell me a scandalous story he had sworn never to reveal. The conversation grew more convoluted as the purpose of his mission emerged.

Sohn Alpet wanted Roger and me to buy him an outboard motor for the whaleboat he was building. He and his family commuted regularly between their homes in Madolenihmw and Kolonia; overland travel was impossible. As administrators of the project, however, Roger and I had a budgetary dilemma. Although the government research grant was generous, it was restricted by category. We were allowed to rent boats we needed to complete the project, but not to purchase a boat or outboard motor. Here is the solution for both sets of problems Sohn Alpet proposed: "Loan me the money for the outboard and I will repay the grant by renting the boat, motor, and drivers back to the project." We drew up a contract.

Later that week his family staged a twilight dinner in the feast house with pork, cucumber salad, mangrove crabs, and yams and taro in various styles of preparation—fried, baked, and cooked with coconut cream. We invited everyone who had worked with the project and seated them next to the guest of honor—a new outboard motor. Proud, Sohn Alpet had carried it in himself and wiped specks of mud from its shiny surface. In the middle of his standard oration about the meaning of our project, how it would help people around the world, he made an announcement.

"Henceforth, this generous American woman, Mrs. Martha, is my mother. I am her devoted son." Never mind that my new son was more than generation older than me. Many Peace Corps members prided themselves on being children of the family with whom they lived. But children, we all know, have less responsibility than parents do. Mothers take care of their sons. Because Sohn Alpet had a real mother in her nineties and a number of aunts whom he addressed as mother, this meant I had financial and feasting responsibilities far in excess of the filial duties a fictive daughter owed. I could not in any language with all the tactfulness at my command disavow this honor.

"What kinship relationship does the new outboard motor have?" I managed to joke in response. To my relief family members laughed. "It is your younger son. Assign its elder brother to care for it," they responded and instructed me to avoid eating eels, the taboo food of the Lasialap clan of which I had become a new member.

But why, I wondered for a split second, had Roger been excluded from this expensive honor? Did Sohn Alpet think I alone was in charge of the project budgets? Then the lessons of anthropology kicked in—I had become an adopted mother in a matrilineal society. The rules of kinship are: first, mothers and sons always belong to the same clan, and second, you never marry anyone who belongs to your clan. Ergo, Roger was an in-law from another clan. Sons in Pohnpei take their status from high-ranking mothers who pass on subtle benefits. Sohn Alpet was thanking me for the boat deal and piggy-backing on my status. Little wonder he extolled my virtues and the worth of the project in his public speeches.

With the troubled trip to Wene behind us and with access to an outboard motor, the four of us scheduled visits to an area of Madolenihmw near Sohn Alpet's homestead to work on the organization of and census for the blood pressure research, as well as other ethnographic projects. The frictions and economic stress that so marked Wene seemed muted, even absent in the hilly region of Wapar. Instead of funerals, we attended a series of feasts to honor weddings, new titles, trips abroad, and the yearly obligations of the section to its titled leaders. Most of the children and adults used our first names. I heard little or no high language spoken, although the people of the area were conscientious about respecting customs and their duties to the Paramount Chief.

Our host, with whom financial arrangements had been straightforward, laughed easily and, with friendly grace, enjoyed the presence of foreign anthropologists. Souehdi and his wife had nine children, yet the number of children in the household never added up to nine. Souehdi's eldest sister, wife of the Paramount Chief of U, had adopted one of their daughters. Two sons were at boarding school, and another lived with his paternal grandmother who needed help on her homestead. A perky little girl about eight years old was a distant relative who had come for dinner several years earlier and never left. Other children dropped in to play with the chubby, cheerful baby of the household who was never out of someone's arms; some remained for days or weeks.

Although I planned to talk to women about their lives, my anthropological training up to that time had given me few theories, questions, or methods to study women except as adjunct to the lives of men and children. When I asked questions, I received stock answers: "You should ask my husband about that," or "Men know about things like that." "I'm baking bread; come and watch." "I wash clothes; let's go to the river." Sometimes they said, "That question reminds me of a story about Lord Kelekel. It's a good one." The women gossiped and talked about their children, but they did not regard their lives or opinions as significant. On the other hand, their unguarded friendliness made it easy to follow the rhythm of their days. Women are expected to work less arduously than men do; they say, "that is just how women are." I thought of cultures where the incessant labor of women ages and kills them and people say, "Of course, that is just how women are."

In addition to the main three-room house that was too hot to use in the daytime, the family had a large feast house and a small feast house, a cooking house, and a sick house built for a relative lovingly cared for until his death. Near the cook house was a copra-drying shed, suitable for drying clothes in the rain if one does not mind the smell. On the path leading to the Protestant church was a small store and another small tin building. A rocky path led to the spring used for bathing, washing, and collecting water for cooking. On the edge of uncleared woods were outhouses and on the opposite side, the decorated graves of family members. At the bathing pool, a short walk down a path from the homestead, pigs and a water buffalo wallowed in the muddy side. On the clear side, I bathed to the giggles of little girls who had never seen foreign ladies bathe. "Naughty, naughty" they whispered as they clutched each other for support—naughty not in reference to their snooping, but to my awkward use of the bathing slip, my inexperience in handling water buffalo, and my inability to chase away young boys who climbed coconut trees for a better look.

The sounds of children raking the yard awoke us before six o'clock each morning. During the day, Roger and I either sat in the feast house as men came to visit and talk or we made calls in the neighborhood. Although children were a constant presence, they were not disruptive; they played about but did not interrupt adults or cause the disturbances that mark most Western households with even one child underfoot. They did not ask questions nor vie for attention. Night and day, they followed and watched me, but refused to carry on a full conversation.

One evening after a delicious supper of freshly-caught reef fish, we sat in the light of a kerosene lantern as the children dropped off to sleep one by one. Relaxed from a good day's work, I was unprepared as Souehdi announced designs to restructure my life. "I think my plan will work well. You can take one of the boys back to America with you. I promise you that whomever you choose will work very hard in school." Sohn Alpet had introduced me as "my mother"; Souehdi wanted to adopt me as grandmother to his children. I was the right person to help at least one of his bright sons attend school in the United States, he repeated, and my mind flashed on the cost of higher education and occasional trips to the Trust Territory to maintain the bonds of friendship and family. I tried to imagine a sexually precocious Micronesian teenager following the custom of night-crawling in a New Orleans middle school or in the neighborhood where Roger and I lived. I declined another opportunity for Micronesian parenthood.

Some imagine that people in the tropics take advantage of the sun-softened days to nap each afternoon. True elsewhere, perhaps, but not in Pohnpei. I followed Souehdi through two weeks of activities; like other men of his generation he worked hard. On Saturday, he organized his church congregation to give a feast for the visit of the Paramount Chief or *Nahnmwarki*. He harvested his own foodstuffs from his concealed gardens and organized relatives and neighbors to work. On Sunday he acted as lay minister at the church service, then ritual leader at the feast afterward, and last, host of a large family meeting at his feast house. On Monday, he went to the District Office, where he was secretary and treasurer, work that provided him with a boat and motor and a small salary.

Tuesday, Souehdi paid taxes—that is, he donated his labor to the Paramount Chief of Madolenihmw who was building a massive feast house. Everyone was required to contribute what they had—money, labor, supplies, or prepared food. Wednesday, he worked long hours on his own homestead, his gardens, and the tiny store in his front yard. Thursday, he went to Kolonia by boat, did business for the church, shopped for his family and store, and represented his district at a meeting. All day Friday, he made preparations for his daughter's wedding, and Saturday, held the wedding feast. Sunday was church again, a little rest, and another family meeting. Monday, he gathered his extended family to raise the frame and thatch the roof for a new house for his mother. Everyone worked in the manner of barn raising on the American frontier; she moved in by nightfall.

Souehdi's work ethic had a purpose. He had a high title beyond what his clan affiliation, birth order, or family connections would entitle him and was in line for better one—titles in recognition of his zeal in working for the Nahnmwarki (or Paramount Chief), church, clan, and the general good of the community. Some people are born into the nobility; others earn it through hard labor. At one point in the construction of his new feast house, the High Chief of

Madolenihmw grew irritated that no one had fed the laborers who had donated their labor. Souehdi organized his family to serve pigs, yams, and other foods on such a huge scale that the pleased Nahnmwarki promised him a high title when the aged incumbent died. Thus it was expected that at the memorial feast for the old man, the Chief would confer the vacant title on his loyal subject. Although Souehdi would respond with modesty—"this title should belong to my clan seniors; I am unworthy"—the High Chief would persist.

Some men achieve status in both the traditional and modern political systems. Being a lay preacher or an elected official are routes, though expensive and laborious, to success. Sometimes men had difficulty finding a path to achievement or economic stability. Josep, a teacher in the elementary school and Souehdi's nephew, felt pulled between additional education and personal ambition, and the traditional ways of family-centered mobility.

"If I have a title or not, it does not matter," Josep claimed. "One night at eleven o'clock the Paramount Chief gave me a title but I left to go home. I didn't care. The next morning at five my fathers [his father, adopted father, and uncles] killed a pig for the Chief. I wasn't even present. They were worried about me and my status, so they made the title payment for me to avoid their own embarrassment."

Elders draw young people into marriage, titles, even land ownership. Men of Josep's generation, trained in the individualistic ethic of U.S. schooling, might achieve success in the modern sector and earn good salaries. Josep wanted to attend trade school in the United States, and tried to save money; yet within a two-week period, he had given more than 50 percent of his salary for a cousin's wedding, the feast house of the Paramount Chief, and the purchase of two pigs. He worked for his higher status uncle several days a week, including the weekdays he took off from teaching. Although he expressed disaffection with the system that forced him to give so much of his earnings and time while the glory went to older male relatives, he had become more and more an active participant in traditional affairs and made no effort to disengage himself. The research question was how work, choices, networks, and the tug between individualism and community life affected Pohnpeians' cardiovascular systems.

In Madolenihmw I heard more talk of yams, pit breadfruit, earth ovens, and community spirit than I did minute features of etiquette, high language, or failures of ancient customs. Had I spent the rest of my life on that island, however, I would not have mastered the technicalities of which titled person of which clan or subclan brought what and sat where at which feasts. The polity or political system of Pohnpei is complex and intricate. Each of the five districts or kingdoms has subtle variations of class and rank ranging from a hereditary nobility through landed gentry to commoners. A Nahnmwarki—Paramount Chief or High Chief—heads each district; below him are a dozen or more high-titled nobles and priests in what anthropologists call the A line. As its complement, the *Nahnken* or "talking chief" leads nobles in the B line.

In a new wrinkle of consumerism, Pohnpeians had begun to spend large sums to fill the raised fronts of feast houses with enameled wash basins—

ainpwot or "iron pots"—they crammed with cooked rice and taro, cans of mackerel and corned beef, loaves of bread with suckers stuck in them, soy sauce bottles filled with pig fat, whole cooked chickens, and lengths of cloth or short-sleeved shirts. The expense is draining many families' incomes, they said, worrying that creeping modernism would destroy their culture.

In the unspoken rules of exchange, each sponsor—family, congregation, or geographical section, for example—contributed everything they could, everything they believed would impress others and show respect to their leaders. Through a complex redistribution system, some returned home with an amount equal to the goods or food contributed. High-ranking people left with more than they brought; commoners who brought much might leave with nothing. The contributions and the redistribution of goods fueled gossip for weeks.

In human cultures people work for a living or in some fashion seek what the Bible calls "our daily bread." They feed, clothe, and house themselves and engage in trade, commerce, business, and practical activities. Beyond that, however, they will also use the fruits of their labor for prestige and status seeking. People can go to work by bike or in a bus or simple car. But some use Cadillacs, Mercedes, or limousines. The prestige factor has little to do with subsistence, survival, or just getting by. Instead, people of all cultures participate in activities that confer status and prestige and provide an outlet for competition. The feasting yams of Pohnpei are in this category.

Pohnpeian yams—not the same botanical species as sweet potatoes—reach legendary proportions. A favorite variety grows nine or ten feet in length and three feet in diameter; two men can carry one with ease. A single yam may weigh a hundred pounds; many are estimated to be over two hundred pounds; prize yams top five hundred pounds or one-quarter ton and require six to eight men to carry them and hang them in rafters of feast houses. It takes twelve or fourteen men to carry the rare ones that grow to the size of Jeeps.

At a feast, a yam grower looks away in faked humility when his relatives display his huge yam. Someone says to him, "Your yam is number one." The owner protests, admires another's entry, and does not reveal his pride or pleasure. His modesty is as much on display as his yam. Boasting will only encourage others to produce yet a bigger yam in challenge, and everyone believes that a man who displays a prize yam can afford humility because he has another bigger one in reserve lest he be challenged.

Men surround their gardens in secrecy. No one with any manners comments on yams growing near the house, much less inquires about places in the forest where a smart man has planted another garden. Yams grow in segments; a single segment several feet long will grow into two or three more when planted. If left in ground that has been dug up and softened, segments keep multiplying. Yams may be dug up, subdivided, or kept intact for presentation at a feast. Yams brought home from a feast may be replanted and are expected to grow even larger for next year's feasts. At the section feast, each head of a farmstead may contribute live pigs, kava plants, fresh breadfruit, fish, coconuts, taro, bananas, small yams, or purchased store goods. However, a man *must* give a large yam grown from a single vine. Pohnpeians know the histories and individual characteristics of more than one hundred varieties of yams, and as much prestige is earned for the introduction of a new subspecies of yam as for an enormous one. Yams are competition and conspicuous consumption that prove a man's industry, loyalty, and generosity.

The last major trip during this middle stage of our research was to the district of U, a seaside settlement called Nan U, home of the Paramount Chief of U. Although I had enjoyed previous day trips there, I was dismayed to learn that Sohn Alpet had made arrangements for Roger and me to live in the homestead of the High Chief. My command of respect language had improved with tutelage, but I wanted to avoid talking with any Chief. Pohnpeians my age were also anxious about exposing their linguistic skills before the nobility. In Wapar Josep had prayed in English one Sunday morning. "Why?" I asked. "I hoped no one had noticed me and no one would ask," he said. "I can't pray in Pohnpeian because I don't know enough high language for the Nahnmwarkis and Nahnkens, much less for God."

To make matters worse, I had collected dozens of examples of respect behavior and avoidance customs to be used in the presence of exalted persons. At one time, it was taboo to touch the Paramount Chief on pain of death. Although that extreme penalty no longer applied, the symbolic removal from direct contact with social inferiors was still in effect. Personal attendants do not look him directly in the face; they speak slowly, and their intonation and vocabulary accentuate rank. The High Chiefs use intermediaries or ritual concealment to enhance their splendid isolation. One practiced respect behavior to show social distance, even when landing a boat or canoe or walking down the path near the house of our host, Johnny Moses, Nahnmwarki of U, also called Sahngoro—Pohnpeian high language for "Your Highness."

The Pohnpeians were bemused, even disbelieving, that people in the United States greet the leader of the free world with a handshake and a "Good morning, Mr. President." Commoners, the status I favored, could avoid contact with their High Chiefs. What if I violated some taboo about dress, food, posture, speech, time, or space? How could I know all the proscriptions? Would my failures jeopardize the project? Sohn Alpet coached us without the nervousness he displayed in Wene. He had requested that Paul Benjamin, a high-titled elder from U, work on the census and other data collection projects. The two of them kept busy, meeting on political plots about title distribution I found byzantine. At intervals I warned them—do not engage in any plans for a title for Roger or me. Peace Corps volunteers were proud of those they had acquired through the intervention of their adopted families.

Anthropologists, I explained, have to maintain some distance or neutrality in order to be fair to their research. I feared that a title from one municipality would compromise our standing and the demands of the project in other districts. As a U.S. citizen, I had no claim to Pohnpeian lineage and no intention of going native. Moreover, I knew that obligatory payments for a title were steep. Sohn Alpet and Paul Benjamin swore with solemn faces that they understood. To placate or distract me, they collected long lists of title holders in each municipality, technical information about the title system we needed.

On the third day after Roger and I had settled into a back room of Sahngoro's house, Sohn Alpet, Roswel, Paul Benjamin, and assorted wives and children arrived at the dock with twelve stalks of sugar cane and a large tin of ship biscuits, the hard unleavened crackers sailors had introduced. Sohn Alpet handed me several sugar cane stalks and Roger a kava plant. We are participating in a traditional ceremony called an *aluhmwur*, meaning "to walk after," he explained. When high people such as Roger and I spend the night with a Chief, the entourage and retainers of the visitors follow within a few days to present their host with sugar cane and a kava plant. A feast with a pig killing, a meal cooked in an earth oven, and kava pounding follows. I entertained the suspicion that Sohn Alpet, who looked pleased with us, was making up traditions. Anthropologists do not want anyone inventing customs, and our sudden promotion to high people was alarming. The sun was too bright for me; I felt absurd and light-headed as I hiked up the hill with sugar cane stalks slung over my right shoulder.

The arrival of our entourage interrupted a meeting of the Paramount Chief with elected officials of U. But the men accepted the interruption with grace, and several began to prepare kava. Although Sahngoro was a Protestant church leader like Nahnid Lapalap (Sohn Alpet) and did not drink it, he expected it to be presented and served in ritual homage to him and to the spirit of the plant.

As the serving men passed the first cups, the Nahnmwarki blessed them; high-ranking elders warmed up for their long speeches. I had been daydreaming when I heard my name called. Sohn Alpet, sitting next to Sahngoro, looked proud—perhaps our public manners on which he spent so much energy had at last pleased him. Then I saw Roger kneeling in front of the Chief who was placing a wreath on his head. "Your new title will be *Koarom en Dohlen Wehien U*," he announced.

"Roger deserves a title." Even as I held that thought I understood how Sohn Alpet had out-maneuvered us—as wife I would have to accept the female equivalent of Roger's title. Before I could devise excuses or strategies to escape my high-status fate, the Paramount Chief summoned me to his feet. Outflanked, I had no recourse but to accept a title with as much dignity as Johnny Moses conferred it. My new title, Sahngoro announced, was *Karapei en Dohlen Wehien U.* Our titles translated loosely as "caretakers of a high peak in U municipality"—which peak in this mountainous region so steep that few live far from the shore, I never knew.

Sohn Alpet, the rascal, regarded the title giving as a great coup. Refusing to entertain my now feeble protests, he began a series of lectures on our new status and the duties we had incurred. We were no longer commoners with an obscure foreign status; our titles were *konnoat*, the royal word for "food"— in English, the "gentry" or minor aristocracy. We were entitled to a share of the Chief's food of roast pig and yams at official district feasts. But with Pohnpeian titles, however, Roger and I were going to have Pohnpeian responsibilities. First, we owed a title repayment feast; Sohn Alpet had already negotiated a plan. Our titles required the equivalent of a medium-sized pig, several hundred dollars in store-bought goods, and traditional produce from the land. But our farmstead produced no yams or kava plants, only worthless cucumbers. Sahngoro, a good Protestant and a lay leader in a church that needed a new roof, would appreciate cash in lieu of a pig or store-bought goods.

The next day, Roger, our aristocratic entourage, and I processioned again to the Nahnmwarki's feast house with cash wrapped in a leaf Paul Benjamin had provided. I should have written down what kind of leaf we used to carry our tribute; anthropologists are supposed to record details like that. But my mind was preoccupied with the category of our grant budget that could absorb the job-related expenses we had just incurred. As we once again entered the feast house under a blazing sun, I selected "public relations." Government bureaucracies accept fieldwork expenses as long as you use their language and explain nothing.

By virtue of our new titles, Roger and I would receive food tribute at the traditional feasts and sit closer to the front of the feast house. I was less nervous sitting under quarter-ton yams that dripped clods of dirt on me than I was by the smoke from the earth oven that filled the feast houses. When I mentioned this at the title repayment feast, the men laughed. "That is the price of advancement. We say that smoke follows the high people. Now you are *soupeidi*, a title holder in the Nahnmwarki's line; you are among 'those who face down toward the earth oven and kava stones.' The smoke will find you."

Although the gap between high people and commoners has closed, the institution of chieftainship and their complex title system give a remarkable coherence and identity to modern Pohnpeians. These customs have always been changing; they are in no danger of dying out. No one has an excuse for failing to serve the Chiefs and high-titled elders. After all, they say, the water in the bottom of the channel is always high enough to bring tribute to rank. Pohnpeians also griped about the demands high people put on followers. High people—it was claimed—do not redistribute their collections in a fair manner. Giving gifts, making flattering remarks, and outright fawning over them are influential. Pohnpeians exhort each other not to gossip about the actions of high people and then complain in the time-honored ways their ancestors no doubt used. Nor would one want to anger the spirits that protect high people. One kind of sickness is caused by a lack of respect for family heads and High Chiefs. The sickness will vanish when medicines and spells placate the offended spirit. If High Chiefs are displeased, their followers and retainers must stage an elaborate ceremony of public forgiveness called a *tohmw.*

Keeping track of children in the High Chief's household was as difficult as it had been in Souehdi's. Because Sahngoro and his wife had been unable to have children of their own, they had adopted and fostered many children. Some of the couple's adopted sons and daughters had children of their own living in the homestead; I lost track of how many and what type of relationship after counting and interviewing seventeen adoptees and as many visitors and young boarders. The habit of adoption is widespread in Pohnpei, as it is in much of Polynesia and Micronesia. The censuses we were finishing for the blood pressure project indicated that at least one quarter of the islanders were themselves adopted, "lifted up," or had "lifted up" an adopted child.

In ordinary practice, biological parents may give a child to another couple soon after weaning. The adopting couple will raise and provide for their adopted child as they would for any natural child; this includes inheritance of both land and status. In return, the child will care for its adopting parents in their old age, as would any birth child. Since Pohnpeians are deeply attached to their land, they must have heirs to honor that attachment through succeeding generations.

In the most common pattern of adoption, the biological parent is a younger brother or sister of one of the adoptive parents and thus owes deference to a childless older sibling. Biological parents who agree to an adoption show respect to older relatives and insure a better portion of land and titles for their offspring. The importance of birth order in establishing seniority within the kin group and the blood ties between siblings are the strongest ties that bind Pohnpeian kin together.

If a man or woman dies, siblings—the man's brother or the woman's sister—will raise the minor children. This is a comfortable arrangement, since those relatives whom Westerners call aunts and uncles are already addressed in the Pohnpeian kinship terminology as honorary "mother" and "father." Because the kinship terminology honors both biological and adopted kin, a secondary or backup parent and child relationship already exists. A spouse's child by a prior union, premarital liaison, or earlier marriage—what Westerners call a stepchild—is called a "discovered child."

No special ceremonies or legalities mark the adoption, although under both the Japanese and American administrations, the agreement can be registered. The two sets of parents (or the single mother with her relatives) meet and discuss the arrangements, often with help of other kinspeople. A single mother who wishes to adopt out her child has full power to make the decision. She will receive compliments, assurances, and full support for a loving and dutiful act. The child grows up knowing the facts of parentage and will probably maintain strong ties with the biological family. No secrecy or stigmas are attached; everyone knows the facts. Adoptions are accomplished with ease, a concern for the child, and an apparent lack of pathology.

Adoption may be an alternative for young couples whose relationship is unstable or for young women who wish to retain their premarital freedom. In such cases, they can postpone parental responsibilities until maturity comes. Others who have embraced adulthood and desire children make better parents. Adoption may provide a gradual way to ease into marriage and adult responsibilities—in contrast to the U.S. custom where the birth of a child to a young couple, a premarital pregnancy, or an adolescent pregnancy has severe consequences for the education and employment of the mother and the health of the infant.

In addition to being made a high-ranking citizen and the mother of an outboard motor, I was tempted with offers of adopting a child. I had become a member of a wide-spread matrilineal clan and the petty aristocracy of U and knew couples delighted to have adopted a baby on Pohnpei. Looking for pathologies resulting from these practices, I found only advantages. Even the rare babies born with disabilities found homes with experienced older mothers who loved their special needs. Emotional problems that may be associated in Western minds with adoption are absent in Pohnpei. On a small island where every third or fourth person is an adopter or adoptee, a child always stays close.

Some anthropologists and foreigners believed that Johnny Moses (Sahngoro, Nahnmwarki, or Paramount Chief of U) was a saint; others thought that he was a conniving genius. Regardless, living in his homestead confirmed my worst fears. His wife, jealous of his royal prerogatives, instructed me in speech and manners. In her presence, I sat silent like a good commoner. Sahngoro, however, wanted to question me about the United States. Although I was never alone with him, he sought opportunities to speak with me and sensed my discomfort, "Let's just talk; never mind high language."

"Look at the incredible machines you Americans have. We see pictures of things we have no name for. I watch the airplane land at Deketik [the landing strip] and I wonder how my ancestors could have built Nan Madol without cranes, bulldozers, ships, or the other machines we have now. Perhaps the Bible was right and 'there were giants in those days' who just picked up the stones and laid them in the lagoon."

"I have heard that you can open a garage door from a distance without touching it. What kind of amazing magic is this? Tell me how it works." I told him one touched a button inside the car and then realized I had no practical idea of the connection between button and garage door.

"Is it true," he asked, "that your countrymen have mistreated Indians, taken away their land, imprisoned them, and killed them?" I tried to explain yet not deny what he knew about the sad history of Indian-European relationships. "If you abolished slavery, as we too did much earlier, and proclaimed that all men are equal, why do you have those terrible racial riots and conflicts between black and white?" He knew the answers; I don't think my fumbling explanations in his language helped. Then, after many tentative tries, he asked the question foremost in his heart, "If Americans mistreat small groups of people whose skin is a different color from theirs, how can Micronesians expect fair treatment at their hands? How can a set of tiny islands hope to negotiate our own political status with a nation of such power and prejudice?"

Although negotiations with the United States about the political future of Micronesia was next to feasting, titles, and exchanges—the most often discussed topic on the island, I had not heard anyone give as much thought to the implications and underlying moral philosophy as Sahngoro did. "What would be best," he asked, "independence, free association, statehood, a commonwealth, a dependency, or some other arrangement? How could Micronesians balance their own ethnic rivalries and protect the interests of tiny atolls or remote islands? Can the people of Micronesia, who had no experience of national unity, cope with freedom, materialism, and international politics? Would powerful U.S. politicians put their need for military bases on the Asian rim before the rights of island self-determination? What leverage did the people of Micronesia have over a world superpower?"

Several months later, I returned to Nan U to check details on the census. I had notified Sahngoro of my visit and agreed to attend him at his feast house. The sun was hot and still; I saw no signs of activity as the boat docked. A retainer emerged from a shady place to announce that the Paramount Chief awaited me and requested that I translate for a meeting he had scheduled with the new U.S. Navy Seabees contingent.

The High Chief was seated with officers from the military unit and members of his retinue. The perfect proportions of his feast house with its traditional lashings of coconut-fiber twine at the corners where the beams joined struck me once again. One could almost believe that only this colorful and mildew-resistant sennit and wooden pegs held the feasting place together as they had in olden times, but I suspected there were nails and screws in the timbers. When polite formalities were underway, the kava pounded and served, and long speeches had begun to flow, the High Chief conferred titles on the ranking officers of the Seabees unit. Their titles were lower than mine; they were not expected to reciprocate in the traditional manner as I had. Sahngoro wanted something else in return.

The U.S. government had sent the Seabees to plan and engineer construction projects on Pohnpei, part of American political strategies for building favor with the Micronesians in anticipation of the status negotiations. They had chosen the Seabees with care, wanting to present the most favorable image of the United States and to balance negative views of foreign policy and the Vietnam War. Tall, wide-eyed, with smooth-faced innocence, the Seabees were breathless with good fortune; they were assigned to a tropical island—far from the gruesome arena of Southeast Asia—with beautiful girls, kind people, and plenty to eat and drink. Gossip attributed the many babies born to single women to these enthusiasms.

The main question that day was what Sahngoro, the High Chief, and other political leaders wanted this smiling arm of the U.S. military to do for U municipality. The Navy men, not given to long speeches, asked the Pohnpeians—what about a boat dock, a school, a special road. I translated. No, they already had enough, came the answer. I knew Sahngoro wanted a new roof for the church in which he was a deacon; Roger and I had already made our private contributions. But I also understood that the Seabees were never going to roof his chapel. The High Chief had asked me about the strange, to him perverse, view of the separation of church and state held dear in the United States. I explained that this principle was written down in our country's founding documents. The people of Pohnpei do not need protection from their religion, he snorted; helping God's churches is the same as serving the title system and the Nahnmwarkis.

We drank soft drinks and ate donuts as the conversation in the feast house drifted. Someone mentioned the progress of the new road that would in time link Nan U with Kolonia. The High Chief mentioned how God had blessed the United States, what we Americans owed Him, and how much our technology had helped the people of the world. The Seabees nodded in the right places, thinking this a secure topic. I believed Sahngoro was building a clever but devious case for a new church roof.

The negotiations seemed at an impasse when Sahngoro drew himself to a regal position, his head higher than everyone there, and announced in a chiefly voice, "The Seabees must make a meaningful contribution to the kingdom of U."

"You Americans," he began, "command the technology of the world. You have just placed a man on the moon, a feat led by your great martyred leader, President Kennedy. Because of your skills, the people of the world no longer live in darkness." Another discussion of our wondrous technology as opposed to our dirty feet and bad manners must be coming; I wondered how to translate his mild insults.

"All the world looks to you because of your power and cleverness," he continued, "but there is much you could learn about making peace. We of Pohnpei used to war against each other, but we have stopped. So you understand machines; we understand peace. In token of that, we [the royal pronoun] shall ask the Seabees for one thing only." The Seabees' officers, ready to construct if not leap tall buildings, grew attentive.

"We request a small piece of rock from the moon." The High Chief waited for the commotion that greeted his translated request to settle and repeated his request in words of escalating humility and modesty.

"We have heard that your astronauts brought back many rocks from that journey. For countless centuries, all human beings have shared the same moon, all have pondered its presence in the heavens. Some have worshiped it. But when you stood there, all of us saw the Earth for the first time. We share that Earth together, and the moon rocks are the symbol of one people on one sphere.

"I shall personally, at my own private expense, take this treasure to all the islands of Micronesia. They will trust my words. I will show them the evidence that the United States of America wishes peace, just as we do. Although we appreciate your offer to build us another wharf, we wish instead to cooperate in bringing a better understanding between the people of Micronesia and those of America. The moon rocks will help people understand that differences in languages and customs are small compared to our unity with each other on this planet."

At that moment, I understood why my ancestors bent their knees to kings. Sahngoro, High Chief of U, was every inch a monarch. The Seabees with glazed looks of surprise and confusion turned to me and to each other. After some cryptic discussion the ranking officer agreed to relay the unusual request to his superiors. With no intention of, much less official mechanism for, honoring his simple request, the sailor engineers left the meeting in the feast house frustrated. The High Chief in his royal sincerity had little idea of the complexity of the U.S. government. At the end I could not bring myself to tell him that the majority of American leaders do not know or care where Micronesia is.

A letter from the field:

Dearest Ones,

Thank you so much for the lovely presents you sent. The sandals fit perfectly, but I must send them back before they mold beyond hope. The manufacturer's instructions in those beautiful blouses say: "Machine wash and tumble dry." Not a word about taking them to the river, pounding them with a flat stick, and hanging them on a bush. No warning that your clothes smell grand, but all buttons and snaps will be beaten to death.

My clothes situation is getting desperate. I have to sit cross-legged for hours, get in and out of boats, and hike up hills without revealing too much leg or knee. Sears catalog sells only "miracle fabric" dresses, which are no miracle out here. Synthetics are too hot, fashions in America too short; and Sears does not realize that coconut milk causes permanent stains.

We served the canned ham you sent at a party. But we are saving the bean dip until a ship brings some chips. The project people in North Carolina sent me granola. I mix it with powdered milk, and it tastes wonderful—what do I know? I have begun to dream about food in 3-D Technicolor. In Madolenihmw, we had wonderful meals—fresh fish (raw, fried, and baked), mangrove crabs, yams cooked in coconut cream, fried and baked bananas, chicken soup, and pancakes. Last weekend, we went to another huge feast, but first we had a lunch of rice and curry. I have discovered that it is better to eat beforehand, because, contrary to expectations, people do not eat much at the actual feast.

Roger and I have great photographs of little kids playing with pig entrails and generally getting bloody and dirty. They have such a good time following the adults around and trying to imitate them. They go off behind the feast house and make a tiny earth oven or carry around machetes taller than they are.

It's winter here in the tropics—the trade winds are stronger and rainstorms more dramatic. But I would have to live here through many more seasons to feel a difference in temperature. It is still hot, hot, hot when the sun is shining. Because of the recent bad weather, the plane had to overfly the island, and we haven't had any mail for two weeks. Since there is no mail delivery outside Kolonia, we are even more isolated from the world on trips to other districts.

A bunch of Peace Corps volunteers and anthropologists had a marvelous time snorkeling off a small island in the lagoon—my first look at the extraordinary tropical fish and coral reefs of the Pacific. Coming back, we ran into the roughest waters we've seen inside the lagoon. Wave after wave came crashing on top of us. Very uncomfortable, but not dangerous. The winds are high in January and February. We were drenched from the rain and waves and stopped on one of those rare sandy beaches to build a fire to dry ourselves out. I was cold—a splendid, rare event. The remains of a former Japanese military installation are a fifteen-minute walk down the beach—remains of war left to rust in peace.

I'm enjoying the company of the Peace Corps people stationed here. The number of volunteers relative to the population of the islands are, I hear, higher in Micronesia than anywhere else in the world. That must be thanks to U.S. leverage and control of Micronesia. I don't know—and they question the whole thing too—how much good do they do? But they are such committed, intelligent kids; in the main they make a great impression on the Micronesians and will be super citizens when they return home.

All of us, Peace Corps and anthropologists, take the rules of etiquette at feasts seriously. You cannot dangle your legs over the side of the platform—no matter what. You must sit with your legs crossed underneath and facing the Chief or highest-ranking person who sits on a raised platform above the main platform. You may not leave without asking permission—in the proper language, please. All walking or moving about is done bent over, shuffling in deference. Keep your head lower than the high people's heads, if only in symbolic gestures.

Should anyone violate the canons of decorum, the Paramount Chief may leave in a huff. In the middle of a feast we attended, just before the food was distributed, the Paramount Chief suddenly bolted out the back door—actually the front door in honor of the High Chief. There were anxious looks and strained whispers; no one could distribute food until the Chief returned through his special door. The second-in-command, the Nahnken, went to see if or how the High Chief was offended. But the Chief had only needed to visit the "little house." Although Paramount Chiefs share that fact of life with commoners, the word for it is different—but of course. Roger hoped the Chief was angry, because there is a special ritual to placate him and seek his forgiveness. Roger wants desperately to see that ceremony performed. Another time.

Yes, we confess. When the Pohnpeians kill and cook dogs at their feasts—an ancient tradition on an island with no protein sources but seafood—we eat some. More for solidarity and courtesy than hunger; it is economical to feed table scraps to dogs and then eat them. Sohn Alpet says that you should eat the ones that bark at night, but not your personal pets. Before pigs arrived on Pohnpei with the first missionaries, dogs were the high-status protein food. Nowadays pigs cost a lot and count as a more serious contribution. But dogs, you should forgive the pun, have a strong traditional flavor and their place at a feasting table.

At a recent feast I spent most of the day watching men and women with quick hands weaving containers and carrying equipment from leaves and vines. They attribute little importance to these implements and discard them after each feast. But I consider them the most beautiful folk art produced on the island. The women of Sohn Alpet's family wove several intricate baskets for me—nothing to it, they scoffed, as they split the rib of an entwined banana leaf and created a perfectly square basket. They are delighted that I sent several baskets back to you all, Mother and Daddy, in exchange for the picture book of plump, yummy-looking dogs you found for them. Thank you for the packages.

Kaselehlie,
Koarom and Karapei

Chapter 5

A Locked Box

For centuries our forefathers sailed throughout the Pacific Ocean without
the luxuries as we know them, but they managed to give us a rich heritage, our customs, and islands we call our own. Destiny has chosen this
generation of Micronesians to decide whether we want to lose our identity as a people and be absorbed into a foreign culture, or remain as proud
and confident people among the community of nations.

—Delegate to the Congress of Micronesia

*W*hen the photographs of our trips were developed in the States and
returned, I gave Sohn Alpet copies. He examined them, shaking his head,
radiating disappointment. "Look at you, this is not a proper way to act. In
the future for pictures and in public, you must tuck your elbows in to your
waist. Proper Pohnpeian women do not wave their arms about. You are permitted to smile a little bit, but not so your teeth are showing. You look ——,"
he struggled for a word. I translate the one he found as exuberant, animated,
or undignified. "Everyone will know how you feel. And that is not done in
Pohnpei," he finished.

Pohnpeians insist that a person's personality is closed off to others. Our
bodies are like a coconut frond basket that hides its contents from view; they
say, a "a man or woman is an attic." Like the shelf built below the house roof
that holds stored and private things, a person's thoughts, feelings, beliefs, and
private selves remain concealed. Human bodies have exteriors revealed in
speech and behavior, but observers must be left to guess what goes on inside.

People say, "Pohnpei is a locked box." They tell many legends about
encounters with supernatural beings, monsters, giants, or dwarfs, or romantic
love stories and animal stories for their own amusement and to instruct the
young. But serious tales—clan origin myths, legends about local gods, the formation of geographical landmarks, magic, and medicine—are traditional

knowledge that remain in the hands of island historians. Although the substance of the stories is common knowledge, only the few specialists know the details—some lore is not only secret but sacred. Some things must remain hidden until the possessor of the arcane knowledge, on his deathbed, reveals what he knows to a successor chosen with great care.

Students often ask me whether people in a place like Pohnpei withhold information, distort their lives, or lie to anthropologists. If Pohnpeians have locked boxes for each other, they inquire, what are they withholding from foreigners and anthropologists? I wish I had a sound theoretical or epistemological basis to separate truth from falsehood. I have no doubt that people lied to, manipulated, ignored, or tricked me. All fieldworkers have these experiences.

Had I gone to Pohnpei with the intention of investigating sorcery, for example, I would not have been able to open the boxes in the attic. What I learned through time came from experiences filtered through nuance and interpretation—smoke and mirrors, whispers of a different reality. No one needed to know the identities, methods, or victories of the major sorcerers on the island; so their secrets when I stumbled upon them were safe with me. Most information I wanted to know on behalf of the blood pressure project was of no consequence to Pohnpeians. They discussed diet, household composition, daily routines, and other nonsensitive topics with ease and intelligence. I doubt that they lied any more than Americans do. On sensitive areas—questions about incest are one example—I looked for patterns, vocabulary, and independent verification, not the wrong-doers, their names, addresses, guilt, or innocence.

In addition to the heart disease project, Jack, Roger, and I were involved in individual and joint research tasks—the first one was to describe and explain how a culture like Pohnpei treated the universal incest taboo that bans marriage or sexual relations between certain categories of relatives. In the United States, Americans think of incest as child abuse and individual pathology. In traditional societies like Pohnpei, incest strikes at the heart of social organization; it is a crime against the blood relationships that bind people together. These facts, however, do not stop either group of people from breaking the taboos of their respective societies.

Lord Kelekel's son was the most prominent Pohnpeian to break the incest taboo. After his father rewarded him, despite disrespectful behavior, with the second highest title on the island, Nalapenian, a precocious youth, began a series of amorous adventures.

> Immediately after Nalapenian's true father appointed him Nahnken, the youth went off to spear more fish. But on his way, his father's sister called out to him. And so he lay with her. This made him late to the walking cup of kava, which was being served in his honor. When the bearers brought the cup, his aunt performed the spell of the walking cup over him.

Never mind the kava. The point of the story is this: after that Nalapenian married his father's sister and she bore him many sons—who under matrilincal kinship rules belonged to the clan of their mother and her brother. Although the oldest son of this dubious match could not succeed his father as Nahnken, just as Nalapenian could not succeed his father, Lord Kelekel, as Nahnmwarki or Paramount Chief, he could become the High Chief by virtue of his clan membership through his mother. And so he did. The sons of Nalapenian and his father's sister had the perfect birth constellation to succeed to high places. The relatives whom Westerners call "aunts" Pohnpeians call by the word for "mother." Knowing these facts, what can we conclude? Is this a tale of incest or ambition?

Pohnpeians themselves are ambivalent. Such stories can illuminate the origin of customs or justify one lineage over another, but on another level they reveal thoughts too dangerous or taboo to voice aloud. Yet whatever interpretation one adopts, the story of Lord Kelekel's adventurous son proved an infallible way to ask people about the incest taboo.

The most general category of incest is called "evil gazing," which means heterosexual relations between clanmates, aunts, uncles, certain kinds of cousins, and in-laws. Pohnpeians define blood relatives in such a broad fashion that they have many temptations and opportunities to break their taboo. The ban against having sex with a clanmate is strong—but nonetheless violated; the more besetting sin is to do it in an open way and incur gossip. Everyone knows people who are guilty of "evil gazing," though no one admits it of themselves. They have a saying, "If you follow the taboos, you die; if you don't follow the taboos, you die."

• The rules of engagement in the "evil gazing" kind of incest are like those for adultery. Couples who commit incest are consenting adults—brothers and sisters, parallel cousins, clanmates, aunts and uncles, in-laws, or grandparents and grandchildren. Perhaps they are alone together and an attraction to each other proves too strong to resist. In common with all extra-marital liaisons, the key question is place—Where do they go where no one can see? Where can an illicit couple be alone? Where can they claim they were swept away in the moment of passion?

At the other end of the continuum is the most shocking violation of the incest taboo—"eating a rotten corpse" or sexual relations within a nuclear family. The worst form of this offense is sex between brother and sister or between parallel cousins, cousins connected to each other through siblings of the same gender, that is, father's brother's children or mother's sister's children. "Eating a rotten corpse" is the Pohnpeian metaphor for the most disgusting acts human beings can imagine. Little wonder no one wished to admit this; the gossip provided few cases.

When I asked people I trusted—"What's this I hear about eating a rotten corpse?"—their response was immediate. "Where did you hear about that? Who is saying these things?" When I repeated what I had heard and asked for clarification, some respondents were analytical; others told of specific incidents. All responses fell into the same patterns. Incest of this type is forbidden and shameful. People who do it are animals; they will suffer guilt, shame, and fear. Their punishment for sexual offenses as well as for breaking taboos about secrecy is "supernatural doom"—sterility, impotence, sickness, asthma, misfortune, and eventually death will come upon them; everyone will know their crime because offenders have dark circles under their eyes. That guilty people will be prey to bad luck, and death is the safest prediction in any culture; in a society like Pohnpei rejection and ridicule remain the strongest social control. I did not hear credible stories in which an adult coerced a child, the type of incest that figures in so many American secrets. In Pohnpeian eyes that violation went well beyond eating a rotten corpse.

During the times Roger's research project on traditional medicine, curing, and sickness took him out of Kolonia for fieldwork, Sohn Alpet and other friends brought assorted female relatives to stay with me, expressing pity for my solitude. Privacy is a bad word in Pohnpeian; no one needs or wants an entire house to himself or herself. Furthermore, the constant visits of people who respected privacy by pretending not to see or hear others in the same room held elements of chaperonage. Married women are expected to have high standards of morality; they should not be left alone. After all, don't the stories recount what happens to a woman and a man when proximity and opportunity are thrown together? Evil-gazing and adultery.

I, however, craved privacy like a physical ache and lusted to be alone. After months of living with colleagues and in bustling households, I wanted to write field notes, read, and work on language study through the cool rainy days.

Besides my lack of solitude, I had another problem common to female professionals. I was holding down two jobs—both anthropologist and housewife. Being domestic manager in a tin shack on a tropical island was a full-time hunter and gatherer life. I went up the hill with an egg carton, hoping the chickens had laid eggs, then down the hill for a loaf of bread. Then I visited the little stores trying to piece rudiments of a meal together. Sometimes at one location or another across town I found fresh fish, fruits, vegetables, or meat. Because I could buy only what balanced on the motorbike, I rigged nylon fish nets to carry my purchases; that meant daily shopping. While on errands, I met people and stopped to chat; soon domestic rounds had consumed an entire day. Even simple meals of rice and canned mackerel or rice and corned beef, staples of our diet, required much more effort than food preparation in the States, and we also had company most of the time.

On top of procurement, I cooked, swept, cleaned, washed dishes, and trimmed wicks on kerosene lamps, refrigerator, and freezer. On the flat stone in the shower I soaped and pounded the laundry, but when it rained for several days my wet clothes refused to dry. Roger and I had only a few changes of clothing between us; clothes that stayed wet too long began to mildew. Pohnpeian women shifted their laundry inside when it started to rain and outside when it stopped, but engrossed in work or out running errands, I forgot.

Sohn Alpet and Paul Benjamin recognized my dilemma and introduced me to Klarines. I needed help, even in a shack, they said; I could use a woman to practice language with, I said. The men I worked with intended Klarines to stay near me night and day; but I balked and we negotiated a compromise. During regular five-day-a-week office hours she could chaperon me and work around the house; nights and weekends, however, belonged to me—even if my reputation suffered. She did the laundry, watched the weather, swept, and performed a task Pohnpeian women think is legitimate work for females—she set traps, collected dead rats, and disposed of their crushed loathsome bodies. I knew in every pore of my body that this was men's work—even one of Floyd's natural laws.

Several times a month I hiked up to a house in the hills above the end of the road and spent a relaxed day with an unusual woman I had sat next to at a feast in Madolenihmw. Iseh was thinner and more vivacious than most Pohnpeian women, and as a widow about sixty years old, she enjoyed a freedom of speech I seldom encountered among Pohnpeian women. The Pohnpeian men I knew questioned me in detail about these trips; the men were protective, perhaps possessive about Iseh and my growing friendship, yet they seemed to accept Iseh as a good person, if not the best companion for me.

It was rumored with quiet respect that Iseh was a favorite of young unmarried men, who formed a line outside her homestead at night. Several young men who had succumbed to her appeal said they were proud to be included in her circle of admirers. One young man gave voice to a common regard: "She is a great friend, experienced and loving. She refuses to remarry and cannot get pregnant. She's fun to talk with, and we enjoy her company."

Later, I asked Iseh about the gossip with as much tact as I could muster—it is difficult to know if one has been tactful in another language. She laughed, patted my knee, and gave me a lecture on the irrelevancies of maturity in making love Pohnpeian style. She claimed that age differentials are an odd American hang-up and regaled me with stories of sexually active older women she knew. "Besides," she added, "it's good for my arthritis."

Iseh, like other Pohnpeians, wanted to question me about strange Western sex practices—hard-to-believe tales, she said. How can two men make love, she asked me each time we met; how can a husband and wife remain faithful to each other all their lives? In return, she recounted some "eating rotten corpse" stories and neighborhood gossip about the sex lives of Peace Corps volunteers and Navy Seabees. She told me about a condition not caused by spirits, sorcery, or supernatural power called "bent penis." This was reputed to happen to men who engage in novel sexual positions with either inexperienced women or very experienced women from the Marshall Islands. Some women are alleged to be so skilled in intercourse that they can bend a man's penis—easier to do if they dislike him. Pohnpeian men can name unfortunates whom they know for a fact have been victimized and deformed. The cure is oral massage by non-Pohnpeian massage specialists.

Some Pohnpeian men as well as anthropologists I know categorize bent penis as a genuine medical condition with serious symptoms and the need for special treatment. Others believe that it is a great joke on gullible people. Iseh said that men worry about it too much and that a bent penis is not serious or painful. Sohn Alpet said we could not discuss such stories because of our clan relationship to each other; Klarines, the only Pohnpeian who did not interrogate me, claimed—in words to this effect—that men were only imagining a problem where none existed. Akina and Ioannes laughed and agreed with Iseh that men like the cause, the symptoms, and the treatment.

One day Klarines and some other women we knew began to worry what would happen to them if Pohnpei voted for independence in the status elections. U.S. money would stop and the flow of American-made products on which they depended would end. "Soap!" they exclaimed. "We can eat off the land, but gardens don't produce soap. U.S. soaps are good but too expensive; we use them up too fast and don't earn enough money to buy more. We have to clean clothes, babies, hair, floors, and kitchen equipment. Lots of people in Kolonia have no stream in their back yard." Then Klarines asked, "Do you know a recipe for making soap?"

My pioneer grandmother talked about how women on the Oklahoma frontier boiled wood ash and animal fat to produce soap. Pohnpei had plenty of wood and pig fat. After the third discussion about soap, I wrote friends and relatives. "This sounds crazy, but I need a favor. Could you send me a recipe for making soap like our ancestors did? Check your local hippie commune, Appalachian folk customs, or the library."

When we had recipe and supplies in hand, Klarines labored for a long time and produced a tiny amount of lye soap strong enough to take the finish off cars. I had a new respect for the work of both pioneer and Pohnpeian women and wrote my friends in America to send soap of every kind they could find. In return, the women who dropped by my homestead gave me a recipe for ridding hair of head lice. The formula has helped in good stead in New Orleans where head lice infestations are chronic.

> Put a bottle of olive oil, coconut oil or other oil in hot water until it is warm. Apply the hot oil to the hair thoroughly. Wrap head in a hot towel and do something else for an hour. Comb out carefully, strand by strand, with a fine-toothed comb. Leave oil on for several hours or several days, then wash out.

One day several men dropped by to talk to Roger about his traditional medicine project. After one short glance Klarines stood up and left, averting her eyes. She refused to reenter—"one of the visitors is my classificatory 'brother,'" she whispered. "I'll explain later." The terms "brother" and "sister" include siblings born to the same parents as well as people Westerners call cousins. Relationships between true brothers and sisters and cousins within the same clan are intense and special; there are strong taboos—no jokes between them, no sitting near each other even in public, and sex between them is the worst kind of incest Pohnpeians can imagine. Such relatives must not come into physical contact with each other; it is unwise to be in the same room, Klarines explained, because the relaxed sexual banter and teasing that marks some conversations is offensive in front of brother and sisters. Yet it is impossible to maintain strict distance for all kin and classificatory kin. So a young boy is assigned a younger sister or a junior parallel cousin (one linked through siblings of the same sex, such as a mother's sister's child or a father's brother's child) with whom contact is taboo. This relationship of avoidance, called *pedel*, is part of the glue that holds Pohnpeian society together.

Sohn Alpet had not been well through this period, although he continued to work every day and make weekly payments on the loan for the boat's motor. Roswel's wife was expecting a baby, the alleged reason for his irresponsibility when not under Sohn Alpet's direct supervision. He had done a good job on the census, but he did not have enough maturity or personal authority to help us administer the questionnaires. Roger and I had to devise a better system than hiring young men if we hoped to complete the questionnaires before the medical team arrived.

With Sohn Alpet as pivot, we had hired four more high-titled elders who represented each of the four districts included in the study. Among them, they had little English and even less social science training; but they had *manaman*—authority or presence. Each one was a lay leader in his own Catholic or Protestant church, spoke the high language for Paramount Chiefs and God, and was married to a woman whom others trusted. Among themselves the five interviewer-elders knew every traditional, secular, or church leader and every family on the island. When such a man asked for assistance, no one could refuse.

Paul Benjamin, literate in Pohnpeian, had been a schoolteacher and councilman during the Japanese administration and had worked with earlier anthropologists. He quickly assumed a leadership role, and his extraordinary tact and knowledge marked the rest of the project. In another world, Paul Benjamin would have been a college professor or a diplomat. He possessed the gift, as a few people in every society do, of standing outside his own culture, looking back in, and seeing its patterns and pieces. Although he valued and observed the customs, he was less concerned about conformity to etiquette; he was fascinated by how and why his society worked and wanted to assist Roger and me in understanding it too.

Developing rapport with this unusual group took time. They had never worked for a woman and needed reassurance that their high statuses would not suffer. Sohn Alpet and Paul Benjamin had been right—the titles they had arranged for Roger and me tipped the balance of acceptance. Although doors opened and I had more freedom rather than less, the high-titled men soon began to mold the blood pressure project in their own image. They had a mission to manage it Pohnpei-style; they were not just doing jobs under a foreign grant.

In their view, Roger was the number-one chief of the project, and I was number two chief—Nahnken, head of the B line, the "talking chief." He—she in my case—hears all the problems, frustrations, and special requests that cannot be taken directly to the Paramount Chief. A number-two chief has special claims to intimacy and confidentiality with which to present the problems of his subjects to the Paramount Chief.

But the division of labor that they had assigned to Roger and me was not the same one we used in our American-style marriage. For example, they expected me to negotiate the substance of a transaction and work with all parties to their satisfaction. Then Roger was to sign official agreements and checks and not concern himself with details. That meant I heard all the daily disgruntlements or changes in plans, and he felt left out of decision making. Sometimes, he and I duplicated each other's work, reached opposing decisions on the same issue, or omitted an important problem. Many times I muttered to myself in both languages—my husband is a croaking frog during the day who expects to turn into a prince at night.

The Pohnpeian language speaks with eloquence about directions, ownership, and respect, but it lacks vocabulary for explaining social science. Regardless of my explanations about the rationale and methodology of the research project, the five interviewers developed their own rationalizations—elected and traditional leaders, farmers, and research personnel all do "God's work." Our work together reflects international and local cooperation; it "helps people." When they prayed at length in church for the research goals, I was grateful to be writing the reports on the project. Try telling Washington bureaucrats or statisticians that God creates the budgets for heart disease research.

Researchers in North Carolina needed a questionnaire that tapped into what people of Pohnpei worried about and what they, themselves, saw as major problems and solutions in their lives. We had to be certain that results of the questionnaire did not unconsciously project our American assumptions and values. The usual type of questionnaire limits responses to what the researchers consider important. To an anthropologist, however, variables, categories, or issues are what the respondents or culture bearers say they are. Take the notion of "achievement motivation"—how were we to translate this abstraction into Pohnpeian terms? Research in the United States showed a possible relationship between high blood pressure, key personality variables, and reactions to stress. In the United States, researchers believed some people are inspired to get ahead, achieve, succeed, excel, or better themselves; for them achievement is often equated with individualism. To find success, such a person needed to minimize family responsibilities in order to be mobile and self-sufficient.

To Pohnpeians, by contrast, ambition is a respected, even ancient idea, one not tied to job status and education. Dedicated work for the Paramount Chiefs and loyalties to a geographic section and district are signs of worthy ambition. Far from alienating an individual from his roots, ambition strengthens his family. In other words, an individual is ambitious through and for his or her family. An upwardly mobile man will have proof of success in higher titles, more prestige, and a larger share of food distributed at feasts. To do this, he must mobilize his wife, her relatives, his relatives, and their children to meet the persistent need for cash or products of the land—pigs, yams, kava—as well as donated labor. A man advancing through the title ranks pulls his hard-working relatives, male and female, up with him, just as his older relatives lifted him.

The traditional island system fosters striving for success as much as any urban society, but does so without sacrificing family loyalties and the strength of affiliation with others. The question was whether the Pohnpeians' mechanisms for balancing interdependency with others protected them from individual heart disease. So the questionnaire reflected what Pohnpeians told us about "modernization" and the stresses they felt as individuals in rapid social change. The pain and pace of change—everyone had sturdy opinions they were willing to repeat—was a staple of conversation among Americans each night at Stewo's restaurant, and among Pohnpeians at every feast. Those who defended life in Kolonia complained about the rural areas; of the countryside, the city dwellers said:

"The roads are bad."

"Those people do not observe the hospitality customs of old Pohnpei. They always want to be paid and to charge others, even their own relatives."

"Too many family members drain resources; in Kolonia a person has less family responsibility."

"They worry too much about customs that are not important, like respect language, and etiquette at feasts."

"They drink too much kava."

"There is nothing to do when you get there."

"The weather is bad; there is too much heat and rain."

To people in the rural areas of Madolenihmw and Kitti, the metropolis of Kolonia was the epitome of urban evils:

"The roads are bad."

"The people there do not observe the *tiahken sapw,* the customs of the land. They make mistakes at feasts and cannot talk in public because they never learned respect language."

"They always want to be paid and to charge others, even their own relatives."

"There are too many ethnic types, out-islanders, and foreigners."

"Kolonia is the same as America—cars, noise, crime, and big buildings too close together."

"The residents drink too much foreign kava—beer and alcohol."

"The weather is bad; there is too much heat and rain."

Regardless of weather and bad roads, the overweening problem islanders named was juvenile delinquency. Community leaders, including ministers, priests, the district administrator, and other prominent men had formed a Juvenile Delinquency Planning Council and sponsored a series of public meetings. All sectors of the community, from the judges to the youthful offenders, had decided that crimes, offenses against the common good— stealing, drinking, breaking and entering, violating curfew, and brawling—

were increasing, a dry rot that threatened the society's collective future. As people in the United States did, islanders blamed families, schools, and churches for failing to exert the proper influence. At each meeting speakers connected the so-called "crime problem" to the "economic problem," to the "education problem," and to the "breakdown of traditional authority in the family problem." When I walked up the hill to the island jail, prisoners and policemen alike offered long interviews and impassioned opinions.

POLICEMAN: Teenage boys do most of the thefts. Those who are influenced by Western culture, movies, bars, and gambling have the most criminal activities. Drinking causes the assaults and troublemaking. The parents of children who get in trouble do not go to church regularly.

PRISONER *[with ten short jail sentences from drinking to grand larceny]:* I was thrown out of school at 16 for drinking. I liked school all right. I just like drinking more. I was thrown out so as not to be a bad influence on the other kids. I really would like to go back to school. I don't have any land. I do not enjoy the traditional customs. They cost too much. You contribute pigs, yams, and kava. You get nothing in return. I have both municipal and section titles. My mother's oldest brother has a high title. I want to stay in Kolonia and get a job. I want to try and get my wife and kids back.

POLICEMAN: I have been a policeman for thirteen years. During that time, crime incidence in general has steadily increased. Most of the prisoners in jail now are teenagers arrested for theft. They usually steal money, clothing, and alcoholic beverages; only occasionally do they steal food. These are kids who have a lot of free time. The families of these children don't make them do chores around the house or tend crops. Corporal punishment would be the best thing for cutting the crime rate, and I say so from my own experience. During Japanese times, I was beaten and it really hurt. I was afraid to commit crimes, so I know it keeps people in line. I think the traditional leaders should have authority in the criminal process.

PRISONER: I was arrested the first time because I was drunk in a bar and assaulted a man. The other guy started it, so I hit him with a bottle. Three months' sentence. After I served that term, I stole some liquor from the club. I served that term and got out and stole some more liquor from the club. I escaped from jail and went to my girl's house at night. I knew I was going to get caught.

POLICEMAN: Giving authority back to the traditional leaders might work, but you have to change many things back to the way they were before. Think of what it would be like for people to start wearing grass skirts again tomorrow, just as people did a long time ago. Pohnpeians feel they are under the Americans and expect to be judged and punished by them or by people whose authority comes from the Americans.

PRISONER: I quit in the sixth grade because my teachers were cruel. The first time in jail, I was convicted of theft. Seventeen dollars. I planned to buy clothes. The second time I was arrested for taking a dangerous weapon—a table knife—into a bar and the third time was for stealing money from the Catholic mission. Five hundred dollars. I can't make copra, my family gave me no money, I had no job, so I stole.

Policemen saw the U.S. sponsored administration of justice, with its jails, judges, a civil and a criminal code, public defenders, and prosecutors, as the problem. The Council on Delinquency called for more counselors, more policemen, better schools, or better parent-teen communication, while acknowledging that such measures did not work in the United States. Women, in particular, blamed the abuse of alcohol for juvenile delinquency and the instability of family life. They fretted about feeding their families when husbands spent their income on drinks or about the embarrassment of sons "doing very bad things" while under the influence. They insisted that foreign kava—imported alcohols, such as the popular 151 proof rum—has a different history and physiological effect than Pohnpeian kava does. A group of women petitioned the district administrator to ban the importation of alcohol on the island; he ignored them.

Meanwhile, the suicide rate particularly among young men had been climbing not just in Pohnpei but throughout Micronesia; there were reliable vital statistics and serious public health concerns, but no answers. Roger and I attended a funeral service for a teenager; the speakers attached the same complex causality to his suicide as they did for juvenile delinquency—modernization, breakdowns in traditions and in family life, pernicious Western influences, lack of community support systems, personal failings, and a decline of the work ethic.

Pohnpeian elders belong to a romantic and worldwide club chartered in the conviction that in the golden age of the past, before modern vices changed everything, adolescents toed the line and respected authority. Elders believe that in traditional times, teenagers worked hard on the land and eventually received the rewards of industry, as they themselves had. They look back to a past when clan leaders, chiefs, and relatives, not impersonal courts and judicial institutions, punished serious offenses as a blot on the family name. Yet Micronesian folktales and legends offer many stories of young people who had hurled themselves from cliffs, sailed off in canoes never to return, hanged themselves from coconut trees, or had otherwise taken their own lives in fits of unrequited love or thwarted ambition.

It also is true, men and women conceded with a rueful look at each other, young girls are always sassy to their elders. Girls want lots of attention and pretty things; they make babies. But girls did that in the past too. Elders laugh about the fun they had night-crawling and remember youth as a time to sow some wild oats before settling down to adult responsibility. They are willing to overlook youthful pranks, practical jokes, and occasional wild behavior.

During this time, I heard rumors at Stewo's restaurant about another anthropologist working in Micronesia, asking questions about islanders' satisfaction with the current administration of the Trust Territory; the CIA or the Department of Defense had sponsored the research to gain an advantage over Micronesians in the political status talks just beginning. With the Vietnam War at its peak, paranoia ran high, and anthropologists had condemned colleagues for doing secret research that cannot be published in professional journals or other sources available to taxpayers or scholars. Research that remains classified or secret has the potential to hurt local people who do not know how to manage or manipulate the information they give. Those of us working on the blood pressure project had taken elaborate pains to explain our purposes, sources of funding, and standards of confidentiality, and to follow values appropriate to social science. We were asking questions about people's feelings on modernization and the status talks; we did not want to be confused with projects Pohnpeians claimed were spying missions. If knowledge is power, then covert research, like sorcery, has the power to hurt. The gossip and paranoia about spies and spying paralleled the feelings Pohnpeians have about sorcerers and sorcery.

Furthermore, most Peace Corps volunteers, anthropologists, and other liberal foreigners identified with the Micronesians. Having learned the language and having lived with Micronesians, we saw their viewpoint. We too were disillusioned with the shape of colonialism on the islands and with the potential for the destruction of native cultures at the powerful hands of U.S. business and military interests. Anthropologists are conservative in the sense that we often champion the values of traditional societies over modernization and colonialism running amok. We have seen other indigenous cultures with their richness destroyed forever. While people survive as individuals, the structure and traditions that give life meaning vanish.

The signs of loss and potential loss were everywhere, depending on your point of view. Pohnpeian elders, as elders everywhere, were dismayed by what they saw as the breakdown of traditional authority. Young people, educated in the U.S. system, did not want to learn the skills of farming and fishing or participate in the traditional feasting and title system. They preferred foreign food, music, clothes, houses, and vices, or so the older people claimed. The U.S. policy of pouring money into Micronesia—checkbook administration some called it—resulted in failed development projects and a type of welfare state with top-heavy bureaucracies and make-work jobs to which only younger males could aspire. Among themselves, Micronesians argued many conflicting points of view. Some looked for ways to have material progress without selling out their traditions to an alien culture. Others wanted independence, arguing that islanders could tame and control U.S. power on their own. Many wanted material progress and consumer goods regardless of the conditions or price.

Their concerns about crime and malevolent foreign influences reached a crescendo when a pair of brothers, drunk on a Saturday evening, attacked two policemen. One of the policemen died, the first such casualty in the island's history—a terrible turning point, people said, beyond which there was no retreat. This is a symbol of what is going wrong on Pohnpei, they repeated, and voiced older fears of clan retaliation between the families of the slain policeman and the young men. Although officials in the Trust Territory's legal system took immediate steps to punish the miscreants, Pohnpeians did not trust foreign law to prevent local revenge and decided to take matters into their own hands.

With anxieties pouring over the island like mountain streams from the highlands after rain, the Paramount Chiefs of several districts stepped into the grief and blame and evoked traditional customs of penance and forgiveness in a ceremony they arranged for the families of the slain policeman and the brothers who killed him. No one can say "no" to a Nahnmwarki who requests the presence of his or her family at a feast of healing. The parties drank from cups of kava in each other's presence, pledging to forgive and to ask for forgiveness. The magical power of kava brought peace and reconciliation and averted terrible acts of blood revenge. However people felt in their hearts, in secret thoughts and moments, would remain a locked box forever.

Throughout this middle period of our project Pohnpeians stopped me on the street to add points about juvenile delinquency they believed they had failed to make. They added more interpretations about the Micronesian status talks to what they had already told me. Some recounted the story of the dead policeman and the young men who caused such an uproar. A few, including our five high-titled interviewers, suggested that our project had solutions to the questions they kept asking us and each other. Quite the contrary. A locked box holds not only secrecy and privacy; it also contains the awful dilemma of raising children amidst forces no one—certainly not researchers—can control or understand.

Letters from the field:

Dear Parents, Siblings, and Friends,

Today has been the most unusual Easter that Martha and I ever celebrated, and I want to write it down while it is still fresh. Before the altar of the Catholic church in Kolonia, priests and Pohnpeian elders placed a kava stone. There, in full ritual splendor, they pounded and drank kava. The lifted communion cup was a coconut bowl—no wine or bread, only the sacramental juice of the pepper plant. The priests wore vestments, and the Pohnpeian men wore traditional loincloths and grass skirts. As the incense of frangipani blossoms filled the air, the celebrants anointed each other with coconut oil. A servitor sat cross-legged before each of the two priests.

What happened, as I have reconstructed the reasoning, was an extraordinary melding of rites of forgiveness and reconciliation from two ancient cultures. The church leaders had held long discussions to fit the theological meaning of Easter into a Pohnpeian worldview.

Following the invocation and Scripture reading, members of the congregation came forward one by one to whisper their confessions into the priests' ears. That took about 15 to 20 seconds for each confessor. Then the kava was presented (this has roots in secular traditions, but I won't go into all the details). The first cup of kava went to the priest who prayed, "Our hope is not in this plant but in God's mercy and in the actions of Christ on our behalf. I will drink it in God's name as a sign of the pardon promised to all who believe in Christ." That was the cup for the Paramount Chiefs. The servitor then offered the second cup of kava to the other priest and took the third ritual cup himself as a symbolic surrogate for the high-titled people present. Since four cups are ritually correct, the fourth cup went back to the senior priest.

The touchy part of a traditional apology ritual adapted to modern times was the difference between the church's view of forgiveness and the magical power Pohnpeians attribute to kava. When islanders present kava in the feast house to ask pardon of the Paramount Chief, he must accept it whether the offer is sincere or not. Such is the power of kava. In church, however, the priests were at pains to say that only true penitence and inner faith will bring forgiveness. Kava alone does not improve matters or atone for sin.

In the Pohnpeian view, correct ritual procedures are more highly valued than evidence of good intentions and a promise to mend sinful ways. In the Christian view, God is less capricious or subject to manipulation than is the Paramount Chief. God is said to offer forgiveness only for true repentance and does not punish mistakes in the rituals.

I have been interviewing extensively about the rituals of forgiveness and the role they play in Pohnpeian society. You remember that I wrote you about the kava and forgiveness ceremony after the killing of the policeman, which ended a potential blood feud and brought public forgiveness. I could write twenty pages on these matters of theological interest, but I want to turn this letter over to Martha.

Dearest Ones,

Imagine, if you can, an Easter Sunday service that climaxed with stick dancing. Visualize several hundred people on bleachers in front of the church. The women are seated in the front, holding twenty-foot-long boards across their laps. The men are lined up in rows behind them. Each person holds two short sticks. As they sing, they cross the sticks against each other and against the boards to produce a complicated rhythm.

Women keep their elbows in at the waist, moving only their wrists and hands throughout the dance. The men's gestures are equally restrained. This is no "let's get rhythm and let it all hang out" occasion. They are dancing sitting down. I tape-recorded the entire performance, but I wish I could have made a movie of it. I have this gut feeling that many elusive meanings of their culture are revealed in those careful movements of hands and eyes.

Klarines and several friends have been at the house all week, working on their costumes for the service. I will send pictures, but for now, you will have to see in your mind's eye how they looked. Men and women wore bright red skirts, flower headdresses, zories, and coconut oil. Some women added black bras, white bras, or dark sunglasses. I loaned that dreadful red Maidenform bra to Iseh. She looked great. That's better than having to wear it myself.

Do you remember long ago when that missionary family came to church and told us about living on an exotic tropical island? Then I was a frustrated teenager in a rural Oklahoma Protestant community who wanted to escape the restrictions of small-town life. You should have told me to be patient and that someday I would be a grown-up anthropologist attending a Catholic Pohnpeian Easter Mass on the very island those missionaries talked about. The Hanlins are back here at the Protestant chapel and send their regards to all of you. Isn't life interesting?

Blessings and Peace.

Chapter 6

The Ends of Canoes

Paddle left and paddle right, paddle mightily! Our boat goes fast.
Watch for roots on the crooked path. And you there—Listen.
And the next one listen. And you, third man, listen,
To what the first one says!

—Canoe song

*E*arly one morning, another distraught delegation from the hospital awakened us. Sohn Alpet, hospitalized several days for tests, had without warning entered a crisis. The doctors believed that he would die unless evacuated to more sophisticated medical facilities on Guam. Apart from practical questions of whether the seaplane could land in the lagoon or whether his condition could be stabilized for the long trip, the family knew of no diagnosis, Pohnpeian or foreign, that explained his illness. They feared he would die in a strange land without the comfort of family beside him.

As the doctors at the island hospital worked on Sohn Alpet, the family into which I had been adopted continued their frantic discussions. "Perhaps sorcery has caused this illness," some of his relatives whispered to me. "We cannot ignore that possibility." "We try to be good Christians," others noted, "but the old ways still work; they have a hold on us. Sometimes we're afraid." A few relatives believed that an evacuation to Guam would take him beyond sorcery's reach. Other relatives argued that removal put him outside the range of curing ceremonies that had the power to lift curses. It did not help that the doctors at the hospital offered no better explanations to assuage the families' fears.

By noon Sohn Alpet's condition, though critical, had stabilized. The doctors radioed the medical evacuation unit on Guam with their request and reported the weather conditions on Pohnpei; Roger and I located transportation to take our very sick colleague and his family across the causeway to the airport the moment we received the signal the seaplane was landing. His tormented wife, daughters, granddaughters, and haggard, silent sons and grandsons, brothers, and sisters waited first at the hospital, then at the landing strip for the plane to taxi to the dock and load on his stretcher. They took their leave, forgetting his injunctions not to show emotions; we watched the seaplane bank over the Sokehs cliffs to race the setting sun to Guam. Late that night, I realized I had just celebrated my thirtieth birthday.

Early the following morning, Roger and I gathered with family members at the hospital to await the radio call from Guam. Sohn Alpet had been comatose at departure and beyond the help of Pohnpei's medical resources; Michael, the American doctor, had prepared us for his death.

So when the radio call came in late afternoon, I interpreted it as good news—within the hour of arrival on Guam, Sohn Alpet had rallied. "No," his family said, "that is bad news, a confirmation of sorcery." When the seaplane landed, he was near death; no one could explain why he was so sick, they insisted. Why would he have recovered so rapidly unless he had been freed from malevolent influences—sorcery or curses—coming from someone on the island? His apparent recovery was the evidence they needed.

Senior family members called in a curer, a lay leader in the Protestant church on Pohnpei, to conduct an investigation and prepare the necessary ceremonies. In public the man they hired claimed to have given up sorcery-lifting rituals in favor of a Christian worldview. In private, however, his reputation for success in the traditional ways remained strong. The day after the radio call from Guam, the curer found a curious stone beneath Sohn Alpet's sleeping mat. Was the object mute testimony to the fear that someone jealous, covetous, or afraid had put a hex upon him? Pending Sohn Alpet's return and an official diagnosis, the family, pessimistic but desperate enough to try anything, began preparations for a "healing ceremony." Although I retained a naive trust in the effectiveness of Western medicine and had counseled for Sohn Alpet's medical evacuation to Guam, my experiences in Wene and the feast of curse-removal led me to appreciate their fears.

After two weeks Sohn Alpet returned—alive but unable to walk. The hospital in Guam wired a diagnosis of lung cancer and gave him less than a year to live. Western medicine had given up; but the family had not. Sometimes Pohnpei medicines bring about miraculous cures, particularly if the cause of the condition were also Pohnpeian. Following the impulse to which humans in pain and grief are so prone, we decided to try anything.

The fact that islanders took sick relatives like Sohn Alpet to the hospital first did not indicate lack of faith in traditional curing systems. Quite the contrary. The hospital was free, a form of socialized medicine, a gift from the United States government; after all, the diseases that foreigners brought to the island required a foreign cure. Western doctors had little luck or skills in treating "Pohnpeian sicknesses." Islanders understand that antibiotics work well, and many diseases do not require a more expensive local curer. They also understood that sick people received excellent care in Kolonia while relatives solicited a diagnosis from the traditional medicine system and planned for island-style treatments.

Indigenous healers made their hospital rounds at night. Once they had determined a diagnosis, they could often perform cures from a distance. "When a person becomes sick, traditional curers look for an oracle, divination or omens, to determine how the man became sick," the man hired to help Sohn Alpet said. "Someone prepares the oracle from various leaves of plants. Then one could determine why the sickness was there. Perhaps a spirit had been angered. Then one kills dogs, large pigs, and brings much kava as an offering and prays to all the spirits. The sick person will either get better or die."

Sohn Alpet's son, a sophisticated administrator educated in the United States, supported the sorcery theory of Sohn Alpet's illness and had been instrumental in hiring the curer. "Western medicine can diagnose cancer but knows no cure or no cause," he explained. "How can you cure something if you don't know the cause? The Pohnpeians want to understand both the diagnosis and the cause. Sometimes with our treatment, people get well spontaneously. This is no longer an American disease; so we will try Pohnpeian methods."

The two curing cycles—four days each—cost as much as a major feast. Roger, in his professional manner, collected data on the plants, chants, techniques, and theories of treatment. I organized financing to pay for our mandatory contributions, arranged for food, and shared some of the emotional responsibilities illness brings into a family. The family focused their concerns and joint resources on Sohn Alpet. For the length of the feasting cycle they set aside conflicts common to all human groups. To me, the intensity and concentration of our plans held curative powers; at the least, they reassured Sohn Alpet of affection and honor.

By contrast, the curing ceremonies resembled ordinary family feasts. The men pounded kava; the women brought flowers and food. The speeches were long, flowery, filled with honorifics and compliments and, like those months earlier in my little feast house, worded in a delicate manner—no one made specific accusations of sorcery or offered guarantees of a cure. On the last evening of each cycle, the family invited people from the community, and we killed a very fat and expensive pig. The piles of food and store-bought gifts grew high at the front and sides of the feast house.

I saw, or think I saw, a shift in Sohn Alpet's attitude after we completed the curing cycle. On his return from Guam, he was pessimistic and depressed, denying that the biopsy had shown malignancies. His moods fluctuated with flashes of uncharacteristic anger. When the curing cycle was completed, however, he seemed immersed in reservoirs of calm. He organized activities for teenagers at his local church and met and talked with friends, elders, and relatives. I wanted to believe him—"I'm getting stronger," he claimed. "We will all work together and be able to finish our important project to help the people of Pohnpei." Although Sohn Alpet had trained his successors well, I missed his sense of humor, reliability, and constant involvement in supervising my Pohnpeian education. All of us wished for a healing miracle.

Through the spring, the project had entered a new phase. Roger and I completed the census with the visits to Wene, Wapar, and Nan U and had hired and trained interviewers who were to administer the long questionnaires. The threat of a dock strike on the West Coast of the United States made us nervous since the bulk of the printed materials we needed had been shipped by sea mail. As we waited for the boxes to arrive from North Carolina, we prepared for the arrival of the medical team and the final stages of the high blood pressure and heart disease research project.

I had spent months collecting long lists of titles, clans, subclans, and the rankings islanders assigned to them as well as long lists of jobs, job descriptions, pay scales, and sources for household income. We wanted accurate measures to help us determine a person's traditional status so we could compare it with his or her status in the so-called modern systems.

Research questionnaires like ours usually measured "modernization" by education and job level. In the United States, jobs are classified into broad categories of administrative, professional, managerial, secretarial, technical, service, skilled, and unskilled labor. In contrast, Pohnpeians classify jobs by analogy to traditional work and the degree to which the job is "advising" or "helping people." Thus, jobs producing or distributing food are accorded the same status as agricultural work—a more valued category in Pohnpei than in America. Cooks in schools perform community services equal to those of teachers or similar professionals. Appointed administrators or bureaucrats are not seen as "helping people," regardless of salary levels or status.

A typical answer to our questions about their work might be: "I work with the Catholic fathers in Madolenihmw, helping them and the students." Additional probes might elicit a description of the specific tasks performed in this job: "I give advice about boats and carry gasoline drums and take people places." Only independent inquiry and the accumulated knowledge of the panel of experts would determine whether this man was self-employed, a part-time boat driver, or a trained mechanic who owned a shop or fleet of boats. To complicate matters, respondents were reluctant to brag about themselves to others. The heavy value on modesty restrained them from revealing how much money they made or what status their jobs had.

We also asked participants how many people were under his or her supervision. To people in the United States this question means, "How many people consider you their boss and report directly to you?" But Pohnpeians have a larger sense of corporate responsibility. Teachers counted their students, credit union employees counted their investors, nurses counted their patients, traditional chiefs and their wives counted everybody in their district or section, and policemen counted all the prisoners in jail or on probation. Everyone added their spouses, children, in-laws, every relative younger than themselves, and all aspirants to traditional titles lower than themselves.

When we asked about sources of income over a month's period, our prepared categories ranged from the possibility of no monthly income to work on the land, salaries, wage labor, or family contributions. But the statement "I have no money of my own" violates the value system and seems to be the equivalent of a serious insult, "That person has no yams of his own." Therefore we found no people without money. People with no cash income still have money because they can solicit it from working children, in-laws, siblings, or other relatives. Poor people on Pohnpei are those who are unable to mobilize the resources of an extended family in their own interest. One man with a wife and five children regularly gave more than a third of his income to his father and stepmother. Another man, having no salaried job, mobilized his two working nephews to buy him a new boat and outboard motor, each worth more than $500. The nephews complied, though they could not afford such luxuries for themselves. These networks, affiliations, and the sense of connectedness made Pohnpeians different from people in the United States who responded to the same questions. The interviewers on the research team became adroit at analyzing job descriptions and translating them into recognizable U.S. equivalents without violating Pohnpeians' own sense of status, the worth of work, and necessary humility. The research team speculated that these interrelationships would protect them from high blood pressure and the stress diseases so prevalent in the States.

Meanwhile, Roger and I kept losing subjects, people we needed to interview and test at different stages of the research. Names in our code books taken from the original census in each district did not match names on questionnaires we were collecting. Only when we sat down in desperation with Paul Benjamin, Sohn Alpet, and his brother, Abner Olter, did I understand how our methods had gone wrong.

In common with many societies around the world, Pohnpeians change their names from time to time. They may have a baptismal name, a nickname, or a name to mark a new stage of maturation or to express some whim or personality change. In a matrilineal system, family identity is inherited from the mother's side, so there is no pressure on a woman to adopt her husband's name at marriage or need for children to use their father's name. Through contact with Spanish colonists first, then German, Japanese, and now American, Pohnpeians have loosely borrowed the patrilineal principle— a man's wife and offspring take his family's last name. The Trust Territory government preferred the patrilineal naming system; many Europeans or Americans have difficulty in imagining any another way of naming.

Having several sets of naming precedents available, Pohnpeians changed all or part of their name or Westernized their previously Japanese names. We found women who used their mother's name at marriage, adopted their husband's name, dropped it when they dropped him, and then assumed their father's name—or made up a new one they liked better. The children retained the last names of their mother's former husbands. A careful analysis of name-changing would probably show that these practices are not random or fanciful but reveal cognitive aspects of social structure and follow a complex set of rules. If this were not the case, many respondents would have been lost in our research. If the project had depended on my local knowledge of genealogy and identity, the whole enterprise would have been doomed. The interviewers, however, knew who had used a different first or last name at some stage of the research project.

Lack of a uniform spelling system complicated our problem. Pohnpeian was a largely unwritten language apart from scripts and alphabets the Spanish, Germans, Japanese, or Americans had introduced. The name "David" appeared as Dapit, Dapid, Depit, and Tepid. Spelling variations made alphabetizing impossible. Furthermore, in traditional Pohnpeian social settings, it is not polite to use an adult's name, nor can one boldly ask, "What is your name?" Instead, one may inquire of someone else—"What is that person's title?" Titles are the correct and preferred form of address. But titles change as men and women move up and cannot be used in a survey. So our code books had to list participants under all their known names and titles; interviewers managed to find them through intuition and inquiry.

Pohnpeians also take a fluid view of what Westerners call family or household, and they move about the island at will. Seventy-five percent of our census households included persons other than members of a nuclear family. Only two individuals in the sample lived alone, and their situations were temporary. With extensive kinship ties and a housing shortage, an individual can live with some part of his or her family in each district. Many Pohnpeians resided both in Kolonia and on their lands in another area. Married couples did not go on honeymoons and return to establish separate residences. They resided with one set of parents—when they were not living with the other set. The composition of the family varied in each house from season to season. For long periods, an individual or couple might live away from the area they claimed as home while they attended school or funerals, or cared for sick relatives, or worked at temporary jobs. At no moment in time would all family members, whoever they were, be residing at their true homestead, wherever that was.

The movement between zones, the fluidity of family formation, and the temporary compositions of households undermined our hypotheses that people in different areas of the island had a different set of experiences with modernization and corresponding differences in healthy hearts. The medical research, conceived in North Carolina, had used Western assumptions about lifestyles and living arrangements; Pohnpeians gently confounded our ethnocentrism.

A letter from the field:

Dear Len, Joanna, colleagues in Chapel Hill, and all supporters of high blood pressure,

I should entitle this letter, "The Defeat of Social Science at the Hands of Ingenuous Micronesians." I have had the hardest time persuading our interviewers about the concept of "sampling." To them the idea of selecting some people and not others is sheer perversity. Just when I thought I had convinced them to interview only the people on the lists we spent months developing, I found a questionnaire of a Mortlockese and asked Paul why he had included a non-Pohnpeian and a non-sample person. He looked at me with innocent brown eyes. "This man is like my brother. I live with him, and he respects our work and wants to be included." Businesses here fail regularly for "just like my family" reasons.

I think that the concept of a sample is the most serious gap in our respective worldviews. I swear that all Pohnpeians believe that the dual criteria of need and worthiness outweighs representativeness, and they dismiss the notion of randomness. In their collective mind, healthy people should not be given preference over sick ones. Young people should give way to their elders. Those who do not take either church attendance or traditional Pohnpeian customs seriously should also be excluded from research that helps people.

Remember how hard we worked to promote the idea of blood pressure and heart disease as sicknesses that cannot be seen. Now I lecture on sampling. But I wonder if they aren't right and we're wrong. Maybe there is no point to sampling procedures. I know, too, that your statistical experts back in Chapel Hill writhe in agony every time I use the word sample; they suspect that we have just included the people we can locate again. Remind them that formulas and computer programs look very different when your feet have turned permanently auburn and you are washing clothes on a rock.

To solve the public relations problem created by these divergent outlooks, I have authorized complimentary interviews to deserving but non-sample Pohnpeians. The medical team will have do the same for the physicals. I have coded these in the code book so that they will not affect our sampling procedure. Rest assured that your computer will never see these.

Kaselehlie.

A month after the curing ceremonies, I paid my last visit to Sohn Alpet. In a house by the stream where I had first visited him, he lay on a woven mat. Fresh flowers and evidence of loving attention surrounded him; women moved without sound through the house, engaged in their graceful rituals of comfort. His daughter had prepared a soup of papayas—the fruit contains a soothing enzyme and is a favorite folk remedy. The simple house held no look or smell of sickness.

I had gone through unusual channels to find supplies of drugs to relieve pain, thinking to offer this last solace. But he smiled and refused—"My relatives know the ancient recipes," he said. At that time I knew nothing of the hospice movement, of organized and caring people who help those who are terminally ill to die at home with dignity. Years later, the power of recognition poured over me when I visited an American friend in hospice care. The women of Pohnpei, as women everywhere, must have been practicing this heartbreaking art for countless centuries. Caring for the sick and dying was a part of their lives, which I had taken for granted, not realizing the commitment and knowledge they had.

As always, Sohn Alpet had something he wanted to teach me. "I am going to die, and we"—he used the dual form for just the two of us—"must say good-bye."

My capacity for denial is immense, and no one had ever spoken to me like this. "Oh no, Nahnid, don't say that. We"—the inclusive form meaning everyone we knew—"haven't tried everything. You won't die. You can't die." And so forth. I did not want to hear him talk about his death. I was comfortable with helping to solve practical problems, but not with the intensity of my feelings.

He persisted.

> Karapei, be calm. How many times have I told you not to wave your arms around, raise your voice, and reveal your feelings? I have taught you respect, so you must listen once again. I have had a good, long life and die surrounded by my family. You will have to learn to say good-bye to those you love and to accept that death is part of life. This is a gift of the spirit few are granted; it is called "to make the inside well"—to bring the power of consolation and peace to those who grieve, to sit with those who know their death approaches. This is the last thing I can teach you.

I cried, tried other avenues of defense, and finally relented to listen as I had on so many less painful occasions. Through the still afternoon, we talked about the arrival of the medical team, the trying trip to Wene, the beauty of Wapar, great feasts, little feasts, and other inconsequential topics. I told him of the financial arrangements I had made about the boat motor so his family would not inherit his debt. Pleased, he made provisions for its inheritance. He said that all of us who had worked on the project were like the ends of canoes that travel in single file with the bow of one canoe close to the stern of the one ahead. This is the meaning of work and fellowship.

We laughed, joked, and spoke together of death. He was right; barely thirty years old I had much to learn. And then we said good-bye.

The following morning his family moved him out of Kolonia and across the lagoon to his homestead on the high hill in Madolenihmw overlooking the ocean. There they brought his ninety-one-year-old mother, herself frail, to join them in waiting. Moving one old and one sick person up the rocky paths was difficult. But a combination of litters, Jeeps, and many strong relatives accomplished the task. He was home and beyond the reach of modern medicine. If the curing ceremonies had accomplished only an acceptance of death and the loving care of his family, they were worth it.

In Kolonia, the work of the blood pressure project had reached its climax amid unresolved conflicts—the demands of medical research and the determination of my island associates to mold the project in their own image. In graduate school I learned that the ideal interview is conducted in private with identically trained and objective interviewers. The respondent does not know the questions in advance and does not receive any help in forming answers. But on Pohnpei everyone was curious and eavesdropped or interjected whenever they could; they wanted joint conclusions, a convincing social consensus. Husbands were the worst offenders, although wives often asked them what opinions to hold or permitted friendly intrusions from children and other relatives. If an interviewer tried to take our "respondent" to a private place—assuming such a place existed—inquisitive friends, kids, and relatives went with them. How could privacy be desirable? they asked. What does social isolation have to do with research?

In addition to problems of confidentiality and disclosure, we were facing the more treacherous logistics of distance. Some people we needed to find lived in difficult-to-reach mountainous areas. In the inevitable wet weather, an interviewer might spend half a day walking to a house where no one was at home. Moreover, were anyone in residence, Pohnpeian standards of hospitality demanded a shared meal and attention to good manners. At that rate we were completing only one or two interviews per day.

Everywhere we went, local people gave feasts for us—a tribute to the interviewer's high status they claimed, but to me, time taken from our real work. When our frustrations over the pace of our schedule peaked, Roger and I called a meeting. The solution seems obvious now—Sohn Alpet's work at the funeral in the hard-to-reach hills above Wene during our first visit there was the model we needed.

The new strategy was implemented: Send an interviewer from the municipality to visit local chiefs and government officials and take them gifts in advance of our arrival. Announce on the radio that the blood pressure study team would be in a certain neighborhood or section on the selected day to honor the people of that area with a feast. Pound kava, hand out sodas and cookies, and serve corned beef and pots of rice. After rounds of speech making, high language, and introductions, the five interviewers went to an edge of the feast house and began to interview eligible participants. I checked the forms, separating those in the sample from those we interviewed as a courtesy, while Roger organized the proceedings. If we needed further information, we did not have to spend half a day tracking someone down, and eavesdropping no longer mattered. However unorthodox, our innovative and culturally appropriate public relations insured us a high participation rate and a place to sleep later that night.

On top of the feasts built into the research project, Roger, I, and various interviewers attended several others each week. The pace of feasts had picked up with the artificial infusion of money during the American administration; the amount of money spent on imported goods was growing on an exponential curve. While the traditional feasts centered on kava, yams, breadfruit, and pigs, contemporary feasts featured washbasins filled with mounds of cooked rice, taro, yams, boiled chicken, fish, donuts, bread, pies, and store-bought goods—cookies, Japanese rice crackers, canned mackerel, corned beef, ship biscuits, canned soda, sugar water with food coloring, and soy sauce bottles filled with pig fat. On the top of these large tubs, suckers, Tootsie Pops, and gum were stuck as decorations. At large feasts, I saw brightly colored shirts topping the filled basin and three-foot lengths of cloth wound around the branches and trunks of trees.

Pohnpeians worried about this new form of prestige competition and the inherent dangers it brought to traditional customs. They fretted about the amount of family income they had to spend, even as they were drawn deeper into the exchanges. They felt that consumer products devalued goods from the land. Furthermore, the wage employment that fueled the new standards of redistribution was tied to make-work jobs, the whims of money from Washington, and an unstable political future. I wished for a computer to keep track of all the contributions, where the money came from, and who received what in the redistribution. No one else, however, seemed to need formal inventories, and the rules were in such flux that each feast, like cocktail parties in the States, was an innovation around a loose theme.

For all the food displayed at the huge feasts, people nibbled in small bites. Filled basins were designed to impress and to be taken home, and the rice and taro at the bottom fed to dogs, chickens, and pigs. Children ate the junk food.

I had long since learned how to sit cross-legged for hours on a hard floor and to accept a half-cooked, dripping pig's head from my hosts. I carried plastic bags or aluminum foil with me to feasts to wrap up such gifts, and Klarines taught me a good recipe for pig's head smothered in onions, honey, and soy sauce. Once I received an entire boiled rooster, plucked but otherwise complete with comb, eyes, feet, and tiny toenails the color of mine. It was too tough even for my dog. I doubt we received back when all the feasts were tallied the equivalent of our personal and project contributions; I know we sent back some very strange and contrived budget reports to the grant managers in Chapel Hill.

By this time in the project, food fantasies were consuming Roger and me. More than a year in the field, the two of us had begun to crave what we were unlikely to find—real milk and temperate zone fruits for me, real hamburgers and homemade berry pies for him. Since the research project included an assessment of dietary habits—salt, fats, sugar, and processed foods in particular—I was collecting long lists and inventories of imported foods in ship cargoes, on sale at local stores, and in the daily diets of selected families. The project had hired a nutritionist to conduct a broad survey and analysis of diet and comparative nutrition. Our minds dwelled on our digestive tracts to a morbid degree.

All foreigners who lived as we did experienced periodic bouts of diarrhea, dysentery, and parasite infestations, no doubt related to poor sanitation and kava drinking. These afflictions, too, were a frequent topic of conversation, the details of which I have been urged not to record. Few of us bothered to have these diagnosed or treated at the hospital; instead, we engaged in a variety of folk cures. I swore by a three-day liquid fast of warm bouillon and warm Jell-O or sought herbal help from Ioannes, Klarines, or local curers I knew. Micronesians had developed a number of homegrown cures that I sampled and found effective. I regretted that our research project had no money to fund studies about these chronic problems. Babies were most vulnerable and had to be treated at frequent intervals for dehydration and gastroenteritis. Infant mortality or death rates were high.

There was, moreover, a sharp contrast between the healthy traditional diet and the seductive force of the expensive dietary habits based on heavily salted or processed American foods. One haunting example was the U.S. government's school lunch program. On an island of bounteous harvests, schools served white bread and rice, which children then preferred to breadfruit and yams. A generation of children was growing up to love expensive, imported food while healthy traditional foods rotted on the ground.

Hunger pangs aside, with interviews and feasting schedules in full swing, I also had to prepare for the arrival of the medical team—arrange for housing, food, laundry, transportation, translating, and the miscellaneous needs of eight people for four months. Their schedule was tight; to complete 1,300 physical examinations the team would need to work six days a week. All the research had to be finished by the time they left. The medical team was going to bring with them the high standards of public health and comfort I had lost, and I dreaded to see what they would say to unscreened windows, outhouses, rain barrel baths, and unremitting togetherness. Each one was going to experience cultural shock, environmental shock, and interpersonal shock as Floyd had; I decided to put them somewhere on the other side of town.

Kolonia was packed with people from the countryside and other islands in Micronesia. Housing was in short supply, and the medical team could not live scattered about in local, makeshift housing—they wanted to work as a team. In the year after Ian Prior's visit, I had searched without success for something large enough, suited to New Zealand-Australian tastes, and near the hospital. A few weeks before their arrival, I happened upon the attic of the annex to the major Protestant church overlooking Kolonia's harbor, centerpiece of the old town's architecture—one huge unfinished room with a spectacular view and cool night breezes. I decided to partition off the room into cubicles, make doors from hospital sheets, and leave space for a communal cooking and sitting area.

All my plans assumed a supply of plywood, wire screen, and appropriate contractual agreements with the Protestant church. My letters to North Carolina during this period were filled with budgetary matters, shifting money from one category to another, and anticipating problems that could scuttle the project. I wrote to Ian to remind him to bring lots of sheets, and he wrote back asking technical questions about laundry facilities for their hospital coats—I didn't mention streams. Delegations of Pohnpeians dropped by my house or cornered me on the street, and with high language and convoluted manners requested jobs with the medical team. Each day I wondered why I had bothered to learn anthropological theory in graduate school instead of plumbing and accounting.

The most serious problem was the toilet. Public health professionals like the members of our medical team loathe outdoor wooden toilets. They believe in indoor plumbing that flushes and washes away the links between flies, fingers, food, and feces and saves untold human lives. Protestant members of the chapel on the hill were proud of their almost new outhouse with its mildewed wooden seat and star on the front door; they had no intention of spending church money to indulge the bizarre habits of foreigners. Since I was in charge and had a religious fervor for water seal toilets, I decided to build another one from the same set of plans Roger, Jack, and I had used. At my request the workmen installed heavy handles on either side of the hole so squatting would be less strenuous; they ran a pipe from the church that doubled for flushing as well as an indoor cold-water shower. I commissioned seats around the edges, inside and outside the toilet-shower room, to increase opportunities for socializing. Like the moss-covered stone church, it was to me a work of art.

The previous summer, Ian had decided to import a jet boat, which ran above the water on a cushion of air; it was a boat built for the rocky rivers of New Zealand. The manufacturer of the unusual boat had donated it; the rules of the grant did not permit us to purchase a boat. With such a boat, free of the tyrannies of tides, we could bring subjects into Kolonia for their physical examinations and not have to set up the medical team, heavy equipment, and our operations in distant locations with less amenities than Kolonia had.

Word of the jet boat's arrival spread rapidly and a crowd gathered at the hospital to test its padded seats and admire the roof. The same evening, a Friday payday, the radio announced that a twelve-foot crocodile had been captured in Kitti and was hanging on display in Kolonia. Not native to Pohnpei, the beast had floated on a log from the Sepik River in northern New Guinea. For several months, people in a swampy area of Kitti had been complaining about stolen and lost pigs. Rumors of swamp monsters circulated but were discounted as the fancies of people who live hours from the nearest bar. Finally, an enterprising group, who had baited a trap with a live dog, caught and killed the crocodile. Most of us had never seen a such a beast, dead or alive, and thronged to the hospital to see boat and crocodile. That wonderful payday weekend, bars were jammed; people milled in the streets, and teenagers raced borrowed motor bikes across the causeway to the airport. I collected great "creature" tales about monsters, dwarfs, giants, or sea beings with strange powers.

The arrival of the medical team the next week was anticlimactic, a signal of hard work to begin. Our research duties had more than doubled over overnight; team members had tripled. We had to locate and question 1,300 people about their personal habits—typical day's food consumption, tobacco, kava drinking, alcohol consumption, and their health history—and then give each one a physical exam. Every person needed a fasting blood sugar test, a first-morning urinalysis, a chest x-ray, a lung function test, and a cardiology examination. The medical team measured height, weight, skin-fold thickness, and other variables relating to high blood pressure. Examinations took at least one morning for each subject and two days for those who were part of the special subsamples.

The medical team had worked in areas of the Pacific where physical conditions were easier and tides mattered less. Research conflicted with their clinical instinct—trained to leap in and save lives, they were not schooled to the discipline surveys required. Equipment broke down and replacement parts were not available. The kerosene-fueled equipment was heavy and hard to maintain. Although Roger and I had hired two bilingual Pohnpeians to act as boatmen, aides, and interpreters, the major burdens of translating, organizing, and accompanying the medical team fell on our shoulders.

My main job was troubleshooter; I circulated through the community and listened. On the streets of Kolonia and in every shop I entered, the curious and eager stopped me to talk about the boat, a conversation that seemed to offset their fears about giving blood. For years, medical doctors, physical anthropologists, and other researchers have collected blood samples in remote areas of the world. In this kind of research, a scientist does not have to learn the language or adjust to strange customs. But Pohnpeians picked up from Americans the foolish and harmful folk belief that a person's race can be detected in the blood, that humans can have "white blood" or "black blood." Islanders who had lived under colonial rule for more than a century feared that racial stereotypes buttressed by scientific evidence could be translated into government policy—a logical conclusion. Colonial governments are racist, and Pohnpeians were aware of racial problems in the United States.

I explained again and again that "race," only a cultural category at best, cannot be seen in people's blood, but some life-threatening diseases and health conditions can. I knew I had been successful when I overheard some people explaining to each other that looking at blood is a form of divination or oracles and reveals important information for curing hidden diseases. I heard a rumor at one of the grocery stores that we were collecting blood to aid U.S. war efforts in Vietnam. Pohnpeians did not want their sons drafted to serve in the military and, indeed, did not wish to further that war. I sent word through interconnected channels of information that the syringes were too small to collect blood for military use, and that foreigners on the project shared island opposition to the war.

Pohnpeian ideas of public health did not include answering personal questions, giving blood for obscure purposes, or acknowledging the collection of urine. Every evening the medical team sent the interviewers out to visit those scheduled for a physical the next day. They were supposed to deliver a useless written explanation, answer questions, and give each participant an empty urine bottle to fill early in the morning and bring to the clinic. Impressed with the *manaman* or authority of the project, some respondents asked high-ranking relatives to fill their bottles on the theory that such an exalted project would not want ordinary, humble urine. Others asked healthier friends to contribute. A few substituted water or sodas in poisonous-looking colors.

Despite these difficult factors and others I had not anticipated, the response rate was over 98 percent, unusually high for surveys of this kind. The medical team lived at the Protestant church and worked as equals with the hospital staff; they gave physicals to people outside the official sample, including several Paramount Chiefs, many noblemen, and their wives—they quickly became local curiosities and local heroes. The nurses and doctors spotted a rare but treatable heart condition in a popular leader with a large family, a man not in the sample whom we included as a courtesy. After that the response in his district was 100 percent. People not included in the sample redoubled their efforts to be tested so they could catch a ride on Ian's jet boat. A year's work of radio broadcasts, speeches, feasts, and careful explanations of our purposes was worth less in public relations than one appearance of that boat. If we were not careful, I believed, our response rate would have climbed to an impossible 125 percent.

Letters from the field:

Dear Jack,

Martha and I wish you were here. We could put you to work. Thanks for the wonderful birthday gifts—an advance copy of the Sears catalog and a bottle of that new Clairol Herbal Shampoo were exactly what we needed. I suspect that Martha has gone "island-happy." I, of course, remain my usual calm and rational self. It must be a reflection of how long we've been here that these items seem so glamorous. Within hours, Peace Corps volunteers started to arrive. We all ate ICE and washed our hair with the exciting new shampoo. As we waited for our hair to dry, we avidly read the catalog and planned our purchases. I think, apart from letters, a catalog is the best link with home for us. Even though she has sworn off materialism and loves living free of so many "things," Martha even read the auto parts and home draperies sections.

I am glad to hear that your garden in New Orleans is growing so well. Mine has produced one ton of cucumbers and twelve ears of corn. Several corn ears were a whooping two inches long, and the whole crop didn't make one meal. Martha claims that planting corn in the tropics is derangement, homesickness, and culture shock. She vows never to look at another cucumber. The bean and onion seeds you sent made many snails and a few toads very happy. Lately, I have neglected my horticultural pursuits in preparation for the medical team, which will be arriving tomorrow—if the plane can land. I hope Martha finishes that water seal toilet in time.

P.S. From me. I think I have solved the problem of reading materials. I am desperate. I exhausted the meager resources of the high school library. I traded ICE for books with the Peace Corps and have read everything the government sent them to brighten their exile. I even read Levi-Strauss again. But now I have found a wonderful source of reading material to feed my addiction. On days when the plane is expected, I listen. When I hear it circling, I jump on the motor bike and rush out the causeway to the airport. There I throw myself on the mercy of deplaning passengers and the Continental flight crew. Shamelessly, I beg their discarded reading materials. Last week I got a Sunday *New York Times*! I scored some paperbacks, too. I miss libraries more than Mexican fast food. I have heard that Bronislaw Malinowski had a terrible case of book cravings. If such a great anthropologist can do the things he did to find books, I can chase airplanes.

Dear Len,

I will give you a capsule review of the medical team. This is strictly my opinion, so don't file it with my official correspondence.

Ian never stops work. He is charismatic, generous, unselfish, and probably manic-depressive. For example, he paid for the transportation and maintenance of the jet boat out of his own pocket. But he is frightened of the boat, which frankly does not run well. A headache for him, but running or not, it has certainly helped the project.

Second-in-command, Dr. John, a real epidemiologist, is Australian, a staunch Baptist, and was a medical missionary to New Guinea for many years. He is an amateur but excellent anthropologist, so we have much in common. His gentleness and sense of humor make him a joy to be around.

Cara is the nurse-administrator. She runs the unit tirelessly and efficiently. I have never met anyone with such executive ability. Nao, the nutritionist on loan from the University of Hawaii, and Rosemary, the other nurse, never gripe and do their assignments of cooking, cleaning, carrying water, and other chores around the church and hospital. This is in addition to their professional tasks and the long hours of tedious data analysis.

Christopher, the medical intern from Michigan, is just plain beautiful—high on my list of special people who can be marooned on the same island as me. His gracious manners and competence have revolutionized the laboratory at the hospital—they adore him for good reason.

Which brings us to Eric, a royal pain in the ass. I don't care if his father is someone important who pressured you all to send him over as photographer and handyman. He is homesick but refuses to leave because he never finished anything in his petty, spoiled life. He complains and is rude to the Pohnpeians—both capital crimes. I am perfectly peeved with him because he has never done anything to help as a handyman and strong back—jobs he was sent over here to do. Roger and I do basic carpentry, and Ian, John, Cara, and Rosemary carry water. Last Sunday, they bribed Roger to take Eric off their hands for a day—that's how desperate they are. Now Roger is desperate to avoid Eric. I got stuck with babysitting him last week when we went to U. He disappeared, and we missed the return tide. I was furious, but he said artists can not be bothered with worldly arrangements. Did I mention he avoids all work of any kind?

Of course, you know Pat, your anthropologist, eighth member of the team. I regret he can stay for such a short time.

The medical team brought with them what looks like a lifetime supply of food. They have tinned butter, canned lamb tongues, freeze-dried soups and vegetables, and Marmite, a salty yeast extract they use like peanut butter. Needless to say, I eat with them occasionally.

As a team, they are well-disciplined; but for Eric, they do communal cooking and follow the posted duty roster. I almost wish Floyd were here to see that. Ian won't let them take but one evening off per week to go to a restaurant. He makes them get up every morning to do calisthenics and organizes mandatory group activities on Sunday, their one day off. He prefers to speak Maori, but all of them have learned a few Pohnpeian phrases, and that goes a long way.

Just as I suspected. The Pohnpeians have given titles to the senior members of the medical team. At the feast given for them, I was privately assured that these titles are perfunctory, just to assist the medical team, and are not the equivalent of the honored titles Roger and your faithful correspondent hold. Innumerable people whom I interviewed about the title system formally deny such a practice, but informally affirm that many unfilled titles exist. Giving some out to foreigners who could not be expected to fulfill traditional obligations is a good use for these titles. In fact, it is widely believed that some of the titles are made up and are probably not even recorded anywhere.

The honor made the medical team so happy—and they deserve it. Pohnpeians, however, are uneasy every time they do this, because it leaves them open to charges of selling titles and exploiting their customs for profit. Foreigners who receive titles usually understand reciprocity and make some kind of title repayment. As you can see from the budget sheets, the medical team paid their respects with two cases of soft drinks, a hundred pounds each of flour, sugar, and rice, and many yards of bright, imported cloth.

I spend major segments of my life these days in feast houses, where I eat canned mackerel and ship biscuits and sleep on a woven mat. My professional life centers around them just as Pohnpeian political and social life does. Why is this so much more fun than camping out in the States?

Thank you for your cards and letters to Sohn Alpet. They mean a great deal. It is obvious that he has not long to live.

Kaselehlie maing ko—which translates as "good-bye" in respectful high language.

Chapter 7

The Core of a Mangrove Log

Night after night, in the open hall of dance,
Shall thirty matted men, to the clapped hand,
Intone and bray and bark. Unfortunate!
Paper and pen alone shall honour mine.

—from "The House of Tembinoka," by Robert Lewis Stevenson

A radio call relayed the news—Sohn Alpet was dead and the family was gathering for the funeral. Roger and I packed, contacted family members still in Kolonia, and gathered our funerary gifts—sacks of food and cloth bought and stored for the inevitable. Sohn Alpet had schooled me in the manners of grief and respect; I followed his instructions to the letter. We managed to catch the high tide to Wapar.

Although I had hiked into the area many times, the trek felt difficult, even dangerous. The sun was out, but an early morning rain had left the path muddy and slippery. Pohnpeians with graceful style carried the heavy gifts for the ceremonies. With my usual clumsiness, I slipped and slid along the path, falling behind them. My zories were caked with mud, and I had kicked clingy pieces up to the waist of my dress. When we arrived at the homestead, I was barely presentable and had to be cleaned up by the women who greeted us. "I am not yet a woman of Pohnpei," I said, hoping to diffuse comment.

The ceremonies would, as was the custom, continue for at least four days with little discernible beginning or end. The women of Sohn Alpet's matrilineage and women in the families he created through his two marriages had prepared his body for burial with obvious tenderness and laid him out in a simple wooden box in the center of the room; they covered him with a hand-embroi-

103

dered sheet they had made with the knowledge of death in every stitch. In quiet competence women and children came and went near the body. Despite an intermittent drizzle, the muddy yard was filled with mourners greeting each other and performing the tasks of the funeral. The men gathered in the feast house and began to assemble an earth oven; other men were arriving with kava and gifts to be presented to the high-titled men not yet seated. Roger disappeared into the feast house, absorbed in the men's activities.

Inside the house, older women had seated me in the area reserved for family several feet from the body; two of his grandchildren came and sat on my lap. We hugged. Sitting cross-legged on the wooden floor, I felt conflict between my professional self who should be taking notes and asking questions, and my private self, who mourned the loss of a friend. From time to time a woman started one of the old mission hymns with which all of us had been raised; I sang English words, they the translations. "Rock of Ages" shattered my fragile composure—Sohn Alpet's favorite song, my father's favorite song. I missed both of them. From time to time, close female relatives closed about the casket and began a loud lament that rose to a crescendo of collective mourning. Ritualized, loud expressions of grief are appropriate behavior for women; men must display bravery and fortitude. It is good form to feign grief, but noise-laden lamentations are too intense a display to be maintained; as the laments subsided, women returned to cooking and the demands of hospitality. For Sohn Alpet's youngest daughter, the grief was genuine. "Papa, don't leave us," she cried. "We'll take care of you forever. Now we are orphans."

At dusk, when all the kinsmen had arrived, a Protestant minister delivered a frank but brief eulogy with one important point.

> Nahnid Lapalap was a man who fought for the right even if this offended some. He liked to lecture young people on proper behavior, but that, after all, was the custom of Pohnpei. Sohn Alpet was the core of a mangrove log, the hard center that is left when the soft outer wood falls away; so have old men lost the ignorance and fickleness of youth as wisdom remains.

The basket for money placed at the foot of the casket was filling; everyone understood how expensive this long period had been for the family. The children watched and listened with wide brown eyes; no one shooed them away or shielded or excused them from the duties death brings to a clan and neighborhood.

In the evening when men had pounded kava and opened the earth oven, they buried the casket in the yard only a short distance from the main house. Sohn Alpet's grave site overlooked the slope of a hill leading past mangrove forests and into a vista of lagoon and ocean. I remember the subtle exchange of feelings between the women. It seems strange to say that they took pleasure in my grief. They were flattered, perhaps relieved, that I knew how to participate in customs and in shared mourning. They knew the stories about the boat motor, our trips for the project, and Sohn Alpet's evacuation and terminal illness. Later in the evening, when we were talking among ourselves, a relative acknowledged the friendships made within our families, "Now you are a woman of Pohnpei."

Klarines and I spent the night at the Catholic mission. Before morning sounds or the palest glow of the sun, she shook my shoulder and, gesturing me to silence, led me outside. There we dressed. Bewildered, I followed her swift movements as she led me down a narrow path for some distance to a boat landing that I had never seen. A red outrigger canoe awaited us—it had old-fashioned paddles and a bailer but no sail. Klarines paddled through the still black water of the mangrove swamp, gesturing me for help when we encountered heavy patches of mangrove trees. By the time we reached the opening to the eastern lagoon, the sun was visible. In silence we paddled along the shallow shores of the island of Temwen and into the ruins of Nan Madol.

Here was a Nan Madol I had never known. The screeching of seabirds, an occasional fish jumping, and the sounds of the trees themselves lent immediacy to the thousand-year antiquity of its sacred space. Each watery path opened into several others, like a cobweb in stone. No paths intersected at right angles. Irregular plazas flooded with sunlight opened up at the ends of calm dark waterways. It was as if, in stone and water, the early builders had duplicated the circuitous mountain paths and scattered homesteads of the main island. With the outrigger, the shallowness of the water and the tides were no barrier, and we traveled there as the original builders had intended. I came in awe and would have paid homage, had I known which spirits or gods to court.

On a schedule and with a purpose known only to her, Klarines began to fish. I could have questioned her about the techniques she was using, how had she learned them, what were the names of the fish she caught, what did women do that men did not and why. Instead, I helped. The secure and competent gestures that Pohnpeian women bring to daily tasks flowed from her hands to mine. Without talking, we shared the companionship of fishing. My memories of that day are centered in the wooden seat of the canoe, the scream of sea birds, the touch of basaltic rock, and the smell of fish on my hands. When she deemed the fishing complete, we paddled slowly out of Nan Madol by routes I had never traced.

Directing my paddle strokes, Klarines steered solemnly as we headed up the other side of the island of Temwen. When we landed, she sorted the fish, strung coconut sennit through their gills, and made two strings. Taking the first length of fish, we marched along another coral-strewn path I did not know. By some miracle, I arrived with clean feet at a household that seemed to be awaiting our arrival. Klarines knew or was related to everyone there, and as young women fried the fish and prepared fresh fruit, I tried to sort out the genealogical connections they were reciting, but I had no notebook or pen. During the meal, my host asked me about Heaven. "Do Pohnpeians and Americans go to the same place when we die? Are people in Heaven divided by color as they are on Earth? What kinds of spirits live there?" "In the Land of Heaven," I answered sticking with the values of anthropology more than those of religion, "it is the *tiahken sapw*, the culture and custom, to treat all people with respect and mutual affection. What spirits do you think live there, which have you seen or been in contact with?" I asked in return, regretting my lack of writing tools.

When Klarines and I returned in late afternoon to the subdued kava pounding in the feast house, the funeral observances were still in progress. She told me to place the second string of fish across the mound of Sohn Alpet's grave. How Klarines arranged that day for a canoe and the welcome of people I had not met or ever seen again, I will never know. I do know that for one incandescent day, I lived as a Pohnpeian woman.

The next morning, I awoke late to the sounds of laughter. Stepping outside to retrieve my zories, someone poured a pail of cold water over me! The women in the yard were throwing water and mud over each other. Unrestrained, they made lewd comments about each other's body parts and sex life. I heard outrageously funny remarks about lovers and love-making techniques. I was wet and shocked. This was a funeral: where was piety and grief?

It is the custom, they explained, throwing more mud on me. But they excused everything with a resort to island custom, so that did not help me understand why I was standing drenched in the yard. Years later I understood ritual release—that accepted moments of humor and fun are allowed to break the seriousness of presentations and ceremonies. Since then, I have been to funerals at which survivors tell bad jokes, laugh, or play pranks on each other when further distress cannot be sustained. The women had nursed Sohn Alpet through the long illness, prepared the body for burial, and grieved for his loss. Now they gave themselves permission to play and to relieve their tensions. I joined them.

Another, smaller feast was held later that same day after the High Chief of Madolenihmw and many guests had left. The men asked me to leave the women and sit at the front of the platform because of my connections to the blood pressure project. But this created a dilemma for them—what was the best ritual introduction for a lone female, a foreigner? My name or "the American lady?" At other formal moments they had used "Mr. Roger's wife," "the cooperative boss of the budget on our esteemed project for helping Pohnpeians," or other circumlocutions that recognized my multiple roles. I listened to the debate; they announced me as Karapei—I was proud of my Pohnpeian title, grateful to Sohn Alpet for his constant tutelage.

Only later did I have clues about the men's work during these three days. At the time I probably discounted their activities as secondary to the intensity of women's work. Roger's field notes of the funeral proceedings look nothing like mine—we had not attended the same event. From his notes, comments during the funeral days, and subsequent questioning, I pieced together the tensions that marked men's activities. To the uninitiated, the gatherings resembled all other feasts—title repayments, marriages, or house dedications, for example. Men brought the food and prepared the earth oven, pounded and drank the kava. A master of ceremonies called out the titles of the high-ranking, coordinated the minute observances of proper etiquette, and placated the High Chief when standards were violated. The men worked hard, prepared most of the food, and labored under a ritual burden that could sour in a moment if a high person were offended or if necessary steps were omitted.

At the funeral feast on the day of burial, the Nahnmwarki or Paramount Chief of Madolenihmw had the seat of honor on the platform of the feast house. But in the middle of the ceremony, the master of ceremonies failed to call the title of the Chief's son at the presentation of the kava. The High Chief, a proud and sensitive man quick to anger, noted the error. Someone immediately ran to uproot a small kava plant near the feast house. The Nahnken knelt in front of the High Chief and laid the kava plant over his right leg. With a kitchen knife he cut off two pieces of the roots and handed them to the pounders. In a few humble sentences, he explained that a mistake had been made in error but not in meanness. For the Paramount Chief, already irritated by confusion and noise from the preparation of the earth oven, the ritual error had been the last straw. But his son, over whom this furor had broken, counseled his father: "Try to educate the people in our customs. Don't just fly off the handle as did the Paramount Chiefs of the past." He resorted to the saying, "Chiefs are like hibiscus bushes in the wind." They must be flexible and bend.

A lesser chief made a speech urging the workers to cooperate with each other, to work slowly, and to make no mistakes. Another Chief asked the workers not to be distracted by the discomfort caused by the rain and cold. "Do not think of difficulties but of the heavy responsibilities of this day. Think only of the love we bear this man who has died." The Paramount Chief accepted a cup of kava and said, "I am very sorry indeed this has happened in the presence of people from other districts. They must see how the people of Madolenihmw observe the proper customs." In drinking the kava, the High Chief forgave the error. Spared retaliation, the men in the feast house went back to work.

An offering collected for his new district feast house helped, my notes show, to assuage the High Chief's displeasure. But another tension simmered beneath the surface. A week before his death, Sohn Alpet requested the Chief to pass the title of Nahnid Lapalap to one of his sons. The high title had been awarded to Sohn Alpet as a returning warrior from World War II. Ordinarily, such a high title awarded under special circumstances would not stay in the family. In the normal progression the title should go to another clan; under the matrilineal principle it would not have passed from father to son. People agreed that the title did not belong in Sohn Alpet's family and expected the Nahnmwarki to take it away in accord with tradition. A death bed request, however, merited attention. Speculation about the decision of the High Chief ran high.

Out of respect, announcement of the new title holder was withheld until reciprocal exchanges and kava drinking had ended on the fourth day. When the funeral observances were over, the Chief announced a new Nahnid Lapalap—a man who was not Sohn Alpet's son.

Roger returned to Kolonia after the funeral, and his field notes once again reflect a different experience from mine. "After the burial, which took place at sunset, I returned to Kolonia, traveling on the lagoon for hours after dark. All we had to keep us off the reef was the experience of the boatman and a measly flashlight. This, believe me, was downright scary. Of course, the Pohnpeians frequently drive their boats on the lagoon after dark and don't think much about it. But I don't care to do it again, if I can avoid it."

For me, the trip home on the lagoon several evenings later was peaceful and calm. I grieved for a lost friend, but he had prepared me for his death and the mourning observances had reconciled me to its fact. The moon shining across the water comforted me; I felt at ease with my adopted family. That night, on the lagoon, I decided to have a baby. And the next day, I got pregnant.

Meanwhile, the work of the medical team had accelerated in our absence; they were close to finishing examinations in Kolonia, Nett, and U. Wene, however, had proved too rock-bound and remote even for the celebrated jet boat. The entire team was going to have to mount an expedition for the last four weeks of their stay on Pohnpei; someone would have to duplicate the arrangements we had made in Kolonia. The logistics were daunting—with the assistance of U.S. Seabees and Trust Territory bureaucrats, Roger, Ian, and I had arranged for a barge to carry the kerosene refrigerators, freezers, barrels, boxes, and laboratory and medical supplies. Timing was crucial. The barge could not be loaded until we finished the medical examinations scheduled for the hospital in Kolonia. Sailing had to coincide with the month's highest tide on the other side of the island, so the laden barge would be able to navigate the mangrove swamps and reach the landing dock of Wene.

Roger and I tossed a coin; one of us had to stay in Kolonia to coordinate the problems and activities of the medical team there; one had to return to Wene to supervise local arrangements there—I lost. The Wene team was compact and collaborative; together we had worked out a scheme to recall Eric the Pain, the lead-weight drag, and replace Christopher, the medical resident, who had returned to the States. Sohn Alpet's brother, Abner Olter or Kaniki Ririn, agreed to step in as chief of the interviewers. His wit and intelligence kept me sane while we went to considerable trouble to find chaperons so he and I would not be the target of gossip. My lodging was a cool, private room in the impressive homestead of Oaron Kitti, whose feast house dedication we had attended the year before. Two lovely rock-rimmed streams close to the path leading to the causeway boat dock formed the homestead's bathing pools.

As local arrangements director, I hired—or thought I had—teams of men to unload the barge, load up the water buffalo, and haul everything up the hill to the dispensary. I made arrangements—or thought I had—for housing the medical team at the homestead of Dr. Franko, the homestead where Jack, Roger, Ian, and I had stayed our first time in Wene. The house had two large bedrooms, one for each gender, a kitchen, and a long, enclosed veranda. I negotiated payment for the cold-water shower with sides and a "little house" that met some standards of public health.

Once again I dreaded the arrival of the medical team and the accelerated pace under which they liked to work. Eating was going to be a belly-ache. A number of large funerals had stripped the community of ordinary foodstuffs. Households had not recouped their energy or supplies. As a result of a continuing dock strike on the West Coast of the United States, several months had passed without the arrival of a supply ship. The two tiny stores in Wene had sold out of products from America, and only a few Japanese and Australian goods were trickling into the area. Although the medical team still had crates of canned lamb tongues, Marmite, and corned beef, they needed fresh bread and produce. I had to find a reliable source of flour, a reliable baker, and a reliable delivery system. First, however, I had to negotiate about money—always a headache—at the slow pace locals set, under contractual conditions that shifted with the tides.

On one level, I sympathized with the people of Wene. They lived in a beautiful but remote area where opportunities for cash income, much less economic development, were limited. The decision of the Peace Corps to locate its first training center in this isolated community only whetted the expectations of local people. Now they saw all foreigners, especially Americans, as groups willing to drop bundles of cash on their doorsteps. The payments they expected for various jobs, however, bore no relationship to U.S. pay scales. At night, for example, the radio reported the price of pork on the Chicago futures market. The next morning pig owners in Wene added 10 percent for sentimental value and quoted that as being the worth of pigs they intended to sell us. Never mind that a pricing structure a world away bore no relationship to the laws of supply and demand on remote islands. I seemed to be trapped in constant haggling over room and board and arguments about the worth of labor, pigs, and rent. The generosity and spirit of cooperation that Pohnpeians might choose to show to individual visitors was not apparent in their interaction with large groups. They needed money; we had it.

Then factions that exist in all small-scale communities—two conflicting coalitions I called "highlanders" and "lowlanders"—reared their disruptive heads. The latter group lived in the area near the dock, the Catholic mission, and the little store; leaders of the first group had homesteads spaced far back into the mountains. They insisted I was not to hire for a job without consulting the senior men who managed the labor supply and acted as subcontractors. Most discussions I had with them, however, were subtle harangues against the opposition. "Those people down there—or up there—will not work well. Your things will get lost or stolen. You must trust us instead. Now let us see how much our cooperation will cost you."

The omnipresent Dr. Franko, our official liaison with the Kolonia hospital, had relatives in both factions. In charge of both the one-room dispensary, the only place suited to our work, as well as the only logical dwelling in the community to house the research team, he became demanding. For half the day he ordered me to treat him like an American medical entrepreneur, for the other half he demanded his due as a high-titled Pohnpeian elder. Hints of blackmail began to seep into our all-too-frequent negotiations.

For an anthropologist, rivalries between warring factions or known troublemakers are the bread and butter of our profession. A certain detachment, even pleasure, grows out of understanding cultural malfunctions and contentious individuals. Through such tensions we learn how the society represents its values and how they structure symbols and leadership. But I was working under the dual pressure of the medical team's needs and Pohnpeian certainty that I had access to unlimited funds. In this setting I could not be a dispassionate observer.

Nor was it easy to manage without Sohn Alpet at the rudder. From the moment I arrived in Wene, I had received mild, tactful complaints about Pernando, an interviewer and high-ranking man from another district. It seemed that Pernando, a handsome man in his mid-sixties who looked thirty-five, had propositioned a widow at least seventy-five years old. The story, just pieces of gossip, was confusing because Pohnpeians have a high acceptance of geriatric sexuality, and Pernando had made no secret of his amorous activities during Japanese times or during marital interludes in the American period. Always cheerful and charming, he took a lot of teasing; "I've reformed," he would laugh. At first, I ignored the reports; I needed him to help finish the interviews and contact people for the physical examinations. Then a delegation of serious-looking men arrived at the homestead and insisted that action be taken.

Why, I asked the delegation, should it matter about a little companionship between these two nice old people? I was secretly cheering for the widow. My question made the men of the delegation indignant. Did I not understand that the moral tone and credibility of this important government project on which I was spending so much money was compromised? Why had I spent months "to help people around the world combat high blood pressure and heart disease" only to sink the project in a love affair? So insistent were they that I sent Pernando back to Kolonia to work with Roger.

After Pernando's departure, several men who had vociferously objected to his moral transgressions admitted that the widow was a rich woman. Clanmates, children, and other relatives who would inherit did not want any surprises in the distribution of her land, pigs, and other possessions. Economic fear, and not morality or impact on the project, accounted for the pressure they brought to bear. Later, at one of the nightly kava poundings, I heard gleeful reports that Pernando's wife had had her revenge. She summoned her relatives to his farmstead, killed his pigs, dug up his kava, and feasted her kin with his produce.

The best respite from work and tension was evening kava poundings at my host's house or at neighboring homesteads. Kava gatherings became occasions for patching up differences and forgetting grievances. During this period, I made speeches with kava cup in my hand, explaining once more the purposes and activities of the project. Since kava is said to be good for pregnant women and insures that a child will have healthy, clear skin, and since Pohnpeian women in the same condition drank it, I did not worry.

One evening, I accepted a cup of kava from a gracious young man, "I have respect for the work you and your team are doing because I work for the hospital and I am an outpatient there—in the leprosy clinic." I gulped and added leprosy to the list of twelve or thirteen dreaded diseases that one might get from drinking kava. That evening I had watched the men add water from the nearby stream to the hibiscus bark used to squeeze the kava roots. At the same time, I saw the pigs peeing and people splashing in the stream. God will have to protect anthropologists and other strange people who have suspended their faith in the germ theory of disease.

I should have worried. All of us—Americans, Peace Corps, and regular kava drinkers—had diarrhea. I ran out of my usual cure of warm Jell-O and hot bouillon, and during the first week before the medical team arrived, I acquired an earnest case of dysentery. Although this was an expected consequence of fieldwork, the dock strike in California and our isolation from Kolonia had cut off supplies of toilet paper. With furtive glances, I checked the Catholic mission and other sites where foreigners might have hoarded the precious commodity. Finally, I found a paperback book, Kurt Vonnegut's *Cat's Cradle*, which a Peace Corps volunteer had abandoned. I read a page, tore it out, read another page, and tore it out.

The arrival of the medical team and tons of goods was timed with perfection to the tides. The lowland laborers at the dock and the ponderous water buffalo performed their tasks well, an anticlimax to the dramas of the previous month. But late that night Cora, a nurse, braved the dark path to summon me. A large family had moved into the kitchen of the homestead I had rented from Dr. Franko. Avoiding the nasty toads feasting on pig dung, I tramped up the hill with misgivings. I had spent months negotiating what I thought was a watertight contract with Dr. Franko for the house. When I confronted him, he put on an innocent face, "You didn't say that no one was supposed to occupy the kitchen. In island custom, families like to stay near each other." I had to renegotiate the iron-clad contract and remove the visitors.

Because of my as-yet-unannounced pregnancy, the low-current tensions in Wene were bothersome. It was difficult to be caught between three cultures, three countries—America, Pohnpei, and Australia-New Zealand. Members of the medical team had been living and working with each other for twenty-four hours a day. They did not understand the rival factions or cross-cultural dilemmas of financing the project. Their thirst for privacy and creature comforts coupled with inevitable frictions of close encounters had sent them into intermittent culture shock.

Although I enjoyed the family with whom I was staying and delighted in the atmosphere of the little tropical world, I was ravenous for foods I could not have. Some days the nausea of pregnancy came in heavy waves. I hunted for papayas known for settling the stomach, but none of the trees were producing. I craved milk, temperate-zone fruits, and coffee from the Café du Monde in New Orleans. No one in the community was going to starve, including me, but food appeared in strange patterns. For several days I ate only ship biscuits and mangrove crabs. During periods when the nausea abated, I ate roast dog, abundant after a series of local honor feasts, and Japanese rice crackers, the only edible food the local store stocked. Between times, I ate canned lamb tongues.

One morning I did a terrible thing. The air hung heavy; no rain had fallen for several days. I was hot, nauseated, and worried about the project. The delegations of medical personnel and Pohnpeian elders with their contradictory needs had worn me down. Dr. Franko had somehow united the lowlander and highlander factions and expanded their demands while denying his manipulation. I was sitting cross-legged on the veranda of my host's house, hoping for a stray breeze and trying to write field notes, when I saw yet another group of men coming up the path. They began a litany of complaints—their peers in rival factions had used deception to acquire the contracts for goods and services I should have negotiated with them first. Members of the medical team were not as generous and cooperative as they themselves were. They offered excuses for why they had not kept their agreement to clear the path to the dispensary. As I listened to them, something snapped.

I stood up on the steps of the porch, a breach of etiquette, my head was above theirs. Each one was older and of higher status and rank than I. They deserved and had always received deference from me. Abandoning all pretense of public manners, I denounced their petty intrigues, the subtle barriers, and passive resistance. In closing, I repeated my most inflammatory accusation, "I have yet to see a single example of cooperation in this community." Cooperation or working together is the single most important public value in Pohnpei. It was as if I had accused democracy-loving Americans of behaving like anarchists or fascists.

What I did is an example of culture shock—which did not excuse my violation of acceptable public behavior or lessen my self-condemnation. I had jeopardized the entire research project. I had trampled on the fragile communications we had achieved. The men I had addressed with raised voice, waving arms, and raised head left stunned.

Less than a week later several of them returned—beaming. "How right you were to become angry with us. That is how we realized that you are pregnant." Wishing to be modest and not wanting to have my activities restricted, I had told no one but the doctors on the medical team—how did these near-strangers know. The men continued—paranoia is the chief symptom of pregnancy in Pohnpei. Pregnant women are allowed to say anything they please; they may express anger publicly and make demands on others. Hence, any woman who does this is pregnant. Pleased with themselves and with me, they promised to clear the path to the dispensary; they pledged other acts of cooperation would follow.

In the aftermath of the speech I had given from the veranda and the continuing tensions about contracts, money, and geriatric sex, I decided to take a field break and let Roger spell me. When he arrived in Wene, I returned to Kolonia.

After a week of relative relaxation, I made plans to return to Wene on the semiregular hospital boat. The aides who doubled as boat drivers were several hours late, and we departed in the late afternoon after the tides had peaked. By the time we reached Madolenihmw, about halfway to our destination under favorable circumstances, the tide was ebbing and darkness had fallen. My uneasiness grew as the aides discussed our progress and the strange noises coming from the engine. A chill wind blew off the ocean, and water sloshed around my feet. The laden boat felt clumsy and out of place on the lagoon.

Without warning the propeller of the outboard motor fell off and sank. An aide dove down and retrieved it from the shallow lagoon floor. The other one tried to fix the motor; water was filling the bottom of boat at an alarming rate. Without power, we were in danger of drifting into the open ocean. "Bail!" they yelled at me. I felt around for the bailer—a lightweight scoop made from a Clorox bottle, usually found on the floor of a boat. There was no bailer. I dumped tools from a metal box and used it to scoop water. As the lid flapped and pinched my fingers, I imagined how news of my senseless death would affect family and friends. I remembered stories of naive Americans dead in foreign lands of exposure or thirst, shark or jelly-fish bites, lost without sign or survivors in the middle of the world's largest ocean.

As the aides fiddled with the motor, the shoreline grew distant. When the engine fluttered to a start, my hopes of life resumed. When it sputtered to a stop, my fantasies of death on the lagoon returned. We were making no progress against the tide when I saw a light on the shore. "Let's stop there for the night," I said, "and finish our trip in the morning."

"Oh no," they replied in the same casual manner they had greeted engine failure, "everyone knows there are ghosts on that path. We are much safer on the lagoon."

Although the motor ran intermittently and the danger of drifting into open ocean abated at low tide, we were hours from safety. Chilled and shivering, I curled in protection over my stomach. Recognizing the boat landing leading into a section of Wapar, I once more suggested, "Let's stop here. I know these people and they are gracious hosts. They will understand our need." The aides looked at each other as much as is possible by the light of a half moon. After a period of ominous nonverbal communication between them, one spoke with reluctance, "That is out of the question. Infamous sorcerers live in that area."

Outraged, I stood up in the boat. "Foreigners cannot be sorcerized. I'm not afraid of sorcery," I announced in English—forgetting my earlier experiences. They placated me and continued to coax the motor. I sat in sullen fear and refused to speak Pohnpeian for the rest of the trip and the long, dark hike back to my homestead.

A few nights later at a kava gathering, hoping that no fresh disagreements or harrowing trips were going to arise, I learned the end of the Lord Kelekel legend. An old man who had worked with Jack Fischer when he lived on Pohnpei sat down beside me and spoke in the authoritative tones one reserves for legends that go right to the heart of matters. "One day Lord Kelekel walked up the mountain path to a secluded bathing pool. As he stooped down to enter the water, he chanced to see his reflection in the pool. Horrified at the gray hair and wrinkles of an old man, he committed suicide." Silver-headed vanities are rewarded in Pohnpei, I thought to myself; the pool of water that precipitated Lord Kelekel's self-destructive urge must have been located in Wene.

As our work there drew to a merciful close, I started to believe that major problems were behind us. At a meeting of the entire Pohnpeian, Australian-New Zealand, and American staff working on the project, we decided to celebrate our deliverance from each other with a farewell feast. Islanders who worked with us agreed to contribute the yams and kava if foreigners would purchase the pig. Given our previous difficulties in buying pigs and the money problems in Wene, I should have known better. It would have been easier to negotiate the adoption of a baby to play with the one I was carrying.

One man agreed to sell us a pig for thirty dollars, but when we went to the farm, he had picked out a 128-pound female porker he claimed would cost ninety dollars. He raved about her sweet disposition, lamented the loss of her legendary fertility—"but no honor is too great for your helpful project," he added. John, the Australian epidemiologist, leaped into the discussion. If this man were so eager to sell a producing female, something must be wrong with the pig. He examined her with a clinical eye, "probably sick and certainly too fat to be tasty," he proclaimed. This increased the owner's agitation: "Pigs whose fat droops to the ground are the most desirable," he claimed as he summoned his neighbors to bear witness to the foreigners' treasonous statements. I left to do other errands, forcing Roger to translate and mediate.

That night at the kava pounding in my neighborhood I learned that the foreign buyers and the local seller had struck a bargain based on price per pound and not on a whole live pig. A bad mistake, one that accorded poorly with Pohnpeian custom, in my opinion. But these children of the British Empire had been yearning to deal firmly with the natives, certain that reason and common sense among men of good will were more effective than catering to local traditions.

In the middle of an appalling scene in the dispensary the next morning was a pig carcass and a scale. "The price per pound was for dressed pork, not the whole pig," Ian roared. "A pig is a pig. You have to pay for every pound," replied its frustrated owner. Without warning an irate and enormous woman whom none of us recognized rushed into the dispensary. "This is my pig. My brother has no right to sell it," she insisted. She then named a price triple that of pork futures on the Chicago market or pigs penned in Kolonia. Everyone else had an opinion and determined, but contradictory, points of view. The members of the medical team who were not exhibiting strains on the composure that made the British Empire mighty were worried about leaving the pork in the heat to spoil.

Negotiations about the price started over—with a dead pig on their hands, neither side had a choice. After an exhausting two hours, they reached a price. Or so I thought until the pig man and his sister suspended their kinship arguments and allied with one another to attack the credibility of the scale. "Your machine does not use Pohnpeian numbers; it cannot be used to weigh a Pohnpeian pig," they reasoned. "Your scale is rigged against us." To the sputtering, aghast medical team, the scale was an article of faith, an absolute in a shifting world. If you cannot trust a British scale and the metric system, you can trust nothing. To the pig owners, it symbolized the weight of Western technology against a defenseless Third World.

In the muddle of cultural misunderstandings, Paul Benjamin and Abner Olter brought a quiet resolution to the price of pork—not a happy financial solution, as the budget showed, but one that averted a pig war. The medical team stored the cut-up pig in their refrigerator and presented pieces at the farewell feast we sponsored. Mutual relief made us friendly. Pohnpeians offered lovely speeches about the "ups and downs of human relationships." Several speakers from both highlander and lowlander factions asked us to pardon the mistakes they had made.

But at every meal after the feast we ate the left-over pork—pork with sugar and soy sauce, pork with yams, fried pork, plain pork. Every swallow was personal. The last night after we finished eating the ill-omened pig Roger dreamed that he stood up in church and threw the project's funds into the air, announcing, "Now you can have all the money. Since I have none to fight over, you will have to take care of me or be discredited for not showing hospitality."

On the morning of our departure from Wene, we all gathered for services at the mission. In his prayer, the lay minister thanked God in high language for giving the Pohnpeian people the strength and courage to cooperate with foreigners.

When we returned to Kolonia, I went straight to Stewo's restaurant and ordered the biggest steak on the menu. As friends watched with amazement, I ordered another one and ate it with relish. In a miracle of international marketing, I found canned whole milk and drank every can I could transport on the motor-bike. In light of my outbursts in Wene and eccentric eating habits, word of my condition spread. No one else shared my modesty or reticence. Klarines, Akina, Iseh, Kioko, and the other women who worried about our childlessness and had probably worked fertility spells on me were delighted, their hopes and chants vindicated. In their view, the baby was already a Pohnpeian citizen.

I was writing a report on the trip to Wene when I glanced through the droopy screens of my house and saw another delegation, this time of women. As they kicked their zories off at the door, they shouted, "Are you there, little bird's nest?" They carried machetes, mature coconuts, flowers, and other paraphernalia. I was nervous: should I relax, run, or write it all down? Had I agreed to some ritual I knew nothing about? Properly raised, I served cookies and Cokes while they set to work.

Raising enormous machetes, they halved coconuts in equal pieces with a gesture I so hopelessly sought to imitate. With the same ease, they scooped out the white meat into a hot skillet. As the heat slowly rendered the coconut into oil, we sat on the floor and talked about pregnancy. The women commented on how well I looked for one so scrawny. They predicted a scrawny baby, too. Several began to share stories about their own pregnancies and deliveries. After skimming the residue floating on top of the hot oil, they added the flowers and stirred. Here was the pure, scented coconut oil essential for ceremonial occasions through uncounted centuries.

Still nervous but fascinated, I watched them bottle the oil. Laughing about foreigners, they demanded that I take off most of my clothes and lie on the floor. The first midwife who was giving orders had trained in midwifery at the district hospital and had years of experience in traditional medicine. Her diagnosis by touch confirmed the twelve-week-old pregnancy. The second midwife questioned me as she began to pour the warm, scented oil over my body. I relaxed as her strong hands followed the patterns of massage she had learned from generations of island women. While she massaged, she explained that island women know how to prevent the common problems of pregnancy, such as stretch marks, itchy skin, muscular discomfort, and nausea.

Someone remarked that abortions could also be induced by certain styles of massage and manipulation of the uterus. This method had been used, though rarely, since olden times. They commented on the nausea common in pregnancies of U.S. women and assured me that I would have no more. Having heard about my paranoia and anger in Wene, they complimented me on acting like a Pohnpeian woman and encouraged me to vent strong feelings anytime I pleased.

As the midwife worked, the women talked. They discussed the stages of pregnancy and labor and how the mother's attitudes affect the personality of the child. They explained how I would feel, emotionally and physically, at each new development. Some information was technical and medical, yet nothing I heard contradicted the American view of biological processes or violated common sense for childbearing. Beyond the practical, however, was a wisdom and sharing I had yet to encounter in my own culture. The kind of childbirth these Pohnpeian women practiced and their ancestors had experienced was an aberration in my native land.

The women left me with the oil and instructions for its use. They were right—it did everything they claimed. How can I describe the intensity and delights of the massages? My body tingled for weeks. A woman's world I had rarely seen in Pohnpei opened to me. In this world, women are confident, noisy, supportive, and knowledgeable; they live in their bodies. Pregnancy, nursing, and making love are all points in a sensual continuum. As women lay out the dead for burial, they hope for the quickening of childbirth. Women are related through clans, through dangers shared, and through the knowledge that the circle of life and death closes in their bodies. In the presence of men or in public, these same women may seem deferential in a double standard.

I marveled at the attention I received. My status among islanders soared. Men stopped me on the roads and expressed delight about all pregnancies and babies; the midwives returned for more massages. When I mentioned my prenatal classes to Americans, however, some were upset that I was in the hands of native midwives rather than "real" doctors. Others looked or acted uncomfortable with my pregnancy and seemed to regard the process as a disease that lowered my I.Q. To satisfy my curiosity and the demands of Americans that I have proper checkups, I attended a prenatal clinic at the hospital. In flower-decked, ruffled dresses, the women that day looked six feet tall; they weighed about 200 pounds each and fussed over me: "So short and thin, no bulge to show. Could she really be pregnant?" Questioning me in depth, they agreed among themselves that I was not faking my condition. They talked all at once, then stopped to hug me again; they recounted boisterous stories of pregnancy and childbirth with some sexy tales as footnotes. I wallowed in mellow bliss. With so much acceptance and nurturance, I wanted to be pregnant forever. From my new viewpoint, the clinic was a roaring success. By contrast, American-style medical care involved only a long wait, a short exam, and a prescription for vitamin pills.

Roger and Jack saw my pregnancy as a fine anthropological opportunity for collecting data. Roger wanted spells, chants, ingredients, symptomatology, schedules for treatments, and other technical features of indigenous medicine. Jack wrote to congratulate us and by the second sentence outlined a research project for me. I was to explore the relationship between mythology, social structure, and reality on Pohnpei as revealed through conception and childbirth. Remember Lord Kelekel, he insisted, magically born and reputed to be the offspring of the Thunder God and his clanmate—perhaps his sister. The God of Thunder somehow made her pregnant with sour citrus fruit or raw fish.

Neither believed me when I extolled the virtues of coconut oil, massage, and female support systems. Nor did they appear enthusiastic about catering to the whims of a pregnant woman. Pohnpeian husbands and relatives are expected to arise in the middle of the night and fix the foods a pregnant woman craves and needs for the baby's growth. Attention to the arbitrary and strong-minded desires of a pregnant wife takes precedence over regular routines and career advancement, and should increase with birth and continue during nursing. Nor did I convince them that no woman believes in magical sources of pregnancy, that Lord Kelekel's legend was irrelevant to my new reality, or that the traditional medical practices centered on sound biological information, shared experiences, and the love of babies.

Pohnpeian women were not finished with my training. We had to discuss names for the baby, its gender, its date of birth, and pertinent aspects of its personality and rearing. They taught me how to determine the sex of the baby by feeling the position of the backbone. This can only be done in the last few months, when the baby has determined its own sex and assumes the correct posture. If the spine rests on the right, it will be a boy; on the left, a girl. Together we consulted a diviner—a person who helps others know the otherwise unknowable. In an elaborate system of number divination based on the safe and dangerous positions in a canoe, he first drew a diagram of the crossbars of a single outrigger, then wrote down the question to be answered, and made random marks to derive a series of two-digit combinations of the numbers 1, 2, 3, and 4—certain numbers in key positions on the canoe drawing are auspicious; they foretell the future. He predicted we would have a boy baby—as did each divination technique Pohnpeians used on me, including the backbone method.

The project was nearing an end; the medical team and their public relations jet boat had left with little fanfare. I needed to return to teaching and would not be able to give birth in Pohnpei at high tide on the morning of May 15—the date the midwives had calculated. "When you return home, study the moon and question navigators to determine high tide that morning," they urged. "I'll also check weather reports on television and in newspapers," I added.

We compared labor and delivery practices in our respective countries. They knew about but disapproved of American customs of allowing strangers and men to attend a woman in labor. "You mean that your own mother or sister or aunts are forbidden to help you?" Delivery was the one time Pohnpeians valued privacy—women feared that strangers would report a lapse of courage. In giving birth, women must show bravery and suppress cries of pain. Female relatives encouraged quiet behavior and offered gentle support.

During these sessions, sandwiched between preparations for our departure, they explained the ceremony called "mother's milk," which follows the birth of a baby, particularly the first one. Relatives make a small feast to insure that the new mother has enough milk to feed the baby. Imagine the distress, they said, of giving birth to a much desired child and not being able to feed it. No baby bottles existed in ancient times, and accepting a surrogate nursing mother would be the same as adoption. Akina and Klarines showed me how to shave the top of a drinking coconut to make a substitute baby bottle. Some of the women told me stories about keeping babies alive with coconut milk. I had often seen women chewing bits of banana and taro to place in the mouths of babies.

The United States was not a place to raise a child in the Pohnpeian manner, and I was ambivalent about returning. The war in Vietnam still raged and campus unrest had not abated. Was I ready to rejoin the world of materialism and the domination of possessions I had left behind? Where in the States could I find hours of gentle training, offers of sisterly support, a public acceptance of pregnancy and lactation, and spectacular massages? Would my baby ever experience the freedom and the limitations of an extended family?

The last two months Roger and I spent in Pohnpei centered on the formalities of leaving. We made an honor feast to Sahngoro, the Paramount Chief of U, as title holders are expected to do every year. Interviewers, friends, and the families with whom we had shared so much staged farewell feasts and gave us and each other many presents. We coded the questionnaires by hand, checked and rechecked our code books and naming and numbering systems; then we mailed the last packages of data to the computers in North Carolina. Having arrived with three suitcases between us, Roger and I had to dispose of a household of possessions, a bike, a kerosene refrigerator, two cats, and a dog.

On the last morning, I hiked up a high hill overlooking the town and harbor to watch the sunrise. The smell of coconut husk fires and a distant pounding sound of someone washing clothes hung in the air. The Pohnpeians who shared so much with me do not end their stories with "they lived happily ever after." Thrice-told tales are never simple or naive. Just as they embellish yams and tales with the green leaves of camouflage, they end them with this warning:

"You who hear my tale should listen very carefully and straighten it out for yourself. Sometimes what I say is not straight."

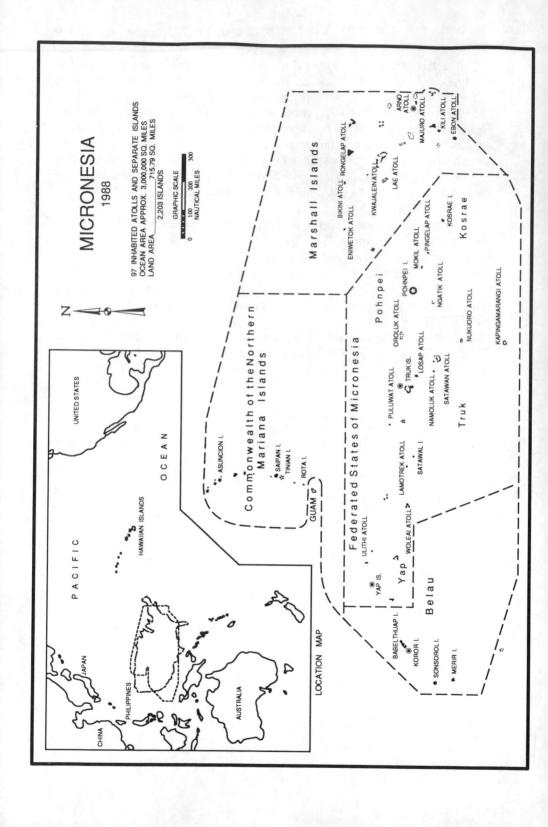

MICRONESIA
1988

97 INHABITED ATOLLS AND SEPARATE ISLANDS
OCEAN AREA APPROX. 3,000,000 SQ. MILES
LAND AREA _____ 715.79 SQ. MILES
2,203 ISLANDS

GRAPHIC SCALE

NAUTICAL MILES
0   100   200   300

N

LOCATION MAP

UNITED STATES

PACIFIC

O C E A N

HAWAIIAN ISLANDS

JAPAN

CHINA

PHILIPPINES

AUSTRALIA

Commonwealth of the Northern
Mariana Islands

ASUNCION I.

SAIPAN I.
TINIAN I.
ROTA I.

GUAM

Federated States of Micronesia

Marshall Islands

ARNO ATOLL
MAJURO ATOLL
KILI ATOLL
EBON ATOLL

BIKINI ATOLL RONGELAP ATOLL
KWAJALEIN ATOLL
LAE ATOLL

ENIWETOK ATOLL

Pohnpei

KOSRAE I.
Kosrae

MOKIL ATOLL
PINGELAP ATOLL
POHNPEI I.
NGATIK ATOLL
NUKUORO ATOLL

OROLUK ATOLL

KAPINGAMARANGI ATOLL

TRUK IS.
LOSAP ATOLL
PULUWAT ATOLL
NAMOLUK ATOLL
SATAWAN ATOLL

Truk

LAMOTREK ATOLL
SATAWAL I.

ULITHI ATOLL

WOLEAI ATOLL

Yap

YAP IS.

Belau

BABELTHUAP I.
KOROR I.

SONSOROL I.
MERIR I.

Chapter 8

Between Times

$\mathscr{P}$ohnpeian predictions about the gender of our child were wrong. Marlowe was a beautiful little girl, not a boy. Just as they foretold, however, she was born at high tide on the morning of May 15, and they are forever right about the joys of raising a child. In returning to the United States and its impersonal, bureaucratic, technology-centered customs of giving birth, I sorely missed the warmth and human knowledge I found young and pregnant on a tropical island. In America there was no one to sponsor the "feast of mother's milk" in honor of my first-born child or my new status.

Trite as it sounds, living on Pohnpei changed my life. When I think about teenage pregnancy, adoption, incest, childbirth, head lice, homeless people, elderly ones, peeping Toms, sex, sensuality, toilet training, or a hundred other topics, I ask—what would Pohnpeians do? How do island cultures define and handle these situations?

I maintained contact with the island in various ways. Roger returned for seven months in 1973 to work on his dissertation; I was teaching at the University of New Orleans and raising a baby. A group of Pohnpeians on a State Department tour connected with the status elections visited me in my home. When I answered the door, they greeted me, then rushed past me to pick up "our baby," and did not put her down for the remainder of their stay. They reported on political struggles, deaths and successions to high titles, the growth of alcoholism, crime, and suicide. They asked me to drive them through different sections of New Orleans and their State Department hosts to take them to an Indian reservation—wanting to see how the United States treats people of different colors and cultures. They also reported that after I had left, my adopted family gave a feast and ate my plump dog—he did, after all, belong to them and had been only on loan to work for us. From time to time I caught up with the family of Pedro and Kioko Kihleng, Sohn Alpet's daughter and his grandchildren. Paul Benjamin became Nahnmwarki of U, and I heard that he reigned there as a gracious, forgiving Chief.

Word reached me through the years that kava still tasted like slimy mud, and kava "bars" had sprang up where one could buy a cup or a bottle. I missed the bitter pepper beverage, missed the graceful sight of men pounding, squeezing, and offering a coconut cup with crossed wrists to those whom they respected. I wondered what kind of market there might be for a product that causes a temporary paralysis of the legs, numbs the mouth, dulls appetite, and tastes like mildewed boiled okra.

I heard that dating customs were changing. Young couples hold hands and eat together in public. Young people who left the island returned having experienced movies, restaurants, bars, and separate young-adult lifestyles. Young men are feeling pressures to be engaged and get serious; young girls just want to have fun. Young people with good educations cannot find employment. Parents pay relatives for babysitting. There are disturbing reports of drug use. Pohnpeians must adjust to growing numbers of foreigners and to out-islanders who claim Pohnpeian citizenship and kinship without full participation in the title and feasting systems. Worries about the future of their children, loss of custom, and seductiveness of foreign ways continued to surface when I spoke to or about islanders.

Each time I talked with colleagues who had returned from fieldwork on Pohnpei, they emphasized how the obligations of feasting had grown. The products of the land—yams, pigs, and breadfruit—are more and more matched with the products of wage labor and capitalism—basins full of cooked foods and stacks of consumer goods. At the same time, the same themes of respect for tradition and high people, cooperation, redistribution, prestige striving, and conspicuous consumption remained vital. This is, we said to each other, yet another example of the genius of Pohnpeian culture in keeping alive traditional systems by incorporating new elements.

The most sweeping change I watched from my distant vantage point was the political fortunes of the island chains of Micronesia. Divided by language, ethnic rivalries, distant ecologies, and different histories, the island groups had never known political unity, a common language, or mutual self-governance. Yet when people discussed the future of Micronesia, everyone assumed a unified country linked to the United States in a kind of interdependence—whether free association, a compact, a commonwealth, or some other status, no one knew. So the outcome of the negotiations was always risky, contingent on factors beyond islanders' control.

Formal negotiations with the United States began in 1969 and lasted for 17 years. In the process, the old Trust Territory broke into four tiny governments: the U.S. Commonwealth of the Northern Marianas; the Republic of Palau; the freely associated Republic of the Marshall Islands; and the Federated States of Micronesia—its four constituent states are Kosrae, Chuuk, Yap, and Pohnpei. On January 13, 1986, President Reagan signed the Compact of Free Association, creating the new nation. On September 17, 1991, the United Nations General Assembly formally admitted the Federated

States of Micronesia as a full and independent member. With independence won, FSM began to look toward the other nations of the Pacific community.

The Federated States unites 607 islands sprinkled across more than a million square miles of ocean. Even with 65 inhabited islands, the total land area of the new nation is only 271 square miles; its lagoons, by contrast, total 2,800 square miles. Pohnpei has the most land—130 square miles or roughly half. The other three states divide the rest between them. A census in 2002 pegged the FSM population at about 107,000. English is the official language. Pohnpei is now home to the new capital of Micronesia. The FSM government offices are in Palikir, a sterile new suburb on the western side of Kolonia. When islanders use the words "national" or "government," they no longer mean the United States but the Federated States of Micronesia.

Time passed, yet the men who wrote the original grant did not publish the results of our research. I learned through informal contacts that no one had finished analyzing the dietary surveys the medical team did; that meant my collection of ship cargoes, store inventories, and weekly family diet journals were the major sources of data we had about what Pohnpeians were eating in the early 1970s. Staff people on the grant told me before it ended that the medical team had failed to take a vital measurement the research protocol demanded—their results were contaminated and insufficient. In 1983 an article appeared in the *International Journal of Epidemiology*—without John Cassel's name on it. Although its technical language obliterated the research project I had known, I gleaned two slices of information. First, the sedentary and overweight women of the island had higher blood pressure than men did. This was an unexpected result, and the hypotheses, formulated about males in industrial societies, did little to account for it. Second, blood pressures on Pohnpei had begun to rise with age. Yet no one knew why—researchers had no cause, no cure, no insight.

In September 1984, Roger and I separated, then divorced. The stresses of building dual careers had been hard on our marriage. In May 1985, Jack Fischer died in his sleep of a heart attack. Between these two brackets of loss, I happened upon a space that was mine alone and decided to write this book. Things had happened to me on Pohnpei that were not about blood pressure. Since I could do nothing more to help the research team, I decided to tell my own story.

In 2003 my editor, Tom Curtin of Waveland Press, contacted me. "Would you consider writing a second edition of *Nest in the Wind*?" he asked. Like a safecracker who hears the numbers fall into place, like a gambler who strikes it lucky with one toss of the dice, I knew the answer at once. I had to return.

Chapter 9

You Cannot Hate with Kava in You

Pohnpei Welcomes . . . Respects . . . Forgives

—Sign at Pohnpei Islands Central School

The journey of return began—not when the plane landed at its destination—but at the open-air loading docks of Continental Air Micronesia, Honolulu airport, at four in the morning. To the strains of island music, women sat in close groups, wearing bright-colored dresses with embroidered flowers on hems and sleeves. They reached up in practiced gestures, combed, twisted, and clamped their waist-long hair in skeins that held its weight and heat off their necks. Some carried babies, shifting them easily from hip to shoulder to breast as they watched children with gentle Micronesian manners play about them. Bulky, burly men lugged appliance-size boxes, ice-chests larger than I had ever seen, and enormous plastic storage containers in primary colors to the conveyor belts—each marked and sealed with duct tape. The airport and airline staff, island-born themselves, passed the containers through security, check-in, and later, through customs. In an age of terrorism, no one appeared to question the contents of the freight or the motives of the packers. The bulk of homebound Micronesians and their baggage, compared to my earth-tone traveling clothes and small carry-on suitcase, rendered me invisible.

Continental Air Micronesia has lost the funky people's feeling it once had—the airline offers a first-class section but no space for chickens and goats. Yet passengers, decked in flowers, still travel in large groups and treat the airline like a moving van. The drama of departure centered not on terrorism in the post September 11 world, but on weight. The 737 jet must carry enough fuel for the long journey yet land and take off on short runways surrounded by ocean depths. At each stop in boarding and loading, airline staff estimate every person's weight, put checked luggage and carry-ons on heavy scales, and enter these figures on clipboards. Crew members will displace cargo and standby passengers for safety's sake as the pounds mount.

The plane landed on two atolls in the Marshall Islands, crossed the International Date Line, then dropped into Kosrae, a tiny jewel, part of the Federated States of Micronesia. Pohnpei was the fourth stop on the long day's journey. As the plane banked for landing on the now-paved airstrip, its ends covered with designs that recall the looms and woven cloth once central to social life in the Caroline Islands, I recognized the luminous outlines of mountain peaks and harbor. Unpacking my shoulder bag and untying my traveling shoes, I slipped on zories, rubber flip-flops back in fashion in America. As I reset my watch to local time and a different day, I saw signs that alerted me to customs and visa checks at an airport terminal grown three times larger than when I left—I had arrived in a new country.

The next morning I awoke drunk on the smells of Kolonia. Somewhere a coconut husk fire burned. Everywhere the perfume of the tropics rose in waves—rampant jungle vegetation, mildew, molds, a whiff of stale pig urine, and humidity that steals one's breath. I put on hat and sunglasses and walked along the old Japanese-built sidewalks and drainage ditches, capped with cement slabs, down the hill to the Public Market at the harbor's edge. Someone had fished on the reefs that morning—the blue, red, and silver catch kept fresh in ice chests. There were still no signs, no system for controlling flies or odors, and no more regular supplies of fresh produce than when I was a housewife hoping to find papayas, mangos, yams, breadfruit, or taro.

Along the street beside and in front of the Public Market, small stores sold hot donuts in the morning and home-grown sweet bananas, local limes, and drinking coconuts all day. In windows of one-room stores, I was surprised to see fresh betel nuts hanging above counters stacked with packages of powdered lime and green leaves. People throughout the Pacific basin and many Southeast Asian countries wrap the lime and betel nuts in the leaves and chew them. This combination makes a stimulating concoction, a kind of Oceanic mouth play. The young proprietor looked dubious when I bought a set of materials to make a good chew and asked, "Do you know how to use betel nut?" Next door a big sign on another small store said: *MIE ICE CUBE*—There is ice here. The Wall Mart at the main intersection of downtown, by island standards a supermarket, was selling excellent take-out meals. Styrofoam containers, betel nut, ice—these are different.

That first morning I walked parallel to the nineteenth-century Spanish wall, past ball fields and the old hospital, which now houses education offices, hungry to take in the Kolonia I had known and the Kolonia that has become the urban center for a new nation. Everyone in the States asks me about the changes—perhaps they assume there is a standstill culture somewhere in the world or that societies move in predictable directions and at fixed rates. Kolonia has paved streets and a few street signs, but no traffic lights. Even so, the roads are still muddy. I heard the high-pitched whine of weed-eaters and saw men with machetes whacking relentless vegetation along the road. It was clear there is no longer a U.S. Trust Territory or its trappings. Employees of the FSM government work in a sterile, planned complex of office buildings at Palikir, a suburb of Kolonia. A national bi-weekly newspaper cost three dollars; I was to discover, however, that it came out at longer and more unpredictable intervals than advertised and did not chart the changes I had come to find.

When I halted before an improbable stop sign set in the middle of a taro patch at lagoon's edge, a woman called out to me in English from an adjoining house. "Where are you going? Where are you coming from? Can I help you?" When I answered her in Pohnpeian, she introduced herself, invited me to sit on her shaded veranda, called her children over, and offered me a cool drink. "Where do you live?" Christina Shoniber asked. "Why are you out walking? Who do you know? Who are you related to? Who told you that?" Curiosity coupled with courtesy has not changed.

I explained, language skills beginning to thaw, that I worked with the group at the hospital studying blood pressure from 1970 to 1972; I'm returning to see what has happened in Pohnpei since then. Before I could finish my introduction, she reeled off her blood pressure, weight, and cholesterol and blood sugar levels like a modern mantra. "I'm borderline diabetic; I went to Manilla for a hysterectomy after eleven kids; I had one set of twins, and my last one," she said as she pointed to a healthy-looking kid staring in fixed fascination at me, "weighed almost 12 pounds. I used to weigh 200 pounds," she continued, "then I decided to loose weight, learn aerobics, and get a d-i-v-o-r-c-e." She laughed and sang the country music song, an anthem of a woman, who like me, was happy to be single again.

With running shoes and workout pants made of a black stretchy synthetic fabric, Christina was not dressed for the tropical heat. "I've just had my morning run," she said. I was sitting on her veranda overlooking the lagoon, wearing tissue linen, loose pants, and a short-sleeve shirt, the coolest clothes I own. Soaked and dripping from a slow walk down the hill, I panted and guzzled water. Sun screen and sweat ran down my body, puddled under my feet, and made my zories slippery. No woman I had known then would have been dressed as she and I were that day. Our conversation would have been impossible to imagine thirty years ago.

When I staggered in the door at the end of my jaunt through Kolonia, a phone was ringing—not a Pohnpeian sound. The apartment I had rented in the old section of Kolonia exceeded my needs and the standards of earlier island households. Besides a telephone, it had ceiling fans, a stove and microwave, cable television, and a flush toilet. Immense *nara* trees shaded the complex; scavenging dogs barked at strangers. There would be no peepers in this place—I sensed that the curiosity of young boys had been sated. Next door, amidst run-away tropical foliage, a half-built and abandoned building was returning to jungle, and an assortment of broken cars that could not be driven and appliances that would never wash or dry clothes again rested in the yard. On my balcony overlooking this perfect Pohnpeian scene, I had two molded green plastic chairs and a table—a place to write my notes of the day and receive my first guests.

The respect and reciprocity that my mentor, Sohn Alpet, Nahnid Lapalap, and I had planted survived his death in the summer of 1971 and, in the summer of 2003, continued to bear the fruit of our improbable friendship. His oldest granddaughter, Maria Donre, a woman my age and a teacher at the College of Micronesia, knew I had returned and where I was staying. On the phone, she greeted me with all the questions Pohnpeians ask each other— questions that proved I had returned, that I remained an adopted relative within their extended families, that I was welcomed back. Because Maria was attending an important conference at the Pohnpei Agricultural Trade School and wanted to welcome me in the appropriate manner, she had asked her younger sister Catalina to entertain me.

Catalina and I had a thousand questions for each other that night when she arrived with two of her five children and armfuls of drinking coconuts. She asked about the grandfather whom she knew less well than I had. I wanted to know about her eleven brothers and sisters—Pedro's and Kioko's other children. Her husband Joseph drove a taxicab; he and Maria's husband, Ioannes, were brothers. Maria and Catalina's brother, Simon, had died not long before, and the weight of grief was heavy. When she told me about her job with the Land Tenure office, I saw in her eyes the world of balancing household, work, children, family, and community obligations that I know so well from the United States.

"Do you have a title?" she asked in the delicate manner she applied to each question. "*Karapei en Dohlen Wehien U,*" I answered with pride. "Sangoro, Nahnmwarki Johnny Moses himself, gave it to me." "I belong to a woman's group," she reported with equal respect, "the U Council of Women of Action. We prepare traditional foods for church gatherings and to honor national dignitaries, make matching dresses appropriate to the occasion, earn money for group projects, and operate a savings lottery," she said, joining us in women's work across the planet. "What women's groups do you belong to? What projects do you do? How we can improve our group?" Her questions rained gently.

The next morning Catalina and her daughter Connie picked me up in a station wagon for a woman's day on the town, an orientation to the past and present. Each time I spotted signs in English or Pohnpeian, we stopped so I could take pictures. A bilingual sign, courtesy of the International Red Cross, advised about safe food preparation—"Cook It. Boil It. Wash It. Peel It. Or Forget It." There were global messages of public courtesy and safety—"No Smoking." "No Littering." "No Spitting." "Drinking and Driving Don't Mix." On the airport road, a sign showed an obviously pregnant woman holding a cigarette in her hand—I translated, "Smoking Cigarettes May Cause Your Baby to Be Born Too Small." Public health messages like these are international, but—*Pohnpei Sarawi,* "Pohnpei is a holy place"—what impulse prompted that sign? The banner in English quoted at the introduction to this chapter welcomed off-islanders to an educational conference at the Pohnpei Islands Central School. I understood the warmth and respect—but what did Pohnpei need to forgive? On the main street waved a high banner in both languages, the theme of yet another conference—"Embracing Cultural Diversities in Pohnpei." Outside Kolonia a more ominous sign in Chinese and English said—"FSM Pilot Farm Funded by the Peoples Republic of China." On bulletin boards about town, someone has posted a notice for revivals and meetings of the Seventh Day Adventists and the Church of the Latter Day Saints. Other notices said: "Computers for sale—make an Offer," "Yoga classes at the community college," or "Pigs for sale—$1.99 per Pound." Everything but the price of pigs was unexpected.

On our drive I saw suburban-looking houses with pastel-painted stucco over cinder blocks, clean-cut manicured yards, porches, patios, and sometimes, carports—a new class elite of Micronesians from other places, rich businessmen and elected leaders. Most have washing machines and clothes dryers; no wet laundry was hanging under carport roofs. What women on the island want most—Catalina explained over lunch at the Joy Hotel—is a clothes dryer. Water for washing is available, but laundromats and personal machines are expensive now that everyone is on the formal energy grid. Perhaps her women's group could buy one, she remarked, then share the costs and benefits within its membership.

As we drove through town, waves of culture shock swept over me—how could I take in, much less explain, so much excess? The Pohnpeian esthetic, the logic of the tropics, is more exuberant than ever. "Things" have their own social life—red rusted tin against jungle green, irregular but artistic stacks of cinder blocks, fifty-gallon baskets of discarded aluminum drink cans, a Japanese battle tank in someone's side yard, plastic buckets and ice chests in bright colors, stacks of coconut husks, fishing nets hung over handmade boats, mildewed ruins, unfinished shells of buildings, and Christmas lights not taken down. Large green dumpsters offered space for the booming trash, although I saw no evidence of dump trucks or regular pickups. A store was painted in supercharged colors—each side half purple and half turquoise, the front half teal and indigo with orange doors and deep green trim. Teenagers dressed in stand-out, Day-Glo T-shirts played volleyball in silhouette against a magenta and lime building. Abandoned cars, many covered with plastic tarpaulins, sat everywhere. Self-trained mechanics will use the auto parts as transplants to keep other cars alive, because replacement parts for all machinery are both difficult to find and expensive to ship. Tropical sun and rain will over time claim and recycle the earthly skeletons of cars just as it is rendering the battle tank and pop-top cans into brittle dust. While this happens, islanders will rest from the heat and humidity in companionable groups, talk, spit, and drink sodas, beer, or kava.

At the beginning of my third week, Catalina and her husband Joseph invited me to a kava gathering at Nan Paradise—"In the Perfect Place"—a homestead tucked into the hills of U municipality. Leaving the younger children at Maria's house where they had relatives to watch them and cousins to play with, we drove in Joseph's taxi along the new road that now encircles Pohnpei. The evening was cool after a heavy day of rain; a quarter moon offered light.

The proprietor of Nan Paradise seated us around a cloth-covered table near the middle of the homestead and brought out molded white plastic lawn chairs with arms. Lightweight inexpensive chairs that stack and do not rust are a boon to the tropics. They permit small intimate gatherings with little need to acknowledge formalities of title and rank. Young Micronesians and aging anthropologists have little muscle memory or cultural mandate for the "good old days" when everyone had to sit cross-legged for hours on the ground or on hard cement. In their new nation, islanders live at waist level, sit in chairs around tables, and work on counters. As I meditated about cheerful molded plastic and looked about the homestead, a woman greeted us, placing glasses of water in front of Joseph, Catalina, their sons, and me.

To my left a tin-roofed patio covered a long picnic table where young people clustered; to my right was a one-room family store with a small stock of island comfort foods—soft drinks, beer, cookies, crackers, cigarettes, rice, and canned meats. Behind the store a terraced slope rose to a five-room cinder-block house. Next to the dwelling and across the open space in front of me, in daylight a drive and parking place for cars, was a formal open-fronted feast house where four high school students bent over a kava stone, which like all the stones I had seen on my return, rested on an old tire. Young men pounded kava for the guests of Nan Paradise after school, on weekends, and on holidays. It was a good job in the new economy—yet they invested their deliberate and hypnotic motions with the ritual grace of ancient times. When they had reduced the roots to a loose mass of fibers, they took it into an adjoining roofed area where other men added water according to a formula that kept the liquid kava consistent through each squeezing. The men positioned the mixture onto an already prepared hibiscus bast, held the filled streamers of bark over a large bucket, and began to twist. Then they strained the kava to remove woody fragments, and poured it through large plastic funnels into washed and empty wine bottles.

The kava steward carried a bottle to our table, wiped it with a cloth, and held the soft brown liquid up to Joseph with the respectful flourish waiters perform in fine French restaurants or Native Americans reserve for peace pipes. He poured half into a green plastic pitcher, shook the bottle with care, and poured the rest. Joseph stirred the contents of the pitcher with respect and a hand-carved wooden spoon as he explained kava etiquette—males drink first in order of age, then women in order of age. He poured kava from the pitcher into a hand-polished half of a small coconut shell that rested on its round bottom in a paper pedestal next to the pitcher. He lifted the cup with both hands, drank, then poured more, and with wrists crossed and eyes averted in the traditional manner he handed a full cup to his teenage son.

"Drink as much or as little as you wish," he explained as my turn came. "Close your eyes tight to honor the kava." As I lifted the common cup gratitude rolled over me—to Jack Fischer, for bringing me to Pohnpei, and to Sohn Alpet, Nahnid Lapalap, and Johnny Moses, Nahnmwarki of U, who modeled manners, respect, and honor for a foreign woman. In many Pacific island societies priests use kava as an *entheogen*—a substance taken to induce an altered state of consciousness, a mild trance that allows communication with spirits and ancestors. Kava is not a hallucinogen, an intoxicant, or a stupefacient—a substance that makes one act stupid. Kava is not the antianxiety medication for which Westerners search. It is only a temperate narcotic, a gentle psychoactive drug like a tranquilizer, a diuretic, an analgesic or pain reliever on the order of aspirin, a relaxer of major muscle systems, and a leveler of emotions. The earthy, peppery flavor is an acquired taste and not worth drinking for the drug's effect alone. Young students rarely believe me or the scientific evidence—anymore than they believe adults who try in vain to talk them out of smoking cigarettes and marijuana or binge drinking. Their denial does not alter the social fact that kava promotes peace, companionship, and communal exchange and that it is a practical and spiritual alternative to hostility and anger that calms irate chiefs and vengeful citizens. Kava in its Pohnpeian manifestation enhances interpersonal universalism and good will. In low light and soft sounds, drinkers "listen" to the drug and hear the voices of their ancestors or the spirits of place—"You can't pound kava alone," people say, "you cannot hate with kava in you."

For me the teenagers there that night were evidence enough of kava's magic. My hosts' son, Jesse, wore baggy pants that hung down to reveal his underwear, a muscle shirt, and arm bands like urban gang members in the United States wear. A head rag that bikers favor covered his long bleached braids. Jesse had dipped a seed from an Areca palm into powdered or slaked lime, laid it on the leaf of a plant known for its interactive narcotic effect, and in a contemporary twist, added a third of a cigarette to create island snuff—betel nut as the concoction is called throughout the Pacific. His right cheek bulged to its fullest extension; he salivated in copious amounts and spit into an empty beer can. Jesse, his brother James, and the other young men their age looked fierce that evening. Although they wore the fashionable uniforms of American teenagers, they lacked "attitude" and could not imitate the sullen, alienated, or infuriating qualities of adolescent rebellion and growth I see in America. In the presence of kava and parents, the brothers were full of courtesies and curiosity. From his neck Jesse removed a necklace he had carved from an ivory palm nut—a perfect marijuana leaf—and handed it to me. "Do you know about Negro stuff?" he asked, and I knew what he meant—the electronic paraphernalia, high-fashion clothes, and loud entertainments that mark urban ethnicity in the United States. "Can you please send me some?"

In the past older men would offer a young man like Jesse a few sips of kava at a big feast or at a private homestead. Then Jesse owed reciprocity and, in the absence of ways to return the favor, could attend few such events.

At Nan Paradise, however, he can pay a dollar or two and drink in shared company—meet his age-mates, male and female, in kava courting and friendship. Women drink kava with men and as much as men do. In the new Pohnpei State, kava remains at the core of respect and feasting systems; it has also become a democratic and recreational drink.

People walked by our table; we greeted each other and mentioned how everyone, including me, was in some fashion or another related. In the gentle conversation and courtesies, I felt no urgency of rank or fear of formality. An oasis of soft electric bulbs within the forest clearing offered lights that did not intrude, blink, or blind. Someone had tuned a radio to the local station; I heard island music, written and recorded here, creative songs not too loud or geared to one social group, one age-set, or the exclusion of another. Kava gatherings, respect, Nan Paradise, the tropical night—these things added up, and Pohnpei felt balanced, somehow to scale.

In intervals of drinking, Catalina inquired with delicate care about my well-being, asking the classic question of kava—"Do you feel good yet?" Although I reassured her, I found no words for the waves of memory and gratitude that swept over me each time I accepted the coconut cup from Joseph's hand. Could I explain that I loved the jungle and the mud as much as I loved the libraries and archives in which I had spent the best part of that week? Far-sighted people are collecting old photographs, unpublished materials, health reports, minutes and reports from thousands of consultants and conferences, books, journals, movies, diaries, dissertations, and all materials they can find that tell of island life. At the Library of the College of Micronesia, a sign says: "Don't bring betel nut in here or spit anywhere." At Micronesian Seminar, I left my zories at the door and walked barefooted through their extensive collections. Thirty years before none of this richness existed; little wonder I was full of gratitude.

Each time I swallowed kava's peppery calm that evening, I remembered and remarked about our boat trip to the ceremonial site of Nan Madol and the journey by car we had taken the week before. Determined to circumvent the island on the fifty-odd miles of road not in place on my last trip, I had negotiated with Joseph to drive Catalina and me in his taxi. Their kids wanted to go as well; soon we had a caravan.

The national highway is rugged and rocky, and part remains unpaved. Bridges, culverts, and slices of road wash out in heavy rains. In places people live so close to its edge that cars are trespassers through homesteads. In other areas the jungle sends out its feelers, relentless in its search for fresh territory to reclaim. The road has no signs, center stripes, or shoulders; yet from the tops of its hills, the view offers forest, swamp, lagoon, and fringing reefs, and I was free to imagine as the entire Pacific Ocean spread out before me. In the transformed and prosperous community of Wene, development initiatives seem to have taken hold. Thanks to the Peace Corps of my generation, the water seal toilets there will work for hundreds of years—no smell, no flies, no fuss. There is an unpredictable bus for workers and students to commute to town. A graceful concrete bridge crosses the Lehnmesi River; on rocks below, however, women wash clothes and bathe children and themselves as we once did.

"What else do you want to see?" Joseph and Catalina had asked before we had embarked on our circumnavigation. "Pohnpaip ['Upon the Stone'—a rock formation about 100 feet long and 90 wide on an upland plateau at the heart of the island]," I replied. I had found a description of the ancient rock carvings or petroglyphs in a Japanese guidebook. The carvings date from centuries before Pohnpeians built Nan Madol and were probably records or markers of their contacts with the spirits. Island legend says that a pair of brothers went about creating local landmarks. After constructing two water-falls, they stole a bed sheet from a house in Kitti, which the ghost Lapango, the same ghost who is said to have used his penis to dig the freshwater chan-nel at Sapwalapw, helped them transform into the stone. Later immigrants sighted the rock and acknowledged spirits through numerous carvings of sun, moon, footprints, swords or dance paddles, and imagined creatures.

To get there Joseph had to stop and ask directions a half-dozen times. At last a man on the path slung his machete over his shoulder, extracted three dollars from me—the price of passage across private land—and gestured to a path only a Pohnpei eye could discern. I used to give lectures to students on my university's Alpine programs—never, never hike without sensible shoes, I cautioned them. Yet there I was in zories—only flimsy flip-flops, rubber shower shoes—hiking through grass up to my waist, climbing up steep rocks with the aid of a walking stick, and stepping across the monument's mossy face to take photographs. The Donres had never seen the carvings their ances-tors made; we rushed from one to another, locating bigger illustrations etched in stone, first exclaiming in wonder at their preservation on the extraordinary rock face, then beckoning each other to admire the sweep of mountain, jun-gle, and ocean views. Catalina told her children—no yelling and running on this sacred rock in the presence of these spirits. They minded her.

She had given them the same instructions on our boat trip to Nan Madol earlier that week. I had last been to the ancient archaeological site on the third day of Sohn Alpet's funeral, the day Klarines and I caught fish for his grave, the day before I became pregnant. You have to go back there, fellow anthropologists insisted. "We can rent the boat that the U Council of Women of Action owns," Catalina told me—reminding me of trips and negotiations I made with her grandfather. That morning it took more time than she and I planned to assemble food, children, gasoline, drivers, and boat. We arrived at the entrance of Nan Douwas—"In the Mouth of the High Chief," the double-walled enclosure surrounding a stone burial vault, the main fortress of the city, a place to pray to the spirits of the island—just past the peak of high tide.

We walked through Nan Douwas along rocky but well-marked paths. A couple of hardy tourists came and went; one had a map to the site, but there were no information signs, no bathrooms or concession stands, and no tour-ist infrastructure. At the edges a young man cleared trees and bushes with his machete. The children swam like a school of fish, played with the boat, brought us drinking coconuts—I marveled at such easy, competent mothering in action and easy, competent children at play. Pohnpeians were my model for raising my daughter, yet I doubt I was ever as relaxed and capable as women like Catalina appeared. In the shade of the great stacked basaltic columns, the measure of place to people and of stone to water felt in balance, once more to scale.

Had we driven to the site and parked, we could have paid three dollars and hiked in and back out through mud and mangrove along a rugged coral path, a mile or so each way. The transit and parking fee, whose worth Pohnpeians debate in heated language, helps maintain the rough path through the swamp. If vegetation is not cut and crucial repairs made, the entropy of the tropics will prevail; the mangrove swamps will have their way. FSM, the United States, and the United Nations have recognized the importance of the site to the spiritual and historical legacy of Pohnpei as well as the cultural heritage of the entire planet; they are investing in Nan Madol as social capital.

As we waited for the tide to rise and float our boat out of the lagoon city, Catalina explained how her Pohnpeian ancestors had worked at upland stone quarries cutting away the columns from the mountain, then building rafts and floating them to the site. To lift log columns weighing several tons, each three stories high, and balance them on top of each other, weaving alternate ends for strength, men lined up on each side. They sang a magical song to the spirits of the island and to the souls of their forebears—we mortals have done everything possible, and now we need your help. Although I could see the visible evidence, I had not heard this story of how the ancestors had achieved such majesty. Catalina repeated the story again that night at Nan Paradise to the delight of her husband and sons. They boasted about the achievements of those who had built Nan Madol—a good omen for nationhood and for the preservation of sacred sites.

Joseph and his sons, in accord with ancient custom and in common with most men on the island, have elevated the act of spitting to an art form. Both kava drinking and betel chewing increase the production of saliva and offer pieces of moist matter that must be expelled with a dramatic flourish. Cab drivers like Joseph can race at 60 miles per hour in a 25 mile an hour zone, drive with one hand on the steering wheel, open the car door with the other, and spit with enviable style on the road. When one drinks kava, spitting is an acknowledgment of or a gift to the supernatural, a return of its blessings to the earth. Spitting may be an enticement, an invitation like a knock on the floor, a hand clap, or the posture of kneeling—a physical act that stands on its own merit. In this way it may serve a higher spiritual purpose than clearing one's throat and mouth of debris.

The kava gathering at Nan Paradise is one of many held every night on the island. Governmental authorities in the Pohnpei State have licensed the "bars" as they call the places where kava is sold. Owners and operators must adhere to strict standards; they must wash the roots before pounding, add a uniform amount of water, and maintain consistency from first squeezing until the last. Pohnpeians review the "bars" or "parties" to each other in the same manner my friends in New Orleans recommend or criticize its world-famous restaurants. A place gains a reputation for price, flavor, and its congenial atmosphere. Joseph assured me—the price of kava at Nan Paradise, $2.50 U.S. for one bottle, is the cheapest. Between us we drank four wine bottles of kava that night. He drank a beer purchased at the little store; a can of Coke each and a few crackers lasted Catalina and me all evening. The island world held the same density of colors, smells, noises, tastes, and good companionship as earlier in the day. No one was drunk, hallucinating, tripping, or high.

The kava gathering at Nan Paradise helped me understand how islander ambitions have followed and failed to follow the laws of unintended consequences. In 1986 when independence came and the U.S. Trust Territory of the Pacific Islands ended, when the Compact of Free Association and the Federated States of Micronesia began, planners and consultants looked into the future and predicted three major economic supports for the new nation—tourism, fishing, and agriculture. I was able to track the three hoped-for initiatives, the development or lack of it, through the archives and libraries of Pohnpei, discussions with many citizens, and time-honored techniques of observation and participation.

On and off during my stay, I played at being a tourist, and concluded that Pohnpei is a destination suitable only for those with money and a lust for adventure. The island is expensive and difficult to reach; it offers too few enticements for honeymooners, families with children, or those who love packaged tours to larger and more varied places like Hawaii. There is no cheap transportation for international adventurers, the backpack crowd, or travelers on a budget. There is no shopping or organized entertainment, and there is little tourist infrastructure on Pohnpei—locally managed businesses that offer tours were often unavailable to answer their phone calls. Postcards are difficult to find, expensive, and can only be mailed from the post office—a faded and dented metal building on main street left over from American days. It would be difficult for a tourist to attend a kava gathering at Nan Paradise or a traditional feast in which baked dogs are served to high-ranking dignitaries, men in grass skirts carry a half-ton yam into the ceremonial platform of a feast house, and ageless women perform the thousand-year-old rhythms and restrained movements of Pohnpeian dances. Diving in the magnificent reefs and lagoons is the tourist activity most worth paying the high fares for a long trip on Continental Air Micronesia. Even *Lonely Planet*, the ultimate guide for travelers off the beaten path, is cautious in recommending Pohnpei as a tourist destination.

A Hollywood version of the tropics is available on Saturday nights to tourists at the South Park Hotel overlooking the scenic sunsets of Sokehs Bay. Young girls wear brassieres or bikini tops, made from small coconut shells or scraps of colorful rayon, and grass skirts in the style only men wore in the past. They dance to music written and recorded on the islands, but their movements are tourist stereotypes—come-hither, suggestive gestures of arms, wrists, neck, torso, and hips, which owe more to mass media or American cheerleading fashions than to the traditions of the islands. The pseudo-Polynesian dance performances are modeled on Western notions of female sexuality and compliance. They carry concerning questions—Is sex for sale? Are Pohnpeians planning to market their young girls, kinship system, and tropical flexibility in return for tourist dollars?

Micronesians wait for travelers to arrive and rescue their bad budget years with cash windfalls. But tourists are notoriously fickle and demanding; tourism torques or twists local culture and promotes manufactured or pseudoexperiences. Host destinations are hostage to changing travel fashions and the world economy. Travelers bring in less money than locals imagine, and in the worst cases, destroy the very traditions and environment they want to experience. Marketing and selling one's own culture is not the same as the courtesies and expectations of reciprocity that hold Pohnpeian life together—Pohnpeians have an ethic of sharing, not one of service. Pohnpei is not yet on the international sexual tourism circuit with packaged tours, for example, geared to men from Japan and China. Environmental degradation—deep wear and tear on sacred places and the trash and pollution that travelers and tour groups bring—has not begun.

Given the gifts of geography and history, the fishing industries of Micronesia should have been a success story, a more certain bet than tourism. In 1979 legislatures created a 200-mile fishing zone around each island. Pohnpei, Kosrae, Chuuk, Yap, and other islands charged foreign-owned fishing fleets for the access and permits they needed to fish in Micronesian waters. Twenty years later, fees and fishing licences sold to foreign vessels were 22 percent of the total national government revenue.

After independence in 1986, however, officials in the new Federated States decided to build a fishing industry for themselves. They knew how to fish; they were people for whom deep-sea tuna was a primary source of protein in local diets as well as a commodity to be traded in the international economy. What they did so well for their families and communities, they reasoned, they would do for their nation. So the newly independent governments purchased ships and built large storage and transshipment facilities to handle foreign and domestic fleets. They then spent the profits from international fishing fees and licenses on local fleets and facilities. The infant industry had a few promising years. Then in the late 1990s the largest fishing fleets, those from Taiwan, pulled out of Micronesia. Japanese fleets failed to survive a financial crunch in their country, and many went out of business. Korea, the United States, and other nations scaled back the size of their fishing fleets in response. Suddenly the revenues from foreign fleets were a fraction of what they had been.

Other unanticipated problems arose. Ships ran aground; some sank. Crew members were injured or caused trouble in faraway ports. The expensive onshore facilities that Pohnpeians built could no longer compete with transshipment facilities closer to the Asian mainland or with cheaper handling and airfreight in other places. Micronesians had no control over the market price of tuna anymore than they did over copra prices, also in collapse. Moreover, the spiritual and personal value of fishing as a livelihood bore no weight on the international maritime scene. The insolvent public-owned fishing company in the Federated States of Micronesia could not compete with private-sector companies. The Pohnpei Fishing Corporation had never turned a profit; it retained fewer employees and had less working capital with each budget year. It carried massive debts that ordinary citizens absorbed in increased electricity rates and other forms of indirect subsidies. Although the fishing industry cost more than it contributed, politicians were not able to muster the will to convert it, sell pieces to private industry, or abandon an enterprise with so much emotional weight.

Agriculture, in marked contrast to tourism and fishing, failed and succeeded in random patterns. In the decade before I arrived the first time, and for the three decades after, consultants, Peace Corps workers, developers, planners, and elected officials talked and schemed about their "great pepper plan." Government agencies in the United States and international development consortiums introduced *Piper nigrum*, a plant in the same genus as and a cousin to Pohnpeian kava. In the volcanic soils and heavy rainfall of the island the bushes produce strong, spicy peppercorns that boutique and speciality gourmet producers love. Over time, development specialists spent significant amounts—millions of dollars by my casual reckoning—on their single-minded mania for this plantation product. Pohnpeian pepper, a niche product with a high profit margin due to the low cost of producing and transporting it, should have sold well; the peppercorns should have established their place along with other tropical agricultural products in the global market. But they failed to do so.

Not one of the pepper companies—despite extensive government and private investment—survived. Black pepper, a cash crop on the international commodity market, never earned more than $150,000 a year, never began to repay its backers for their investments of capital, and never captured the imagination and energies of an island population otherwise eager to work and to earn money. Pohnpei pepper has no value, not even sentimental, to Pohnpeians; it is no great loss to the international spice industry either. After a diligent search, I found a few packages for sale on dusty shelves—six to twelve dollars an ounce. In the Wall Mart, ground pepper sells for 30 cents an ounce.

Meanwhile, the same development specialists and economic advisors projected no potential use for the peppercorn's indigenous country cousin, *Piper methysticum* or kava. To them, if they considered it at all, kava had value only within the traditional subsistence and prestige economy of the island. Nor did anyone—islander or outsider—pay attention to the economic potential of the seed of the Areca palm, the betel nuts I saw for sale and in so many people's mouths.

Betel nut is one of the most widely used mind-altering substances on the planet—only nicotine, alcohol, and caffeine are more prevalent. Thousands of years ago Pacific people discovered that the Areca seed and the leaf of the *Piper betel* in combination are pharmacologically active, more so when combined with slaked lime. The Areca tree and *Piper betel*, the pepper vine, a relative of both kava and boutique peppercorns, grow wild in forests and in cultivated form in gardens. Slaked lime is a soft white powder made from water-softened seashells or ground coral. The betel products on Pohnpei earned a reputation among Asians and other Pacific Islanders as some of the tastiest and most potent anywhere on earth. But Pohnpeians themselves did not chew betel until independence. When people from the Philippines, Southeast Asia, Guam, and other Micronesian islands moved to Pohnpei to work with the new FSM government, they brought the betel habit with them and passed it on to young Pohnpeians with whom they worked and attended school. Soon garden plots expanded with pepper vines and Areca palms. Betel is a boon to the local economy—easy to produce, cheap to buy, and legal to sell. It makes ecological sense, does no harm to the environment, and requires no government investment whatsoever in promotion, cultivation, or marketing. Many chewers mix a third of a cigarette into their betel quids for the added enhancement of nicotine.

Betel chewing has much to recommend it, if one is able to ignore or excuse the appearance of those who enjoy its benefits—bulging cheeks and bright red saliva. Chewers have the startling, fierce look of someone who has just eaten slabs of raw meat or is bleeding from internal injuries—they must spit the excessive saliva they produce. Pop-top soda cans work better than anything made of clear glass, but most spitters make use of the rich brown soils of Pohnpei, which do not show the scarlet stains of betel.

Mildly addictive, betel leaves users with a pleasant minty mouth odor. If they choose to quit, the withdrawal is similar to that of cigarettes, or so the experts who want to discourage the practice contend. Health educators hate habits like betel—I heard or read claims that it causes tooth decay, learning difficulties, and a lack of motivation. Now that more young people are chewing it with cigarettes, it may be possible to make the same linkage as those between smokeless tobacco and oral cancer. Nonetheless, no one claims that betel quids in the mouths of adolescents or adults lead to depression, car accidents, homicides, suicides, outbursts of uncontrollable anger, or other problems of drug use. Chewers have the same kind of buzz I would get from strong coffee and a smoke—but no one fights or kills after chewing betel nut. Sharing betel with teenagers and other young people made them relaxed and the conversation easier; I began to carry a supply with me.

When I walked through Kolonia on Friday and Saturday nights in the two years I lived there, I was never out of earshot of at least one of the twenty bars in town. There was no escape from the noise or the groups of belligerent young men hovering drunk along the edges of island social life. "No good will come of all this drinking," adults used to moan. Now they say that alcohol consumption is way down. The loud bars have disappeared; young guys are drinking less "foreign kava"—beer or expensive imported alcohol. I walked through Kolonia at night and could not find a noisy bar. Islanders still consume beer and cigarettes, more as supplements than necessities. In a progression of events no one predicted or planned, they have switched to betel nuts and kava.

In 1982, El Niño, a sporadic weather pattern in the Pacific, caused a persistent drought on Pohnpei. Kava plants in the lowlands began to die of thirst. Farmers had to harvest the plants before they perished, consume as much as they could, and sell the rest. Kava became, for the first time, available to everyone outside ceremonial contexts. As the demand soared, farmers began to clear vegetation from rainier and unpopulated forests in the highlands of the island. To their delight, the kava they planted grew faster—two to three years for maturity as opposed to three to five years in the lowlands. Many claimed it tasted better. Since 1982 kava has exploded—a cash crop controlled for and by native-born Pohnpeians. Kava gathering places like those of Nan Paradise have replaced conventional bars; the traditional beverage is so popular that its price increases every year.

Kava offers a certain, fast return on the labor invested in it. Farmers clear, then plant, returning at intervals to weed before they harvest. Although it is difficult to collect reliable economic statistics under the circumstances, officials in the Pohnpei State say that more than a million pounds of kava per year are harvested and sold at the going rate of a dollar a pound. About one-tenth of the harvest is shipped frozen to Pohnpeians living in Guam, Hawaii, and the Marshall Islands, or to other places with exiled populations thirsting to drink kava. A smaller amount of dried roots—including tasteless branches and bark of the plant—is sent to Europe and America and made into herbal preparations. This means at least a million dollars from kava circulates in the island economy per year.

Pohnpeians receive income in foreign sales for something only a few people in the world are producing, yet they are not selling their culture. A small investment of labor produces an impressive yield per pound, the highest income per workday of any cash crops in the Pacific, more than vanilla, ginger, coffee, or cocoa. Commercial kava is a lucrative export that owes nothing to foreign businesses or government bureaucrats. Its small-scale operations have low start-up and labor costs and no advertising expenses. It does not depend on an educated labor force, specialized technology, or heavy machinery with easy-to-break and hard-to-replace parts. Kava was already part of the traditional economy—now the traditional leaders have sanctioned the use of the sacred crop in this commercial manner. Once again, the scale feels right—kava, an easy-to-grow sacred plant, produces income. A drink of hierarchy, honor, and forgiveness has added democracy and universal good will to its consumption.

Kava is the ultimate performance of meaning and cultural understanding on Pohnpei, an emerging icon of identity and unity. The coconut serving cup appears on most of the Pohnpei State insignia—the state flag, the state seal, and the seals of the governor and the supreme court. Policemen, jailers, and other civil servants sport a simple version on their state vehicles. At feasts and celebrations for national holidays and inter- and intraisland events, men with flower garlands and grass skirts form processions, carrying the kava bush, roots forward, boughs behind, over their right shoulder. They decorate the plant with green leaves and lift exceptional plants onto a litter. Priests and Pohnpeians pound kava, the beverage of atonement, at the altar of the Catholic church; High Chiefs, ambassadors of foreign countries, and elected national officials drink from a shared cup at rituals of solidarity within the Federated States.

Back in the United States I drive to a local health food market, an organic and earth-centered store, where I buy "kava" in pills, liquid extracts, and in mixtures with other alleged calming substances. I open a bottle, break apart a capsule, and put the light brown powder on my tongue or use a dropper to squirt the milky gray liquid in my mouth. The astringent, almost bitter, taste feels the same as that of the kava I drank on Pohnpei. The front of my tongue goes numb, then the back of my throat. This is kava—but only its echo, a signature in place of a real person. I feel no power, no connection. In Pohnpei I felt the synergy of social and ritual elaborations coming from plants grown over centuries and mixed with an active ingredient in the inner bark of hibiscus plants used to squeeze the pounded roots—a synergy that no commercial products can achieve. The kava fad in America is artificial; it rips the woody remains of roots, bark, and branches alike from their homeland and the collective social setting of consumption; it expects machine-rendered twigs to carry the weight of healing and helpfulness. The purchased products have no smell; they do not taste of flower garlands, coconut oil rubbed on sweaty bodies, ringing stones, honor, respect, or ancestors. Several Pohnpeian men laughed about the kava sold in stores in the United States—"Those people are grinding up branches and leaves. It won't work for them."

It may not work for islanders either. The traditional-to-modern botanical success story has built-in problems. Kava grown as a cash crop in fragile and finite ecological zones to fill expanding, perhaps infinite, needs may harm their environment as well as their social relationships.

Cash cropping is a dangerous endeavor, a short-term gain for long-term loss. Farmers are tempted to clear more jungle in the highlands and plant another crop. But the poor tropical soils will soon wear out; wash off the steep slopes; clog rivers and lagoons; kill fish, reefs, sea life, and beauty; and destroy the reasons for which tourists visit. When the shallow upland soils are exhausted, nothing will grow on the volcanic rocks that remain. Pohnpei's single most important asset is the island itself—clear, clean waters, a sustainable garden and forest economy, and a gently managed beauty. This inheritance from their ancestors, that which they preserved through four colonial occupations and into nationhood, is theirs to ruin.

After independence the Pohnpei state legislature passed a wise but highly contested law that turned almost 40 percent of the total land area—13,000 acres of highland forest and 15,000 acres of mangrove swamps—into a conservation zone. The act restricts traditional or commercial use of upland forests, prohibits access to homesteaders, and establishes a goal of sustainable development. International agencies like the Nature Conservancy, the Asian Development Board, and various South Pacific development groups favor the law. Native-born Pohnpeians, however, do not share the same premises. In common with many indigenous peoples around the globe, they have not put foreign environmental concerns high in their priorities. They want to farm, sell as much produce as possible, and have clear title to their own property. They want to work hard in the day, earn enough money to buy imported goods, and drink kava at night.

Pohnpei is a small, finite island with giant questions of land tenure—who owns or has rights to spaces like forested land in highland areas, islets in the lagoon, or waterfront property, for example? Four colonial powers and one independent nation later, laws about inheritance and land titles remain chaotic and confusing. Land is distributed through leases or "gifts" rather than outright sales or direct inheritance. This means it operates much like the sale of pigs—high and unrealistic expectations, sudden disappointments, elaborate schemes, claims and counterclaims. Public lands continue to fall into private hands by lease or title transfer. At the same time many families are homesteading land to which they have only some or no hereditary claim.

Pohnpei is a garden. Its rich volcanic soils, equatorial sunshine, and heavy rainfall mean that no one has to work under extreme or harsh circumstances. There are no crop failures, starvation, brutal colonial appropriation, wage-labor entrapment, or any of the bitter conditions that mark agriculture in other places. Pohnpeians have problems—the island's economy and environment, and the islanders' physical well-being and health are the two greatest. But they have kava—a balm for the ordinary frictions of community life, a sacrament for its extraordinary moments. And they have found a way to divide up work and work's rewards between women and men.

Chapter 10

It Takes an Outrigger
to Float a Canoe

Much attention and respect is awarded to the females at this island, and
they are not made to do any work but what rightfully belongs to them.

—Andrew Cheyne, shipwrecked sailor, 1840

"*I* bet everything has changed." "So what changes did you find?"
"What has changed the most?" Although questions and comments like these
are well meant, change is a poor word to use about my return visit to
Pohnpei. Major events and adjustments happen every year, every decade, yet
the island felt more like itself than ever. It is I who have changed.

On my first field trip, I was not yet a weaver, a writer, a mother, a
divorced woman grateful for the women's movement, or a person grown into
networks of kinship and friendship. I could not see the worth of women's
work in Pohnpei because I could not see the worth of my own work. I did not
participate in women's exchanges, and only when I became pregnant did I
begin to experience women's lives. Pohnpeian women replied to my questions—"ask my husband about that"—not because they lacked answers but
because I asked the wrong questions.

By the time I returned I was connected to island life through a variety of
personal and professional women-centered lineages that began with anthropologist Suzanne Falgout. She had been an undergraduate in my classes at
the University of New Orleans; then she went to the University of Oregon for
graduate work, and from there completed extensive fieldwork and a dissertation about Pohnpei. In time, Suzanne became a friend and mentor for a graduate student from the University of Hawaii—Kimberlee Kihleng.

Kimberlee was also "related" to me; she had met and married Simeon Kihleng, grandson of Sohn Alpet and one of twelve children in the household of Pedro and Kioko Kihleng with whom Roger and I had lived. Her initial visits with Simeon's family, his grandmother, mother, and sisters as well as other female relatives convinced her to become an anthropologist, to do fieldwork and research on the lives of Pohnpeian women. Kimberlee's dissertation, like Suzanne's, reveals the way matrilineal kinship and female-centered work and play command much of island activities. For several years Kimberlee, Simeon, and their daughter, Emelihter, lived in Saladak in U municipality, and as family member and anthropologist, she attended feasts and participated in the exchanges that dominate Pohnpei's social life. Over the years, adoption, marriage, and anthropological kinship had turned Suzanne, Kimberlee, her sisters-in-law Maria and Catalina, and me into a women's support group.

When I spoke with them, with the director of Women's Interests in Pohnpei, and with people anthropologists call "agents of change"—administrators, teachers, priests, Peace Corps workers, and politicians—each was quick to inform me that the discourse about "rights" in American feminism is not a proper fit for Micronesian women. Equality is not our goal, each person insisted. They worked to convince me, citing similar claims from the published literature about Pohnpei, that the social roles between men and women were in the past and continue to be "complementary." The sexes are not competitive, hierarchical, patriarchal, or even postcolonial, they insisted. "Complementarity" means that women and men do different but equivalent work in kinship, households, agriculture, offices, and at feasts. In a complementary system men and women do not have the same privileges and rewards or take the same risks—they are not mirror images of one another. Women do the work of women just as men do the work of men; each are rewarded by both men and women, but in different ways. In every conversation, people reminded me that the matrilineal principle is still at play in island affairs. I had doubts, or certainly confusions.

True, I saw women at work everywhere I went. Women play basketball and volleyball. Women drive cars and trucks. Yet I know that colonialism and capitalism are forces that shape women's work in world cultures and assign low values to it regardless of what islanders think happened in the past. Historians and anthropologists point to manufactured and foreign goods or agricultural products that give weight to money and male prestige. Others think it is easy for Pohnpeian men to model themselves on American male behavior, the dominant model for three generations, in which women act less as complements and more as adjuncts or assistants—wife, secretary, mistress, mother. In the contemporary wage-labor economy of the Federated States, patterned after the United States, women earn lower salaries than men do. Few women run for public office and even fewer win. Women cannot aspire to be Nahnmwarki or Nahnken. Although no one complained, I imagined subtle barriers to land ownership, unequal access to education and job advancement, second-class citizenship, and subordination of the kind that spurred the women's movement in the United States. So why do women on Pohnpei—unlike my friends in America—seem cheerful, even enthusiastic, about the principles of complementarity?

Look to the feasting and title systems for your answers, said each anthropologist I spoke with or whose works I read. Pohnpeians establish and validate each other's prestige, standing, and honor through exchange and reciprocity—even within capitalism and nationhood. The motivations to sponsor a feast, colleagues like Kimberlee and Suzanne insisted, have exploded in the new Pohnpei. Although traditional chiefs can no longer compel anyone to take part in the feasting rounds, Pohnpeians find more and more reasons to participate. Here is a list of contributions to a High Chief one woman organized, purchased, or traded for on behalf of her brother's dedication of a new feast house.

Material Goods: futon, mat, seven pillows, 18 pieces of fabric, large mirror, 12 embroidered skirts, 5 sheets, 10 embroidered handkerchiefs, 1 aloha skirt, 2 dresses, 9 plastic buckets, 5 plastic washbasins, large glass plate, 5 smaller glass plates, pitcher with cups, and 22 flower garlands.

Foodstuffs: 2 cases of flour, 9 cases of Japanese soup; 21 50-pound bags of sugar; 4 22-pound bags of rice; 7 cases of soda and a 12-pack of beer; 3 large boxes each of snacks and sodas; 4 cases of frozen turkey tails [a popular item]; 2 cases of frozen chickens; case of corned beef; 70 assorted cans of mixed meats; 4 dozen eggs; 15 bags each of bread and donuts.

Traditional Contributions: 1 kava, 1 pig, and many breadfruit under a large palm frond (Kihleng 1996:177).

This outpouring bears no resemblance to the gifts I gave my brothers when they bought new houses. Most Pohnpeians, certainly most households on Pohnpei, will be involved in a dozen or more similar events during a calendar year.

In the past women wove the social fabric of Pohnpei society. They handcrafted fiber skirts, belts, headdresses, mats, and baskets central to all feasting and exchanges—the core definition of wealth on the island. Pieces of cloth that survived reside in museums and have earned women of the island an international reputation for artistry and craftsmanship. Women made all clothes, bedding, and jewelry for everyday use; they wove sails for canoes and thatch for houses, and spun coconut sennit twine, the bindings that were the equivalent of nails or glue. Women twined flower garland headdresses and cooked fragrant coconut oils to decorate and anoint their bodies. They grew and harvested sugarcane, the female ritual equivalent of kava. Practical artists and producers of personal services, they tattooed the elaborate body art that spoke of the wearer's affiliations and ambitions. Women controlled the social lives of "things."

Today women use imported fabric and metallic threads for machine-embroidered dresses, skirts, blouses, half-slips, sheets, pillow cases, and other prized goods. They add value through imaginative sewing done on machines relatives have sent them from the mainland. They crochet intricate lacy trimmings and store their cloth wealth awaiting an inevitable funeral or a feast to honor a high-ranking chief on a public occasion. Hand-decorated goods will adorn the bodies of the dead and impress leaders with the donor's skill and generosity.

In the past women grew and prepared dryland taro, an important food crop that had little ceremonial significance and required little work. Then, men did most of the cooking for household consumption; in the postcontact period, however, women have taken over the bulk of these tasks. Processed white rice has replaced taro as the core, everyday food. Men continue to make earth ovens and pound kava; women, however, control the supply and distribution of imported foods and other foreign goods. At funeral feasts, women's degree of kinship to the dead person propels them into a four-day frenzy of food preparation and distribution. Although men supervise the pounding and distribution of kava, the centerpiece of shared mourning is the women's ainpwot, "iron pot"—long boards or picnic table bursting with platters, basins, bowls, and trays of food that kinswomen of the deceased have collected and cooked. Over a four-day period everyone who attends will eat at least one plate there and take another home.

Women work a variety of jobs and use the cash they earn to buy ice, sodas, donuts, or canned meats for funerals and exchanges. They raise chickens or catch fish to sell to local markets, stores, and hotels; to bring to formal and informal gatherings; or to supplement their household diet. Sometimes they prepare special dishes for an ainpwot—grated tapioca or ground taro mixed with ripe bananas and coconut cream, cooked in a stone oven. Within the calculus of exchange they anticipate relationships and mutual indebtedness. At a feast to honor receipt of a new title, the wife of a nephew of the person being honored may contribute an ainpwot of cooked rice and a can of corned beef. A married couple with matrilineal ties to the person being honored would be expected to contribute more—a 22-pound sack of rice, a carton of frozen chickens, several bags of donuts, and a kava plant would be appropriate. Over time, the food they give in profuse unselfishness—whether cooked, raw, store-bought, or land-grown—returns to them in the same manner. The currency of exchange and most important commodity on Pohnpei are a person's hard work and contributions in such generous quantities that no one can keep track. Anthropologists call this the "ethic of generalized reciprocity."

The morality of generalized reciprocity on Pohnpei is stronger than the ethics of individualism or male-centered achievement. Women strive for social symmetry, for honor, and to be able to say—"I'm an active member of this community, a good neighbor, friend, and relative." The gifts they organize on one occasion give birth to further exchanges in a continuous circle. What Sohn Alpet and I gave each other through our work on the blood pressure project returned three decades later and drew me into yet another cycle.

If we define "exchange" as short- and long-term cycles of gift giving in the form of food, commodities, services, and relationships, then we see at least three clear cases of cooperation not dependent on hierarchy or competition—they are sibling bonds, adoptions, and women's church work.

The *pedel* or special sibling bond, like those between an older brother and a younger sister close in age, continues to be strong. When people marry they gain in-laws, not just mates—a woman is sister and wife as well as sister-in-law to her brother's wife and her husband's sister. Just as natal cross-sex siblings are bound together, a woman is bound to her husband's sisters and he to her brothers—same-sex in-laws or *mwah* are a special category of regard and investment. Groups of sisters-in-law cooperate in labor exchanges particularly for feasting and farmwork. When a woman has obligations or troubles, her sisters-in-law are her best allies. They visit each other and give gifts. They form the organizing committee for family-centered celebrations; the primary ones are marriage proposal feasts, "tied by the church" or wedding feasts, "mother's milk" feasts for first births, and first-year anniversaries of family members' deaths.

Pohnpeians continue to "lift up a child," that is, to adopt each other's children, making gifts of kinship, transactions in parenthood that connect adoptive parents, biological parent or parents, and an adopted child throughout their lives. The FSM Census in 2000 revealed that 84 percent of households on Pohnpei had at least one, sometimes more, adopted members; one out of every three people is adopted or "lifted up." In Kimberlee Kihleng's (1996) study, she found that the majority of such transactions in U municipality linked matrilineal kinfolk—sisters, sisters-in-law, sisters and brothers, maternal nieces and aunts, female cousins, mother and daughter, and grandmothers—to each other. In his earlier study Jack Fischer (1966) identified the same degree and type of adoptions, but he traced them through males. To me, this is proof of complementarity in fieldwork and in social life. Across generations and gender, two anthropologists found the same pattern—long-term cycles of giving, the kinship of solidarity, and obligation. Both anthropologists found the same motivations to give a child in adoption—an unmarried mother too young to take on such responsibilities, a childless couple who needs an heir, a divorced couple whose parents or siblings are in a better position to raise the children, parents with more children than resources to raise them, parents who respect older siblings, a boy to round out a family of girls, or a girl for a family of boys.

Pohnpeian women practice another form of generalized reciprocity and exchange in their respective congregations. Whether Catholic or Protestant—there are about equal numbers of each—church organizations mirror the traditional hierarchies of chiefs, feasts, and titles. Foreign missionaries in the nineteenth century gave machine-made metal needles and iron pots to women already skilled in weaving and cooking—so their material world was enhanced but not changed. When islanders embraced Christianity for its earthy stories of multiple wives, clans, chieftainships, magical acts, and nods to the spirits of place and of nature, they transformed the foreign churches into something Pohnpeian, something that validated extreme social cooperation. Women seized the missionary models of clubs or Christian sororities to build organizations that turned an alien religion into an ethic of mutual obligation among kinfolk and long-term reciprocities among community members.

The Protestant organization, "Women of Friday," commemorates the special place of women in Christ's death, thus in Christianity. Catholic women belong to a counterpart called the Mercedes Group. Both groups, however, do fund-raising, serve as hostesses, and prepare traditional foods for interisland religious and cultural exchanges, special government events like the inauguration ceremonies for the president of the Federated States of Micronesia, United Nations Day, and major national gatherings in Kolonia. Women from island congregations staff and attend government or local conferences on health, children, or nutrition. Protestant and Catholic women alike celebrate together in the month of May—for Mary, the mother of Jesus, and for woman as mothers; they stage sacred and secular celebrations at the New Year, and cap their ceremonial calendars with the gatherings of Easter week. Church women of both denominations accumulate material goods and foodstuffs; they organize formal presentations, songs, dances, skits, and prepare huge platters or wash basins of food, flower garlands and head wreaths, perfume, and perfumed oils for the exchanges. Expending enormous labor during these ceremonial times, women engage each other and their congregations in a continuous dance of competition through cooperation.

It would be difficult to claim that conversion to Christianity has devalued women's lives or work. On the contrary, missionary activity seems to have empowered Pohnpeian women in personal relationships and in the public arena. Women's groups, secular and sacred, flourish as the tropical vegetation does. Kimberlee worked with nine different ones in U municipality alone—not counting formal church bodies and informal work groups. Maria and Catalina are active in church organizations, leaders in their matrilineage, founders of and officers in the U Council of Women in Action. In their cooperative, members earn money for collective assistance—they cook and serve traditional food and prepare gift packages for churches, government events, and other women's groups. Sometimes individual women earn commissions through unusual endeavor; sometimes the group helps a member in difficulty. The U Council owns the boat I rented to take us to Nan Madol and the gardening tools the members use to clear, clean, and plant. The group runs a benevolent revolving lottery: Once a week each woman makes a contribution of five to twenty dollars to a drawing. One name is drawn and that woman takes the entire collection home. This round goes on until every woman has had her name drawn; then they start again. The principle of exchange—what they contribute in the long run is equivalent to what they take out in the short run—ensures a group savings plan.

Pohnpeian women claim that they have not experienced a loss of authority within households and communities. Unlike myself and my friends, they do not talk about personal freedom, sexual identity, independence, or equal pay. They speak of interdependence, cooperation, and connections. As they told anthropologist Suzanne Falgout (1993), the emotional qualities a wife brings to her marriage matter. A woman's character and reputation help her husband's social prospects. Her connections within her matriline and the standing of the matriline itself double a groom's social networks and determine their children's chances for advancement. Suzanne concluded that women's work for wages enhances her husband's status beyond the household budget. Pohnpeian men pay more attention to a woman's achievements as a wage earner and less attention to her social background. A woman with an education and a salary can purchase imported goods, free her husband to work in agriculture or other traditional realms, and aid both families in exchanges and title striving.

The Pohnpeian paradox is this: a man can be the male head of household and a woman can be the female head of household—for the same household. Pohnpeians say a wife is the outrigger for her husband's canoe, steadying him for their shared journey—without her, the vessel will go nowhere. Women work for salaries—as secretaries, nurses, store clerks, babysitters, and teachers; they earn money for their work in fishing, cloth production, and hospitality services. Often self-employed, they bake bread and donuts or make quick-serve sandwiches with fresh fish or chicken. Women are partners in exchange networks and economic coproducers with control over household budgets; they are not consumers who have to rely on men's wage labor. A household in which either husband or wife works in traditional agriculture and the other in the cash economy is said "to give birth to money."

Joint male-female survival activities and matrilineal kinship, according to anthropologist Elizabeth Keating (1998), have not led to inequality or subordination but to *power sharing*. She videotaped, transcribed, and analyzed hundreds of hours of oratory from public speeches that women of chiefly rank made, and she gathered similar materials from more ordinary occasions in which they used high language and honorifics. She concluded that traditional roles for both men and women have shape-shifted, eroded, and wobbled on their axes. Men and women, chiefs and commoners, however, continue to collaborate in creating symbolic inequalities through food, ritual, language, titles, and other markers or privileges, and then resolve the contradictions through more giving. A title, for example, determines how much food a person will give as well as how much she or he will receive back when the goods are returned. Titles, called out in descending order of rank at a feast, tally the distribution and provide labels for fairness—not equality. In Pohnpei it is an insult to say —"you are the equal of everyone else." In staged competitions individuals deplete both their prestige resources and their vocabularies for humility and deference. In this way, losing can be seen as winning. High language contains no formal way to "just say no" to a chief; only material and spiritual generosity can oil such social relationships. And in the end, a woman of chiefly station outranks male commoners.

Those who attend contemporary feasts measure the contributions in number of pounds, cases, bags, basins, or baskets; in how many feet high the goods are piled; and in how many people it takes to carry them. Participants estimate the volume of kava plants, pigs, dogs, giant yams, and stacks of breadfruit. It does no good, however, to argue about who does the most work or who has the most prestige—men or women. The Pohnpeian ideal of complementarity does not make female and male equal—it makes them parallel and balanced. No man achieves recognition without his sisters, mother, aunts, sisters-in-law, and a wife and her male relatives willing to work on his behalf, or without a matriline of men to assist him. Women are weaving their contributions to a postcolonial nation with ancient and practical patterns for power sharing. There may have been more respect for women's work and less work to be done in the past. Pohnpeians swear this is true—but accounts of a golden age when cultural customs worked better than they do now are more legend than fact. I conclude that, based on their own cultural values, men and women do complement each other; on island terms, there is a flexible complementarity. Matrilineal descent may not be as important to food or craft production as it was in the past, but it is still the unit that exchanges goods and services, status and prestige, and meanings and metaphors as anthropologist Glenn Petersen (1982) also found.

Another exceptional situation supports the Pohnpeian claim that power is shared between men and women, that their respective social roles are reciprocal and complementary. Since German times the inheritance of land has been based on patrilineal primogeniture or inheritance of land through the male line. This system tends to favor firstborn sons over later-born ones or over daughters. Such a system means land that produces agricultural goods for feasts—the major route of mobility for families and individuals who seek high titles and influence—remains in the patrilines. Yet access to titles and mobility at the section or municipal level remains solidly in the matrilines. Men and women bound together in matrilineal ties promote active rounds of feasting and ritual; they produce goods and present them to the Chiefs—selected on the basis of the matrilineal affiliations. Then the Chiefs redistribute them through the matrilines as though it were a corporate group. The production and exchange of these goods is the core of Pohnpeian collective life.

So Westerners like me will have to bow to different ways of reckoning status and power. Pohnpeians have to be trusted when they say that men and women do complementary work and receive separate rewards, and that they are pleased with their many-faceted arrangement for reaching life's goals. In Pohnpeian logic, when a woman "wins" men will "win" as well. Within the sphere of woman's work, prestige and honor are high. Dancing at formal events, for example, is considered a form of community service, the performance of Pohnpeian values, not the display of one talented individual. In the past kinsmen gathered on donated land and erected the log framework of a house; kinswomen gathered and sewed thatch for the roof. That was complementarity. Today third parties demand payment for supplies and labor, and monthly bills for electricity, water, telephone, or cable TV require two wage earners to pay. This is on top of the claims that funerals, feasts, churches, siblings, or chiefs have on islanders.

So I must also trust my gut feeling that women of Pohnpei in the global, postmodern nation-state are subjects, sometimes victims, of Western-imposed values. They have not been able to bring complementarity into the Federated States, their wage-labor jobs, or the legal system. Instead, the contemporary island order makes them compete with men, but stacks the odds of "winning" in favor of males.

The model of parallel and balanced lives, of complementarity between men and women, and of respect residing in the matrilineal principle that I have argued, breaks down in several areas. One is the rise of nuclear families; the other is the decline of women's overall health.

Officials of the Federated States swear that the nation and its constituent islands value the worth of women. Yet the health of women in Micronesia is worse than it was under the Trust Territory government or in traditional times. According to UNICEF, an agency of the United Nations, "Women's reproductive and domestic responsibilities have led to intolerable workloads, continuous reproduction, malnutrition, illiteracy, the lack of rest and relaxation, and decreased health status among both women and children." The studies cite high fertility, poor diets, iron deficiency anemia, high blood pressure, and diabetes. None of the international health reports mentions the lack of organized health services and the drains on budget, energy, time, and morale that go with caring for family members with chronic and debilitating illnesses. From the statistics we could make a case that women's workloads have doubled since I was last there. Birth rates, while dropping, still mean each woman will likely bear and raise an average of five or six children. The global economy means that a woman will need a job, and that she will work for wages lower than men receive. Women told me that they are sometimes pressured to run for public office, as though winning an election would improve their lives. FSM officials admit that "much needs to be done before women are fully integrated in the policy and decision-making processes."

Women are under severe pressure to change situations not of their own making; they are taking the blame for social problems they did not create. I saw signs in English and in Pohnpeian—"Breast-feeding is best, don't smoke or drink while pregnant or your baby will have problems." Yet I saw no efforts to keep cigarettes, alcohol, or baby formulas out of stores or off the island; no health or education programs to address women in a fair and non-judgmental fashion; or no effort to take into account the unique cultural configurations of island life. Health officials complain that pregnant women come in for prenatal visits only in the last months before birth; yet outpatient attention to pregnant women on the islands follows the Western model—competent but not kind or supportive. And, in community with their sisters across the planet, Pohnpeian women are deciding one by one to spend less of their bodies' capital, time, and reserve energies on breast-feeding their infants. They buy baby bottles and formula, and ignore authorities who try to persuade them otherwise.

As a small example with large consequences, the birth control and family planning programs that the Trust Territory government initiated in 1965 were not then, and are not now, geared to women's lives or needs. The original programs used a low-key approach to avoid conflicts "with relevant and cultural sectors of society"—in other words, men developed a system that would not offend or upset other males. The program failed to reach teenagers or young women, and it failed to offer sensitive prenatal or well-baby preventive care. Older women started to use contraceptive methods when their families reached the desired size—three to six children. As a result, the population exploded in the 1970s; birth rates on the tiny island were double those of the United States and one-and-a-half times larger than those of the rest of the world. This translates into more children than adults to raise them.

On Pohnpei, as elsewhere in the world, the parent-child ratio has declined in dramatic fashion. The amount of work necessary to raise a child to adulthood in a money economy has increased as the number of adults available to do the job has decreased. The multiparent family has given way to two-parent families and to single-mother-headed households, where the difficulties are magnified. Like American consumer goods or junk food, the notion of a nuclear family is seductive, promising freedom, security, and romance in far greater quantities than it can deliver.

I heard stories—as I had not before—of neglected and abused children, of men who beat their wives, of stepfathers and fathers molesting their daughters, and of pregnancies happening to too-young girls in their teens whose own mothers and grandmothers cannot or will not adopt and raise the child as they would have in the past. With the stories came judgments, suggestions that these occurrences are terrible trends—women are failing in their life-tasks of caring for others; young people are not motivated to do right; men cannot control their angers; and society is somehow failing—pathologies connected with modernization that no one expected.

Bureaucrats in health care and social services in Micronesia speak openly about domestic violence and abuse. Incest between father and daughters in the past was a status offense against the lineages and the intricate restrictions governing relationships. Now it is a crime against the bodies and personhood of vulnerable girls. Stepfathers who are not linked into the lineage system are free to prey on those within an isolated nuclear household. The documented increase in the frequency and intensity of beatings of wives and girlfriends is a function of the opportunity structure nuclear families provide—secrecy in the disguise of privacy. The relatives of a married woman or a girl with a "boyfriend" may not live in the same household, and reluctant to intervene, they have no stake in or authority to help the couple. Nuclear families anywhere in the world carry the same logic—they cannot be vigilant enough, cannot punish offenders, and cannot or will not protect daughters, sisters, wives. There have been shocking cases in which husbands have murdered their wives. Pohnpeians deny that abuse, and definitely murder, happened in the past. This is probably true—in those days a High Chief intervened in what Westerners term "personal lives." The offender humbled himself before the kava cup of atonement. Everyone watched to make certain he did not repeat the offense. The solution, like the problem, was public.

Other problems have arisen—suicide, mental illness, neglected children, and alcohol and drug use. Where there are gaps in the safety net a local government like Pohnpei State must step in and act as a "lineage adult." Everyone who comments on these problems—whether in Pohnpei, the United States, or in other countries—uses the same language. They use emotional language—motivations, male rage, loss of self-esteem, frustration, depression, dependency, shame, embarrassment. They speak of victims, perpetrators, court actions, or legal solutions. They advocate education and counseling. Like their counterparts in the United States, they tend to preach virtue even if it does not work, enlist women's groups but not men's, and pass legislation. But like the 250,000 cases of beer brought into Micronesia each year, these problems did not originate locally; they came with colonial powers, international business interests, and the mysterious processes we label "change."

On the first Saturday night of my return, Maria, Catalina, and their respective husbands, brothers to each other, invited me to a feast in honor of the bestowal of a title. I bought frozen chickens at the Wall Mart; Catalina cooked them with rice. When we arrived at the homestead along the highway in U municipality, preparations were underway. Feasts still begin on a logic all their own, a set of signals I have yet to intercept; space and time are organized in the old Pohnpei ways I remember, not on American habits or updated national customs. Already that night several men were preparing the pounding stone. Others brought pails of water; one knocked dirt off roots and reduced them to small pieces with his machete. While another washed them in a plastic bucket, two were stripping hibiscus bark in five-foot lengths to make bast for squeezing. They served kava that night with respectful ritual but no fanfare. Joseph husked drinking coconuts, sliced off their tops with his machete, and laid them in a row on a bench. Women, busy in the yard of the one-room store, had prepared an ainpwot, setting huge platters of food on a picnic table beneath an adjoining roofed patio. Children played at being adults, but there were no inappropriate scenes amidst the shyness and courtesies they practiced.

At this, the first feast on my return, I followed the older women about, asking for a task, meeting the babies, and trying to keep genealogies—who is related to whom and how—arranged in my head. That night, as never before, I watched the women whose invited guest I was. They arranged heaping platters of food, lifted babies to cuddle, sent willing children off on errands, and searched the edges of the gathering to make sure everyone was enfolded into the evening's events. I had come to Pohnpei in my twenties, married, my head echoing with anthropology's cautionary tales about not offending locals, elders, high people, and supporters of our research project. Decades later, I felt little pressure about manners, less fear of making a mistake. A man hawked up a heroic mass from the back of his throat, leaned over the side of the kava stone with a dramatic demeanor, and spit on the ground. "*Karapei en Dohlen Wehien Uh*, come and receive your cup of kava," he intoned in Pohnpeian. Surprised with the thrill of respect that ran through the group at the announcement of my title, I looked to the women. They smiled and gestured me to turn and accept the cup of kava the man in the bandana offered in gentle sincerity.

Then they handed me a drinking coconut and sat me at the closed end of the feast house just in front of the partition where babies nap and clothes are stored. Talking with young girls chewing betel nut and making flower headdresses with practiced hands, I concentrated on my drink—coconut water is delicious and nourishing, but a natural stain that ruins clothes. An older woman sat beside me—you can dangle your legs, she offered—but I folded them tailor-fashion. Even if the structure doubles as a garage and a kitchen when the kava pounding stones are rolled back, it was ritual space that night. The title holder, a modest man, had already presented gifts of kava and imported goods to the section Chief; I watched him receive rolls of dollars, count the total up, and divide it into piles between his fingers. He kept some and distributed the rest; a few men made secondary redistributions. Several made sincere speeches filled with humble descriptions of their own work and exalting words for the labors of their peers and Chief.

A few men, including Ioannes Donre, Maria's husband, sat beside me and volunteered stories about their children who live in the United States, some in suburbs where no one speaks Pohnpeian or knows about island customs. The older woman sitting on the other side of me wanted to talk about economic development. "I used to raise pigs; it's money just growing up in front of you," she said. "I intended to sell them when they were grown, but family members came to me, begged me—'just this once. We'll repay you.' Then someone died; how could I refuse?" Sincere reasons, urgent needs. She quit raising pigs.

On the last evening of my stay, Maria and Catalina invited me back to the same homestead for a going-away feast in my honor. By that time I had talked to people, taken notes in archives and libraries, and traveled every road on the island. I knew if we measure women's lives with "improvements" or "things," that the FSM Census found more houses are being built with concrete walls and tin roofs than 30 years earlier. There are more houses with electricity even in rural areas, more piped-in water, noticeably more lavatories or showers, and twice as many flush toilets, although only half as many as are needed. Fifty percent of the houses are attached to a community water system; the other 50 percent use the same kind of catchment system as I did—a fifty-gallon drum for rainwater. These vital statistics add up to fewer flies, less water-borne diseases, and a decline in infant mortality.

Most of the 7,000 households with whom census-takers spoke use a combination of kerosene stoves, wood stoves, or open fires that burn coconut husks for fuel—that explains the pervasive smell I love. Some cooking arrangements are outdoors, under a tree; others are inside under a roof. One-third of the houses have no electricity; two-thirds have no refrigerator. About 40 percent of islanders own a TV-VCR, a vehicle, or a telephone—land or satellite. Yet everyone has access to these technologies through their communal ties.

By that time I had learned that youthful delinquency receded from being a threat to the social fabric into a mild and intermittent nuisance about which no one worried. Young men who drank too much, stayed out all night, dropped out of school, got arrested for fighting, and failed to assist their senior relatives have not gone on to criminal careers. They were merely going through a developmental phase but not entering a life course. Older men at the feast who went through dysfunctional stages a generation ago swore to me over kava that night that alcohol consumption and youthful troublemaking have declined. "Our sons and nephews are much better behaved than we were," they laughed.

By my last night I also understood the flawed assumptions of major international granting agencies; they assume that the capitalist business model—like the internal combustion engine—will work in any social climate. But the philosophies of outsiders ignore the central conflict in all business development in Micronesia—one that reveals the awkward side of complementarity. How can islanders reconcile family obligations with standard business practices? The owner of a new store must give credit to family members who may not be obliged to repay him or will repay in currency other than money. Loan officers at the bank must be sensitive to local customs. For example, a first-time borrower who is under intense pressure to give a generous sum of money for a relative's trip to Hawaii for medical treatment or for a family member's boat, car, or new house may come to the bank to seek a loan. Micronesian employees must take time off to attend funerals; they must contribute large gifts. Deaths within families, lineages, neighborhoods, and networks undermine capitalist concepts of budgets, long term planning, and savings accounts. Helping a brother or sister with a task, seeing someone off at the airport or greeting them on their return, taking care of an ailing family member, or planning for feasts calls employees away from work and channels their spending in new and unpredicted directions—nothing has changed in this regard since my first visit.

Many people own stores, explained a woman who sat on the small platform beside me. Yet wayside stores rarely earn a profit on Pohnpei despite their popularity. "I keep hearing that, but I don't understand," I said. "Through a store like mine," she replied, "I give my relatives and friends the things they need and want; and of course I give them credit when they cannot pay." "What if the store goes broke?" I asked, knowing that many tiny enterprises on the island do not meet the fiscal standards of capitalism. "If I run a store, it is not a way of making money," she told me. "It is a way to be a better Pohnpeian, a better woman." To her a store is a social investment—not a financial one.

That last night, the women, under the inspiration of Maria and Catalina, prepared only traditional foods in my honor—baked and fried breadfruit, yams smothered in coconut cream, mangrove crabs, and fried reef fish. They had also laid plans to surprise me at the airport the following day with fare-well gifts—load me down with flowers, cotton skirts in the newest island fashion, and hand-woven fans. No matter how much I gave them (mostly money, my own and what I had from the university), or planned to mail them when I returned, they gave me more. Catalina, Joseph, their sons, and I had spoken about reciprocity when we drank kava together. There were items they could not buy, but I could send—running shoes, high-fashion teen wear, men's cologne. Sohn Alpet, Nahnid Lapalap, had five children by two wives; he left fifty grandchildren; his brothers and sisters married and reproduced into similarly ramified webs of kinship. Their families extend to Hawaii; Guam; Savannah, Georgia; San Diego, California; Eugene, Oregon; and between New Orleans, Louisiana, and the Federated States of Micronesia. Reciprocity on Pohnpeian terms did not mean I was used or manipulated. It made me grateful to give what I could, grateful for all that I have, and very self-conscious—I should have given away more money from the blood pressure project when I had the chance.

I should have used more island medicine and consulted more women when I had the opportunity. Female practitioners, healers, therapeutic massage specialists, and midwives who practice household health care and address gender-based conditions—then as now—offer medicines for back-aches, headaches, and disorders or infections of uterus and vagina; they administer special tonics and local herbal medicines, treat spirit sickness, and alleviate the influences of sorcery. Women provide diagnosis and sick-bed care for loved ones; they organize the payments—island treatments cost more than Western-based treatments do. Compensation to indigenous healers for their work is discrete, not to be discussed in public, but it is understood that cash, imported foodstuffs, and consumer goods will, within a short period, follow treatments. Throughout my second stay I told women about the treatments I had received on my first visit—spells to insure I became pregnant, comfort care for an easy pregnancy, empowering advice about my condition, and predictions for the hour of birth. "You were right to trust traditional Pohnpeian medicine as we do," several replied.

"Why did you call your book *Nest in the Wind?*" people asked me as we talked that night. I tried to explain. "The people of Pohnpei greet the occupants of a homestead," I said, "as though they were birds sitting in their airy cradles having built a haven, safe harbor, an oasis to take care of them when the inevitable storms come. Mesenieng, the old name for Kolonia, means 'facing into the wind.'" Pohnpei is an island, we agreed as we talked. It is impossible to hide; dozens of people in official and unofficial relationships know what everyone is doing and will gossip. Each episode of neglect and hurt within a household feels unique, fresh, just as each situation of harmonious cooperation is magnified. Many off-islanders have moved to Pohnpei; they are not moored in traditional harbors of obligations and respect—so Pohnpeians must incorporate them into local ways without sacrificing uniqueness. Above all, Pohnpei is an island, a besieged nest, with the cruel dilemmas of all cultures. How can people keep the core values of their culture safe and still embrace the forces acting on them?

Chapter 11

Our World Itself
Is an Island

All brothers and sisters in this generation,
To build a nation, together we stand.

—Lines of a song broadcast on the radio

*T*axis race through Kolonia—a person who needs to go from the hospital to the Wall Mart or from the post office to the College of Micronesia may phone for a ride or step into the street and wave. So I was able to ride in Joseph's cab for hours, meeting and speaking to everyone he picked up. When I explained in Pohnpeian about working with the "group at the old hospital who studied the movement of blood," most people responded with an instant English translation. Many recited their blood pressures and added cholesterol counts or blood sugar levels—quoting health-care workers who told them to watch their diets, get enough exercise, and lower their dangerous numbers. "What really causes this?" they asked in genuine puzzlement. "Why do Micronesians have so many of these problems?" "Is this happening to Americans too?" "Why don't Americans have a cure?"

From my first morning's walk in downtown Kolonia through the last conversation I struck up boarding the plane to leave, people confronted me with comments and questions like these. When I sat down for lunch in the Joy Hotel, a man at the next table greeted me and explained that his right leg was permanently weak. "A stroke," he told me, using the English word. "Pedro and Kioko died young," their son Simeon Kihleng told me. "They didn't take proper care of themselves." "Why," asked one woman my age, "are so many people getting diabetes?" Another woman, in mixed Pohnpeian and English, launched into a high-energy story about a prominent title holder whose diabetes cannot be controlled. This man cut his foot. In the past his injury would have been, at worst, a painful tropical ulcer that took months to heal. With compromised circulation, however, gangrene developed, and doctors had to amputate his leg. People kept telling me that the most common surgery performed on Pohnpei is the amputation of legs due to diabetes, and official health reports confirm this statistic. I tried to imagine how this man or others without one or both legs will manage on a rainy, mountain island where accommodation for such a disability is not possible. Will the burden of their care consume family members' lives, energy, and money?

Jesuit priests spoke to me of a Micronesian colleague, a priest of his people, whom they had sponsored through ordination and his first assignment. He died of complications of heart disease and diabetes in his early thirties. A high-ranking man I knew from the past commented that prestigious titles seemed to be circulating faster. Men held the ones they had worked hard to earn for too short a time, and many candidates for advancement were ill. Everyone I met had attended funerals of friends and relatives dead in their thirties and forties. "And look," exclaimed dozens of people, "all of us are getting really, really fat."

In the past, infectious diseases—smallpox, influenzas or flu, and childhood diseases like measles to which islanders had no immunity—took their toll. From 1880 to 1945 the population of Pohnpei declined by half or more from its precontact levels. During this time three colonial powers and two world wars brought famines, epidemics, and sexually transmitted infections. After World War II, with peace in the world, with inoculations and antibiotics, the public health system in the U.S. Trust Territory centered on communicable diseases such as those caused by the "four f's"—contaminated food, dirty fingers, flies, and feces. Public sanitation and sewerage systems, a safe water supply, and personal hygiene reduced the burden of these diseases on the population. Although chronic and contagious, these national public health problems are not alarming because they yield to treatment and prevention. Solutions do not depend on convincing people to change their behaviors or the cultural patterns at the core of their lives.

The new diseases are, however, more deadly over time; I call them the "global trio"—cardiovascular diseases that begin in high blood pressure and end in heart attacks or strokes; diabetes, which is difficult to treat and impossible to cure; and obesity in epidemic form.

The average life span of Micronesians has plummeted in the last thirty years. In the decade of the 1990s, the major cause of death for adults under 60 years of age was heart disease and strokes. Next came respiratory failure, lung disease, asthma, cancer, and diabetes in roughly equal amounts. "The reported death rates from heart disease and stroke," an unpublished public health report from Pohnpei states, "greatly exceed those of developed countries especially in those aged 45 to 54. Actual rates may be twice as high because of unreported deaths." These startling facts must be placed against the record of the past. Islanders examined at the end of World War II showed no rise of blood pressure with age and no diabetes at all. No one was obese.

In 1971, when our medical team tested Pohnpeians, their blood pressure, heart disease rates, weight, and incidence of metabolic disease had started to inch up. Thirty years later, every study, from those of island health departments to the ones the World Health Organization produces, agree: coronary heart disease is the leading cause of death and illness in the Federated States of Micronesia. It is two to four times higher than in America, and would be, experts agree, double or triple those numbers if all deaths were reported.

In a survey of chronic diseases on Pohnpei, investigators discovered that more than twice as many Pohnpeians as Americans ages 35–55 were clinically obese. Another survey reported obesity in 72 to 92 percent of people, male and female, in that same age group. Men spoke about weight gain as if a giant hand had reached down and cursed the entire island—not just them—with heavy poundage. Women recited the high birth weights of their babies to me—"But why is a beautiful fat baby a problem?" they asked. Islanders are right about their increased girth. The pictures I took in the early 1970s and ones I have seen of still earlier times show thin, muscular men and full-bodied but not obese women. Today young people in their early twenties look healthy, yet, according to experts, silent problems are beginning to accumulate. Many are in a premature, primary disease process with disability and early death staring them in the face. People age 60 and over have the lowest weights of any group, but that is because they have been left behind as heavier relatives and neighbors die at younger ages.

Diabetes is an ugly disease; there is no cure, no logical or easy prevention strategies, and few ways to monitor its progression. The burdens of diabetes include blindness, kidney failure, disability, and lower limb amputations; by some estimates, Micronesian rates of this life-threatening metabolic condition are nine to ten times higher than rates in the United States. In the ideal medical scenario, individuals with diabetes eat three meals a day on a regular schedule, each with a harmonious nutritional balance to match their condition. They are physically active, maintain a reasonable weight, and do not drink alcohol. They monitor their blood sugar several times a day and adjust their medications. These requirements are difficult for most Americans to follow—doubly so for Pacific Islanders who eat what and when they feel like it, when the food is ready, and whatever happens to be available, and who are unlikely to have either the training and supplies for monitoring complex conditions or the resources for long-term chronic care.

The number of people suffering and dying from this unhealthy trio of conditions is skyrocketing around the globe. People in the United States, Canada, Europe, or other industrialized nations are witnessing ballooning rates of diabetes, heart disease, and obesity. But the rates in Asia, Africa, the Caribbean, Latin America, and islands in the Indian and Pacific Oceans are much higher still. Polynesians; Aboriginal Australians; Native Americans and Asian Indian emigrants to Fiji, South Africa, and Britain; and Chinese emigrants to Singapore, Taiwan, and Hong Kong are falling ill and dying of what many health professionals are calling the "New World Syndrome."

Although Pohnpei is a pinpoint in the global epidemic of obesity, diabetes, and heart disease, it is easier to track cause-and-effect on an island than it is on populated continents. Until the middle of the twentieth century, the cuisine of Pohnpei, like that of other Pacific Islanders, was moderate to low in proteins, fat, sugar, and salt and high in complex carbohydrates and fiber. They had drinking coconuts, taro, breadfruit, yams, bananas, fish, and fruits in season. From what researchers can tell, islanders got enough vitamins and minerals from the foods they ate. Although they have no word for "vegetable," they used green, leafy plants in the form of tonics or medicines and wrapped food in green leaves to cook it. In an appropriate evolutionary balance, islanders used as much energy to find, grow, and prepare food as the energy and nourishment they received from the food.

Today, however, the opposite is true. The national diet of people in the Federated States of Micronesia is high in fat, protein, salt, and sugar and low in complex carbohydrates, fiber, potassium, vitamin A, and many other vitamins and minerals humans need for growth and maintenance. In the face of massive surpluses, people can be stuffed to death on cheap, tempting, and calorie-dense foods. Fat-filled foods alone do not prompt the release of or surges of insulin that lead to Type II diabetes, the failure of one's body to make enough insulin or to use the insulin it has. Fat combined with starches, salt, and sugar, however, does. Chips, sodas, or other junk food, while easy to eat and digest, require large amounts of insulin to metabolize. In Type II diabetes, physical activity helps draw glucose out of the bloodstream and increase one's insulin efficiency. Without the expenditure of energy needed to keep it in check, insulin rises to dangerous levels. A nutritious diet and maintaining a reasonable weight make insulin's job easier. A meal of Spam, Vienna sausages, salted mackerel, or canned corned beef served over white rice, washed down with a can of soda made of water, sugar, and other flavorings, and accompanied by donuts, cookies, sweet crackers, or snack foods and sedentary habits is both commonplace and deadly.

The highest rates of the unholy New World Syndrome are in Micronesia on the island of Nauru, a tiny nation that grows no gardens because the land has been mined away for phosphates, natural fertilizers deposited by a million generations of migrating birds, fertilizers used to insure other nations' food supply. The people of Nauru have plenty of money from the sale of these phosphates, but they must purchase alien foods. They will never starve, but on their postmodern diet their average life span has declined by two decades. A Nauruan who may have lived to be 70 years old in the past can now expect to die before age 50. The second highest rates in the world are on Kosrae, the volcanic island nearest to Pohnpei. The Micronesian Department of Health, in cooperation with the Centers for Disease Control in the United States, screened and tested adults in 1994. They found that 85 percent of people ages 45–65 were obese; one-third of the entire island had diabetes; one-third had high blood pressure. Nauru and Kosrae bracket Pohnpei, where rates are rising and may soon match those of these neighboring islands.

Blood pressure had been a near-perfect thing to study, I realized as I listened to the litanies of systolic, diastolic, cholesterol, and blood sugar levels that Pohnpeians recited to me. The significance of the numbers, the instruments used to measure them, and the power of diagnosis to be read in the movement of blood have not changed. Blood pressure remains the herald, the trumpet's call of warning about sickness, not only in a person but within a population. Our research team had to make up a term for blood pressure—the good or bad "movement of blood"—and one to fit heart attacks as well. Only a few people had heard of diabetes, which they translated as the "sickness of sugar." Strokes were so rare, sudden, and lethal that sorcery was the only logical explanation—a powerful spirit had been insulted, a breach of custom in the presence of a high person punished the offender with death to one side of his body, an argument with a neighbor called in a curse and both people died. But today deaths and disabilities in epidemic proportions do not strike with sudden or random force. Offended spirits and the evil wishes of others do not cause heart attacks, high blood pressure, or strokes.

The anthropologists and epidemiologists who worked on the blood pressure project are dead, most from heart disease. Our research failed in many ways apparent to me now. We spent too much money for too little return to Americans and Micronesians or to science. Funding sources in Washington and the prevalence of heart attacks in men who controlled the research, not the needs of Pohnpeians or the truths of island life, determined the research agenda. Moreover, the fundamental assumptions of the research were profoundly flawed; the sociological interview that Floyd wrote was translated word for word and administered by a team of dedicated Pohnpei men like Sohn Alpet. But the cultural translation made no sense. Theories about Type A and Type B personalities and those of so-called urban, peri-urban, and rural influences were never sophisticated or flexible enough to tap into the experiential realities of Pohnpei lives. In the end we would never have found differences by personality types, achievement motivation, or that strange and unmeasurable variable—modernization. We depended on complicated statistical formulas, computers, and irrelevant hypotheses more than cost-wise and commonsense survey methodologies that public health officials needed then and could still be using now.

Today it is unthinkable to exclude women from health research in contemporary projects, yet the men who wrote the original grant planned to leave females out of the study. Women get pregnant; they don't die from heart disease; they are physiologically unreliable—the principal investigators argued. In those prefeminist days female staffers and I insisted on having women included in the sample and won that round. But when results revealed that blood pressures of women in Pohnpei, who were more sedentary than men and who lived and loved by the standard of fleshly female beauty, matched those of men of America, the researchers did not see the implications of such results. Moreover, the men in control of the project failed to anticipate, appreciate, or warn anyone about the one solid finding we should have achieved—Pohnpei, and all of Micronesia by extension, was a population on the cusp of a massive and deadly health crisis.

As to the "cause" of the deaths and disabilities the Pohnpeians are experiencing today, the scientific and medical literature suggests—for the time being—that personality types and exposure to the stresses of "modern" life, whatever they are, matter less to a person's health than his or her body weight, food choices, and levels of physical activity.

On the original study we took physical activity as a variable in health for granted. This was well before American citizens or professionals developed the concept of "regular exercise." The work Pohnpeians did to earn a living was far more active and muscular than most Americans of our class and color did. In those days there were few cars and no phones to summon a taxi—walking was the best, often the only, way to get somewhere. Outside Kolonia, Roger, the project interviewers, and I hiked for miles on hilly, muddy paths. Sohn Alpet, Paul Benjamin, and others who worked with us walked from the countryside and across Kolonia to our house, not only for the day's work, but to make appointments or to confirm plans—requests and checking that today most do on the telephone.

On my return, I decided not to rent a car—I wanted a "walk the ground" involvement and a return to the feelings of my previous fieldwork. Yet within half a block of my apartment, taxis stopped for me, strangers offered me rides in private vehicles, and people who knew me made a U-turn in the middle of the street and hailed me. "Where are you going?" "Why don't you take a taxi?" "This woman," Pohnpeians said when they introduced me, "speaks our language; she lived here and worked at the hospital." Then to explain what might be seen as their neglect of me, they added, "She really likes to walk." Most people have phones, including growing numbers of cell phones. A car ride is only a call away. It is difficult to tell which came first—riding in cars or weighing too much to walk.

Although I hate big-box stores in my native country, I kept returning to the Wall Mart in downtown Kolonia. Smaller than the size of a strip mall grocery and with no formal kinship with its name-sake, it took my imagination hostage. I felt I was inside one of the stories Pohnpeians tell about their past. A gentle, seductive giant—call him America or Capitalism or Colonialism or Globalism—has brought glamorous, captivating gifts to this tiny land. There is enough cheap soap for every woman to wash everything, bright plastic chairs and basins to hold people and things off the floor, and a splendid assortment of things to eat. The giant does not force anyone to eat his gifts, does not mean to hurt anyone, certainly not the inhabitants of such a beautiful island; he only wants to "do business." But who can resist the tastes and temptations the gentle giant offers—even if they are poisonous?

The only "super market" on the island, an instant landmark in downtown Kolonia, Wall Mart carries goods that mirror the limited inventories of smaller one-room stores in which Pohnpeians shop. There is no visible ordering system and no hint of traditional or local foodstuffs; container ships from

Asia and America unload generic international inventories. Wall Mart sells mass produced consumer goods, the fruits of global capitalism, the food of global poverty and migration—enough fat, salt, and sugar to kill every man, woman, and child on the island at an indolent tropical pace.

The "fresh produce" section sells a few tired, wrinkled cabbages, egg-plants, cucumbers, potatoes, onions, apples, oranges, limes, or green peppers shipped from half a world away. In the frozen food section, I found ten-pound bulk packages of seafood, breaded fish fillets, frozen shrimp from Viet-nam and Port Washington, New York; chopped clams from Chesapeake Bay; pan-Asian pastry wrappers; Chinese taro in shrink-wrapped packaging; and something called "mixed meats," whose ingredients, which were said to con-form to USDA standards, came from China. Most of these packages have freezer burns, signs of thawing and refreezing, or holes in the bags. Multina-tional condiments, mostly Chinese and Japanese spices, have bugs in them. Everything reflects the requirements of mass shipping and storage. No one will ever again run out of spaghetti makings, cheap sodas, potato chips, or canned meats like Black Label Luncheon Loaf.

Mountains of rice, fifty-pound sacks of flour, row upon row of cheap cookies, American sugared cereals, infant feeding formulas from Japan, snacks, snacks, and more snacks dwarf everything. On every aisle, at every turn, wherever I looked, high and low, I found sugared drinks—soda in cheap cans and plastic bottles, powdered, concentrated, or packaged with little straws in three and six packs. At the entrance was a truck-size display of cases of sodas imported from China—30 cents each, a new version of the colored sugar water I was served in the past, now masquerading as fruit juice. The drinks and food are full of cane sugar as well as fructose and corn syrup—lit-tle wonder children and adults alike are addicted to their complex and com-pounded sweetness.

Since the United States inherited Micronesia as a colonial possession after World War II, government administrators have influenced islanders' food hab-its. Candy, gum, other sweet or addictive foods, alcohol, and cigarettes helped to sway a reluctant population to trust Americans during and after the war—and in some ways has kept them hooked. Embarrassed Pohnpeians apologized to me about their turkey-tail habits; the rich, fatty poultry waste, shipped to the Pacific after lean portions of the bird have been sold in the States, remains pop-ular. The supplementary feeding programs of the United States Department of Agriculture mandated lunch programs in all schools under its colonial con-trol—white rice, ketchup, canned meats, and treats like donuts made with sur-pluses of sugar and flour produced in America. By the late 1960s and parallel to the war in Vietnam, U.S. food-aid programs began to flood small islands and replaced local foods with the foods they brought in. School lunches, needy families, elderly people, disaster relief, and hospitals became occasions for serving sugar, rice, flour, canned meats, and refined foods.

The United States is "force-feeding" its own dysfunctional values about consumption to island societies who neither asked for nor needed such interventions. Some critics claim that U.S. policy was designed to create dependencies in Micronesia and thus insure access to strategic sites for military purposes. Other critics cite the need for markets for the manufactured produce of larger nations and point to parallels among poor populations in urban areas or Native Americans on reservations. My students and colleagues predicted that television would be the major culprit in "changes" or problems on the island. They did not know that container ships filled with cheap Chinese sodas—generic sugar and water—held more dangerous temptations than television, which, by contrast, is too expensive for many families.

Pohnpeians and other Pacific Islanders did not choose or develop their new habits in isolation. What they eat and how they live and die are partly the result of *dietary colonialism*. International *Coca-Cola culture* arrived on foreign ships like the sexually transmitted infections of an earlier century. The foreigner's foods tasted good, were simple to prepare, and became linked to both the prestige economy and the daily lives of entire kin groups. Islanders do not have "lifestyles" in the sense that Americans speak of nor do they have "lifestyle diseases." On an island people are not just individuals or a number, a statistic—each person is a part of, a member of the social body. When a virus spreads over the island or the sewerage system fails, everyone shares the danger, the risks. When someone dies, loss reverberates throughout the entire social body.

Health officials are wrong to think that so-called "lifestyle diseases" are not catching or communicable. The global trio is contagious in the same manner that cultural fashions, fads, and obsessions are. Obesity is not an individual choice or a character defect; it is the system-wide availability of foods that entice, seduce, and fill with empty calories; it is schools that feed children turkey tails and Spam. Such foods become social and biological necessities, something at the root of what it means to be Pohnpeian, and the core goods for women's extensive exchanges. One man told me, "If I don't eat rice, I die." Yet processed white rice is the symbol of what is killing many people in the prime of their lives.

Several theories attempt to explain the global trio or New World Syndrome. The "lifestyle" or individual approach is one; another is my theory that the social body is suffering. In addition, many scholars and scientists think that large groups of people have inherited a "thrifty gene" that helps them metabolize every ounce of food and store it up against the day their food supplies fail. This gene orders us around: "Famine and bad times are coming again," it screams. "You will go hungry or die if you don't store up some fat right now. Eat." Under the right conditions, the thrifty gene would be an asset, a way to conserve energy and survive lean times, periodic starvation, famine, or seasonal shortages. Pohnpei is a good example; World War II and Japanese occupation interrupted their food supplies. That is why islanders were slender when doctors aboard the U.S. Navy ship arrived at war's end to check their health. But what happens to thrifty genes when the environment of potential scarcity changes into one of never-ending surpluses, where few people burn as many calories in food-getting each day as they eat? The increase in diabetes, high blood pressure, heart attacks, and strokes results, not from better measurements, but from vast food surpluses and dietary colonialism.

Meanwhile, Micronesians have come to regard health care as a social right, a service the government owes them. In Trust Territory times the U.S. government funded facilities, staffs, equipment, and supplies—in effect, socialized medicine for people who paid only token fees. A visit to a village dispensary might cost a dime. The hospital and smaller clinics provided basic medicines like antibiotics for free. My prenatal visit, for example, cost me less than a dollar.

Even without the unhealthy fruits of the global trio, the medical system of the Federated States would still be in collapse. Since their independence, Micronesians have had to manage the health-care budget of their new nation without the financial help of the United States. Health surveys note that there is little preventive medicine, primary-health or private-sector care, and no individual or group health insurance. The hospital in Kolonia and the scattered dispensaries are not sanitary, safe, well-staffed, or stocked with bare essentials of equipment or medicine. Some clinic positions have become hereditary; like titles, a coveted job sometimes goes to a relative of the incumbent, trained or not. Hospitals and dispensaries cannot recoup the costs of treating patients, buy expensive medical supplies, and train or pay staff. There is no way to make treatments most Americans take for granted fit the scope of the nation's finances and resources. Pohnpei's hospital, for example, cannot offer dialysis for kidney failure, a common complication of diabetes. The machines are too expensive and too difficult to maintain; it is impossible to train and pay skilled nurses and technicians to use them. Even if these problems were solved, demand is so high that rationing would be necessary. Dialysis, like many other treatments, is not a technology of scale for a nation like Micronesia.

The most painful life-death decisions in a sick health-care system are the off-island referrals. With a single radio call to Guam the hospital summoned a medical evacuation seaplane for Sohn Alpet in June of 1971; he received the best care the times provided at no cost to himself or his family. The U.S. government paid the bills for his referral and off-island hospitalization; even I took the service for granted. Cancer was rare, justification enough for heroic measures. Today massive medical interventions are available in the major teaching hospitals of Hawaii, Guam, and the Philippines—but at astronomical expense to the nation's budget. As few as two referrals can drain a community prevention program and force dreadful choices on the social body; islanders often cannot keep up with well-baby and prenatal care or inoculations against communicable diseases and still send a sick person away for expensive treatments that may not work. A few individuals sick with preventable, chronic, or very expensive-to-treat diseases can absorb and spend the FSM's entire health-care budget. When the FSM government tries to limit referrals, families buy plane tickets and pay for medical consultations and hospitalizations out of the funds collected from within their networks. Referrals send Micronesian money abroad rather than circulating it back into the island; whole families can bankrupt themselves for one sick person.

And the consequences keep growing. Medical researchers think that vitamin A deficiency—the most dramatic example of malnutrition in Micronesia—may cause one out of every three children to die on Pohnpei. Without vitamin A children have weakened immune systems; they are vulnerable to parasites, respiratory illness, and other systemic infections. Although the best known symptom is night blindness, in advanced cases daytime vision is so compromised that blindness results. The best solutions—prolonged breastfeeding, completed vaccine cycles, vitamin A supplements, and better nutrition—require public health programming at the expense of referrals.

Beachcombers and shipwrecked sailors in the nineteenth century noticed how strong and beautiful the teeth of Micronesians they met were. In the twenty-first century, observers cannot avoid the sight of dead, decaying teeth and gap-filled mouths—another legacy of dietary colonialism. Women stop investing the time and energy for breast-feeding infants in favor of formula feedings—for mothers it is much easier; babies grow to like the sweeter, fattier taste. They carry the urge for sugar into adulthood creating dental problems, rotting teeth, and gum disease on an island with no dental care. There are no public health campaigns about the burden of gum disease and poor mouth health on individuals or on the social body. Islanders with money must go to Guam or Hawaii to see a dentist. Many rely on betel nut to cover up their bad breath.

On Pohnpei the average household spends about 40 percent of its income on imported food, beverages, alcohol, and tobacco. Mass-produced foods are cheaper than locally grown produce. Eating in Pohnpei is not a private or individual matter. Food is far more than nutrition; it is communal and public, tied to prestige, social connections, and interrelationships; it is the metaphor for status, identity, and life's greatest meanings. I cannot imagine Micronesians with a work ethic about eating—scheduling themselves everyday for quality, quantity, and timing or being able to monitor their blood sugar and adjust it with regular feedings. I cannot see them discussing a "heart smart" diet as my health-obsessed peers do. Men are not going to return to the work of the past in food production and processing or women to several years of on-demand breast feeding. Nor do islanders have traditions of protest or nativistic movements; they will not or cannot confront dietary colonialism and the lure of Wall Mart. I can imagine, however, that an extended family would pool all their resources, including those needed to purchase appropriate food for their children, and send a senior and much beloved diabetic relative or one suffering from congestive heart failure to Hawaii or Guam for treatment—no matter the cost.

In the absence of effective Western medicines, islanders continue to use time-honored healing practices. A number of women told me about local treatments for diabetes, plant medicine they believed would help control the condition. Catalina gathered plants and bark for itchy skin. Many people mentioned *wini en Pohnpei,* traditional medicines and techniques, as the solution for the global trio; but such a drug would be a pharmaceutical miracle, difficult to measure, and impossible to replicate on a global scale. Meanwhile, there are no international models of a nation that has bested the New World Syndrome and restored public health to its people.

The leaders of Micronesia will not be able to promote initiatives that confront the deadly New World Syndrome. They themselves are store owners and importers and share the same lusty taste for sugar, salt, and fat their constituents have. Like church women engaged in endless circular exchanges, they too circulate the giant's gifts through the prestige economy. Despite their own sicknesses or illness among their peers and family members, the elected or appointed leaders of Micronesia are not considering, as outsiders have suggested, a tax on food imports to use for public health programs. They do not question the increase of imported automobiles on an island of only 225 square miles, with only 60 miles of road. In common with American colonizers, the island leaders say that health is a matter of willpower and individual effort, a consideration of character. To complicate matters, the economy or financial body of Micronesia has problems that resemble those of the social body.

"We are a turtle on its back," Pohnpeians and other citizens of the Federated States told Father Francis Hezel, head of Micronesian Seminar, when he asked them how the economy of the new nation worked. In Trust Territory times, having a job meant "working for the government"; otherwise, people "lived off the land." In the 1960s, 1970s, and 1980s the number of jobs the United States provided to Micronesians doubled each decade. Islanders went to school and learned what was necessary to hold such a position; they took government jobs for granted and parlayed them against family obligations and consumer desires. As one woman said, "I've been working for the government since 1984. My parents sent us to school so we'd grow up and work for the government—help our government, help our family." But governmental or public sector spending based on artificial U.S. aid keeps the turtle from turning over and walking on its own. Its shell rests on the sandy beach and its legs wave upside down in weak and futile motion.

The Federated States is bloated with office jobs and agencies; salaries cost the cash-starved Micronesians 80 percent of their operating budgets. "We can no longer afford the major source of our livelihood—the government," some joke. Of the 25,000 ethnic Pohnpeians in the island population of about 35,000, more than half work for the local, state, and national governments. Teachers, legislators, senior managers, clerks, craftspeople, service workers, those who repair vehicles, and those who work in wholesale and retail trade, shops, and markets comprise less than half of island jobs.

Within a few blocks of my rented apartment I counted dozens of offices for Kolonia Town, Pohnpei State, or for the FSM national government. Outside consultants from the Asian Development Bank, the International Monetary Fund, and the World Bank who visit the Federated States make unanimous recommendations—the FSM government is obese and must lose weight or die in slow and painful degrees. Everyone on the island is familiar with the English vocabulary of job loss—downsize, layoffs, budget reductions, forced or early retirement. Some speak about a change of habits, short-term sacrifices, and structural reforms. Others are in denial or bargain to buy time before the axe falls. A few apply for grants and external funding from donor nations or international agencies, but who would give money to a little nation that cannot control its own overweight economy? The citizens of the FSM levee no local or income taxes against themselves. They must find a way to flip the turtle over so that the larger and more stable productive private sector based on exports supports a thinned-down public sector.

At various times from 1978 to 1991 anthropologist Eve Pinsker (1997) did fieldwork for her dissertation; first in Pohnpei, then in the Federated States as it passed from colonial status into nationhood. She identified a national political ideology that she called the "Micronesian Way"—a form of consensus linked to respect and conveyed through language. For example, when people arrive at a meeting at which a formal decision has to be made, they may have decided in private how to vote. However, instead of confronting the opposition, contradicting, arguing, or debating, they listen "until agreement emerges." Each speaks in a guarded and indirect manner, weighing words with care, waiting for a group viewpoint to emerge, using time-honored parliamentary procedures and democratic structures. Instead of a majority-takes-all vote with its minority-loses-all result, they work to find common ground. Consensus does not mean uniform agreement or unanimity of opinion. It means the appearance of agreement in public. In this ethic a person is obligated, not to express his personal views in a public debate, but to work toward reconciling conflicting views in a cooperative manner. The price of consensus, however, is long speeches and many meetings.

By 1986 public debates, long meetings, and doubts about the future political status of Micronesia ended with the Compact of Free Association. The United States agreed to give FSM about $1.4 billion in direct aid and access to other benefits and programs over the first fifteen years, intending to reduce its payments in tune with Micronesia's own ability to support itself by 2001, the end of the Compact.

In the Cold War era, the Compact was a bargain for both sides. Micronesia had funding for its first fifteen years of nationhood. In return its leaders guaranteed that no foreign powers would establish a military presence among the islands—an agreement of "divided sovereignty." But international events have not been kind to Micronesia. In the first Compact of 1986, both sides assumed that the then-powerful Soviet Union would continue to threaten American interests and that Micronesia would continue to have the strategic importance it enjoyed through the Vietnam War–era. By the early 1990s, one-third of the way into the first Compact, the Berlin Wall had come down; the Soviet Union had fallen apart; and the Cold War had ended. Just as the Compact was scheduled for its second round of renegotiation in the fall of 2001, terrorists attacked the United States. The strategic and military importance of tiny Micronesia to giant America slipped once again.

Policy makers in Washington know nothing about the tiny Pacific island nations carved from old colonial responsibilities. The partnerships of their parents' generation no longer matter in the shifts of twenty-first century events. So the second Compact of Free Association with the U.S., signed in November 2003, was not a genuine renegotiation or a bargain struck between old friends and former allies. It was a set of imposed fiscal reforms and bureaucratic demands that offered the Federated States less money and less autonomy than the first Compact had. It created a cottage industry of filling out heavy paperwork to show compliance with U.S. directives. Neither generous nor sympathetic, it reduced funding as both the population and their expectations rose. "Somewhat bleak," one politician/business-owner said.

Pohnpei, for better or worse, has become an international capital. Micronesians whose grandfathers and grandmothers spoke Japanese, who themselves persevere with English, ask if their children should learn to speak Chinese. People who have come there from the Marshall Islands, Guam, Hawaii, the Philippines, and other places in the Pacific or along its rim speak English and rarely participate in the exchanges of Pohnpei life. Four countries maintain embassies there—Japan, China, Australia, and the United States; a number of nongovernmental agencies like the International Red Cross, the Nature Conservancy, and the Small Business Guarantee and Finance Corporation with its cumbersome motto—"Empowering Pohnpeian Small Entrepreneurs by Facilitating Financing through Loan Guarantees"—have offices there. The largest and most sinister-looking building in Kolonia is the FSM Telecommunication Corporation, which handles cable television (the only kind), land and wireless phones, and even phone cards. Given how much islanders pay for television and telephones, and the monopoly the business has, I predict that in the future an anthropologist will be writing about telecommunication-colonialism in the same way I write about Coca-Cola colonialism.

Other world problems threaten the fledgling nation. Being a country of only 270 square miles, land is their most precious resource. If predictions about global warming come true, however, the ocean will rise and drown the low-lying atolls of Micronesia. Entire culture-sites will disappear beneath the water. Those who live on low islands will have to turn to those on high islands for assistance and refuge as they have when typhoons and drought made their tiny ecosystems unfit to inhabit.

When I checked through customs at the Pohnpei airport, officials handed me a pamphlet on quarantine procedures: "The FSM is free of many pests and diseases so HELP keep it that way," it said. Although Pohnpei had no foot and mouth disease, rabies, hog cholera, oriental fruit flies, other insects, or epidemic diseases, quarantine and customs officials know that airplanes, ships, packages, and people can—even by accident—bring in animals, eggs, meat, plants, vegetables, or other produce that can destroy the specialized ecosystem. The most serious threat to the FSM is the brown tree snake, a foreign species introduced into Guam when one pregnant snake stowed away in a container on a cargo ship. Many snake generations later, Guam is a place where no birds sing because the brown snakes have eaten them and their eggs. The native species are gone forever; snakes drop from trees onto people's heads and have attacked babies. On Pohnpei one egg-laden brown tree snake would be worse than a dozen terrorists.

Invasions of other foreign species threaten ecotourism—a major hope of bringing money into the hungry economy. Tourist promotions promise bird-watchers lorikeets and other rare tropical birds, some found nowhere else on earth. Brochures offer travelers the chance to spend the night in a tropical rain forest on uninhabited atolls in the Pohnpei lagoon, or spend their days diving on iridescent coral reefs and swimming in a movie-setting lagoon. These ecological treasures are now hostage to international tourist traffic.

Pohnpei is part of a pan-Pacific consciousness, a sense and vocabulary of building the political body, of taking a small but firm place within the world of nations. In church, on the FSM channel on television and on the radio, in conversations among friends, I listened to citizens talk about their new nation. Each sermon I heard, both Protestant and Catholic, was some variation on the theme of "working together"—collective effort, group cooperation, full-blown collaboration in truth and honesty. Every prayer was eloquent and steadfast, and in high language. The Pohnpei channel on television reran recordings of national and state events—inauguration ceremonies for FSM presidents, speeches before major island sports competitions, church gatherings, educational conferences, and United Nations Day festivities—events I would not have otherwise seen. The programs made it clear they had worked out a way to incorporate traditional Chiefs who sit in comfort and dignity even as the speakers stand in front with heads higher. Participants wear flower headdresses in the Pohnpeian style and necklaces traditional on other islands. The speeches, dances, and food made it clear that the officers of the nation have agreed to invent and promote a new set of "traditions."

Islanders say the four constituent states of FSM are brothers and sisters, using their kinship relations as models for nationhood. I heard no one complain, question, or whine about their problems or social identities. They make calm and repeated assertions of their voluntary and historic partnership with the United States—an alliance not without problems, but one akin to those they form with the High Chiefs.

The feasting and honor system—status and standing through competitive giving—is as strong as ever on Pohnpei. The quantity, even the quality, of presentations to the High Chief or Nahnmwarki—expensive gifts like furniture, and in one well-discussed case, a pickup truck—continues to expand. The authority of Chiefs remains; they embody the highest values of the culture—honor, exchange, respect, cooperation. They hold together a set of islands that has no national media—print, television, or radio—and no national literature or language. Both traditional and elected leaders are topics of gossip; both control, enhance, or thwart the flow of resources around the island. The

Pohnpeian proverb, "Chiefs are the water under cliffs," fits the new government as well. People's complaints about their leaders are like the surf against the rocky shore, noisy and constant. But the cliffs do not move or change.

The FSM government has no way to enforce nationalism or unity, no geographical imperative to get along. Yet Pohnpeians have raised the ethics of generalized reciprocity from the local to the national level; their high standards have become the model for engaged citizenship. In speeches, the leaders of FSM and the other three states acknowledge the generous contributions of Pohnpei State to the greater good. The leaders of the tiny nation acknowledge that Pohnpei does not extort, is not contentious or selfish, and has not demanded money or concessions. They have come to depend on Pohnpei's generosity, their freely given contributions to nationhood—land and labor for building the College of Micronesia and the FSM offices, and elaborate ritual presentations and celebrations at national events.

The Micronesian way, like Pohnpeian tradition, does not have fixed boundaries for ethnic groups. The differences between people—low islanders; high islanders; off-islanders; Pacific Islanders from Melanesia, Polynesia, or the Philippines; Asians; Europeans; Americans—are not something primordial, ordained by God or nature or history, or unchanging. Individuals belong to multiple communities. Their leaders serve many constituencies. Flexible affiliations prevent ethnic fighting. People say with pride, "Pohnpei is not one."

The shared coconut cup from which kava, the drink of forgiveness and social harmony, is sipped has become a dominant metaphor of island life after independence. The exchanges at life-turning events and the prestige cooperation-competitions that women engage in comprise the model for nationhood. Yes, they have problems—economic development, environment, and public health are the biggest. But they have chosen to make common cause. As the Preamble to the FSM Constitution states:

> To make one nation of many islands, we respect the diversity of our cultures. Our differences enrich us. The seas bring us together, they do not separate us. Our islands sustain us, our island nation enlarges us and makes us stronger. Our ancestors who made their homes on these islands displaced no other people. We who remain wish no other home than this. Having known war, we hope for peace. Having been divided, we wish unity. Having been ruled, we seek freedom.
>
> Micronesia began in the days when man explored seas in rafts and canoes. The Micronesian nation is born in an age when men voyage among stars; our world itself is an island. We extend to all nations what we seek from each: peace, friendship, cooperation, and love in common humanity. With this Constitution we, who have been the wards of other nations, become the proud guardian of our own islands, now and forever.

Bibliography

Bascom, William R. 1965. Ponape: A Pacific economy in transition. *Anthropological Records*. Vol. 22. Berkeley: University of California Press. An early work in applied anthropology, the monograph, written in 1946, makes recommendations for development in the newly-formed United States Trust Territory.

———. 1948. Ponapean prestige economy. *Southwestern Journal of Anthropology* [now called *Journal of Anthropological Research*], 4(3): 211–21. An oft-reprinted classic.

Cassel, John, and Herman Tyroler. 1961. Epidemiological studies of culture change: I. Health status and recency of industrialization. *Archives of Environmental Health* 3: 25–33.

Cassel, John, Ralph Patrick, and David Jenkins. 1960. Epidemiological analysis of the health implications of culture change: A conceptual model. *Annals of the New York Academy of Sciences* 84(17): 919–38.

Cheyne, Andrew. 1971. *The Trading Voyages of Andrew Cheyne 1841–44*. In D. Shineberg, ed., Pacific History Series, no. 3. Honolulu: University of Hawaii Press.

Coyne, Terry, Robert Hughes, and Sarah Langi, eds. 2000. *Lifestyle Diseases in Pacific Communities*. Noumea, New Caledonia: Secretariat of the Pacific Community.

Falgout, Suzanne. 1993. Tying the knot in Pohnpei. In Richard A. Marksbury, ed., *The Business of Marriage: Transformations in Oceanic Matrimony*. Pittsburgh: University of Pittsburgh Press. The best study of the marriage system in Pohnpei.

———. 1992. Hierarchy and democracy. Two strategies for the management of knowledge in Pohnpei. *Anthropology and Education Quarterly* 23(1): 30–43. The creation of a new elite through American educational practices and theories has changed the traditional system.

———. 1984. *Persons and Knowledge in Ponape*. Dissertation, University of Oregon. Ann Arbor, MI: University Microfilms.

Feldman, Jerome, and Donald Rubenstein. 1986. *The Art of Micronesia*. Honolulu: University of Hawaii Art Gallery.

Fischer, John L. 1970. Adoption on Ponape. In Vern Carroll, ed., *Adoption in Eastern Oceania*. Honolulu: University of Hawaii Press.

——— 1969. Honorific speech and social structure: A comparison of Japanese and Ponapean. *Journal of the Polynesian Society* 78(3): 417–22.

———— 1966. A Ponapean Oedipus tale, a structural and sociopsychological analysis. *Journal of American Folklore* 79(311): 109–29.

Fischer, John L. with the assistance of Ann M. Fischer. 1957. The Eastern Carolines. *Behavior Science Monographs.* New Haven, CT: Human Relations Area Files. A descriptive ethnography of Chuuk [Truk] and Pohnpei done in the style of the Human Relations Area Files.

Fischer, John L., Ann M. Fischer, and Frank J. Mahony. 1959. Totemism and allergy. *International Journal of Social Psychiatry* 5(1): 33–40.

Fischer, John L., Roger L. Ward, and Martha C. Ward. 1976. Ponapean conceptions of incest. *The Journal of Polynesian Society* 85(2): 199–207.

Fischer, John L., Saul H. Riesenberg, and Marjorie G. Whiting, eds. and trans. 1977. *Luelen Bernart: The Book of Luelen.* Pacific Science Series, no. 8. Canberra: Australian National University Press. An oral history of Pohnpei widely read and quoted on the island. Luelen was a prominent Pohnpeian who died at the end of World War II; he left a manuscript of place names, myths, legends, botanical lore, and advice.

Garvin, Paul L., and Saul H. Riesenberg. 1952. Respect behavior on Ponape: An ethnolinguistic study. *American Anthropologist* 54(2): 201–20. Classic work on high language.

Hambruch, Paul. 1932–1936. Ponape. In G. Thilenius, ed., *Ergelmisse der Sudsee-Expedition 1908–1910.* Hamburg: Friederichsen, DeGruyter. A German scientific expedition went into Micronesia before World War I. Volume 7 (subvolumes 1, 2, and 3) is about Pohnpei, its history, Nan Madol, mythology, and general ethnography.

Hanlon, David L. 1998. *Remaking Micronesia: Discourses over Development in a Pacific Territory, 1942–1982.* Honolulu: University of Hawaii Press.

————. 1988. *Upon a Stone Altar: A History of the Island of Pohnpei to 1890.* Pacific Islands Monograph Series, no. 5. Honolulu: University of Hawaii Press.

Hezel, Francis X. 2001. *The New Shape of Island Cultures.* Honolulu: University of Hawaii Press. A synthesis of important changes in Micronesia drawing on Hezel's decades of direct experience and involvement. See also Micronesian Seminar (in "Other Sources of Information"), which he founded.

————. 1995. *Strangers in Their Own Land: A Century of Colonial Rule in the Caroline and Marshall Islands.* Pacific Islands Monograph Series, no. 13. Honolulu: University of Hawaii Press.

————. 1983. *The First Taint of Civilization: A History of the Caroline and Marshall Islands in Pre-Colonial Days, 1521–1885.* Honolulu: University of Hawaii Press.

Keating, Elizabeth. 1998. *Power Sharing: Language, Rank, Gender, and Social Space in Pohnpei, Micronesia.* New York: Oxford University Press. Examines the etiquette of women's power through detailed analysis of public speeches made by women of chiefly rank.

Kihleng, Kimberlee S. 1996. *Women in Exchange: Negotiated Relations, Practice and the Constitution of Female Power in Processes of Cultural Reproduction and Change in Pohnpei, Micronesia.* Dissertation, University of Hawaii. Places Pohnpeian women in center of ethnographic analysis and examines how they maintain power and efficacy through feasting and networks of exchange.

Lebot, Vincent, Mark Merlin, and Lamont Lindstrom. 1992. *Kava: The Pacific Drug.* New Haven: Yale University Press. Traces the origins, history, botanical properties, and social uses of kava, a plant indigenous to the Pacific.

Lieber, Michael D. 1990. Lamarckian definitions of identity on Kapingamarangi and Pohnpei. In Jocelyn Linnekin, ed., *Cultural Identity and Ethnicity in the Pacific.* Honolulu: University of Hawaii Press.

————. 1984. Strange feast: Negotiating identities on Ponape. *Journal of the Polynesian Society* 93. How ethnic groups of Pohnpei, out-islanders, and Pohnpeians use the title and feasting systems to define their respective identities.

O'Connell, James F. 1972. *A Residence of Eleven Years in New Holland and the Caroline Islands*. In Saul H. Riesenberg, ed., Pacific History Series, no. 4. Honolulu: The University Press of Hawaii. The journal of a not-always truthful, shipwrecked ex-convict who lived on Pohnpei and married a woman there.

Patrick, R. C., I. A. M. Prior, J. C. Smith, and A. H. Smith. 1983. Relationship between blood pressure and modernity among Ponapeans. *International Journal of Epidemiology* 12: 36–44. The only published scientific results of the Blood Pressure and Social Change Project.

Petersen, Glenn. 1995. The complexity of power, the subtlety of kava. *Canberra Anthropology* 18: 34–60. Patterns of kava consumption and the contradictions of its status as both sacred plant and secular drink.

————. 1993. *Kanengamah* and Pohnpei's politics of concealment. *American Anthropologist* 95(2): 334–52. Explores an abstract quality of "reserve," a habit of dissembling and manner of behaving, which Pohnpeians use to exalt their leaders while remaining free of oppressive authority.

————. 1982. *One Man Cannot Rule a Thousand: Fission in a Ponapean Chiefdom*. Ann Arbor: University of Michigan Press. Tight analysis of political processes in Awak, a section of U; particularly instructive in understanding the functioning of contemporary chiefdoms.

————. 1982. Ponapean matriliny: Production, exchange, and ties that bind. *American Ethnologist* 9(1): 129–44.

————. 1979. External politics, internal politics, and Ponapean social formation. *American Ethnologist* 6: 25–40. In common with most anthropologists who have worked Pohnpei, Petersen maintains that Pohnpeians have retained most of their lands, precontact subsistence patterns, and a skillfully modified polity in response to colonialism.

Pinsker, Eve. 1997. *Point of Order, Point of Change: Nation, State and Community in the Federated States of Micronesia*. University of Chicago, dissertation.

Rehg, Kenneth L., and Damian G. Sohl. 1981. *Ponapean Reference Grammar*. Honolulu: University Press of Hawaii. Native speakers of Pohnpeian have standardized the orthography and alphabet, and provided a grammar and a dictionary (see below).

————. 1979. *Ponapean-English Dictionary*. Honolulu: University Press of Hawaii.

Riesenberg, Saul H. 1968. *The Native Polity of Ponape*. Vol. 10 of the Smithsonian Contributions to Anthropology. Washington, D.C.: Smithsonian Institution Press. From his fieldwork in 1947–1948. Pohnpeians and anthropologists alike quote from this early political ethnography that focuses on hierarchy and feasting.

Riesenberg, Saul H., and John L. Fischer. 1955. Some Ponapean proverbs. *Journal of American Folklore* 68: 217–27.

Shell, Ellen Ruppel. 2001. New World Syndrome. *Atlantic Monthly* 287(6), June.

OTHER SOURCES OF INFORMATION

2000 FSM Census and National Detailed Tables of Population and Housing. Department of Economic Affairs. FSM National Government. P.O. Box PS-12, Palikir, Pohnpei FSM 96941.

UNICEF. 1996. A Situational Analysis of Children and Women in the Federated States of Micronesia. United Nations.

Micronesian Seminar. P.O. Box 160. Pohnpei, FM 96941. www.micsem.org and micsem@micsem.org

The Nature Conservancy. 1996. *Pohnpei: An Ecotourist's Delight* [tourist pamphlet]

Lonely Planet. 2000. *Micronesia,* 4th ed. Melbourne, Oakland, London, Paris: Lonely Planet Publications.